PAY ATTENTION

TO THE THIN COW

Roger and Wanda,
Thanks for your support of CornerCap.
May all your investments be thin
cows.

Gene

Gene A. Hoots

This edition published by
Dog Ear Publishing
4010 W. 86th Street, Ste H
Indianapolis, IN 46268

www.dogearpublishing.net

ISBN: 978-145751-147-9
This book is printed on acid-free paper.

Printed in the United States of America

For Ken Hoots –

The first contrarian investor I ever met, and one of the best.

G.A.H.

My grandfather once asked my uncle Ken, "Why do you pay so little attention to the advice of others?" Kenneth answered, "Because I am the only one that I'm certain is working <u>for me</u> ALL the time." He was skeptical about advice, experts of every ilk, and especially politicians. No one was more widely liked than my uncle.

He made a living for over sixty years as a farmer and cattle trader. He was a true contrarian. He told me that at cattle auctions, most people buy the fat, slick cattle – they look healthy and prosperous, and they are priced accordingly. He always bought sickly looking, thin cows. He said there was nothing he could do to improve the fat ones, but he had a fair chance of improving the prospects of the thin ones and selling them for a profit. Investors would be well advised to use his approach in searching for stocks.

July 15, 2012

To CornerCap's Clients and Friends:

While it sometimes seems like only yesterday and then again like a lifetime, seven years ago CornerCap first printed this book about investing, accountability, and a few other things. Readers seemed to enjoy the information. And I was flattered that we needed to make a second printing.

Much has happened to CornerCap and me in that seven years. On the very positive side of the ledger, in 2009, we celebrated a number of milestones – my fortieth year as an investor, Tom Quinn and my thirtieth year as partners, and CornerCap's twentieth anniversary. And there were also negative entries in life's ledger for me. I lost my wife to cancer after a long illness. She was the greatest influence in my life and my best friend for forty-three years.

During these seven years, I have realized that our work has not so much to do with the markets and a great deal to do with relationships. While we do our best to serve our clients wisely in their financial life, for me there has been enormous benefit in just working with clients and CornerCap peers. They have become my good friends, and these relationships have gone a long way to fill a void in my life. These people mean more to me than most of them know.

Our message about investing has never varied, we have always recommended a steady, conservative approach. Although the specific facts and collection of essays in this book may be from time past, the core messages still apply. Since 1999 millions of people's hearts have been broken by the market. For some, it was not just "play money" that had gone missing – it was their life savings. They learned a serious and expensive lesson that will stand them in good stead the rest of their lives. If they learned young enough, it will have been worth the tuition. An investor's most valuable asset is time; given the magic of compounding, even modest investments become great with enough time. Sadly, many people do not have enough time left to regain what they have lost. Investors are still dealing with the aftermath of the Tech Bubble and the Great Recession. They will carry financial scars the rest of their lives. Now, we are gratified to have been more right than wrong, at least about the Tech Bubble. But we do not take pleasure in losses investors suffered.

I do admit to enjoying writing however. Along with the comments on markets, I have yielded to the temptation that comes with age to reminisce, sometimes about personal experiences. I hope you'll indulge me. And I have found a new word that, I'm sure many readers will agree, suits me perfectly:

philodox (FIL-uh-doks), noun: someone who loves his or her own opinion

Our personal message can be summed up in one word – RESPONSIBILITY. It seems nobody wants to take responsibility anymore. Whatever goes wrong - our health, our job, or our investments – we say, "I don't know who was responsible but it certainly wasn't my fault, and somebody's going to pay." The Responsibility theme is tied to two major tenants of our investment strategy: contrarianism - thinking for yourself and not being a part of the herd - and being accountable for your own actions. I often quote two of my uncles who taught me a great deal. Their business philosophies were similar. One of them, Buck Baity, was the original investor in the forerunner of CornerCap Investment Counsel. Kenneth Hoots was the other.

And a quick observation about the themes in the first edition and how events have unfolded: All of the major themes about investing, the economy, and education remain intact. We don't seem much closer to solving the big problems facing us than we did in 2005. We have been through a second investment bubble. We have seen even greater malfeasance in the financial industry. We have yet to solve the issues of terrorism, education, social security, and healthcare.

People never change their investment behavior. They still want us to forecast what the market is going to do (as if anyone knows!). They still want to sell after the market goes down. They still don't want to diversify. They still overpay for poor service and performance. But many of our clients over the years have accepted our philosophy on some of these issues, and we view that as progress.

We hope you find this book helpful, and we welcome your comments on how we might make the next book better.

Sincerely,

Gene Hoots

TABLE OF CONTENTS

I: BEING ACCOUNTABLE

CAUTION

I hope this collection of writings will be of some help to investors. But it is <u>your</u> judgment that is important. If <u>I</u> hadn't thought it was significant I wouldn't have put it on paper, but the author is seldom objective. You must decide whether this quotation applies to me:

The folly of mistaking a paradox for a discovery, a metaphor for a proof, a torrent of verbiage for a spring of capital truths, and oneself for an oracle, is inborn in us.
Paul Valery, poet and philosopher (1871-1945)

1:   PRINCIPLES

It is important to develop a framework for investing your money. It's even more important if you invest OPM (other people's money). We call this framework "principles". They set the stage for all that we do as investors. If you haven't thought through just what your principles are, when the going gets rough, as it most certainly will from time to time, you are very apt to do something foolish.

PHILOSOPHY

Perspective – Time Horizon

You must maintain a long-term perspective. This is one of the most difficult things to teach our clients. Indeed, investors generally have a great deal of trouble with focus; they want to spend far too much time on the minutiae. It is also ironic that the younger the client and the longer time perspective they can therefore afford, the shorter time horizon and less patience they actually have. We profess frustration with many people's lack of patience – because we know that patience pays.

The most dangerous phrase in investing is 'this time it's different'.
Sir John Templeton

John Templeton exemplifies long-term thinking. A friend of ours who had worked for him met with Sir John at Templeton's home in the Bahamas in 1999. Templeton had been cautious on stocks but said that when prices declined he would be a buyer of low P/E stocks. My friend asked, "But what if this time, the economy doesn't recover from the recession and goes into a full depression?" Templeton's answer, "It really doesn't matter. Economic depressions only last about five years."

It is admittedly a bit easier for a billionaire like John Templeton to ride out a five-year depression than it would be for most of us. But the point is - he takes a very long view. He was ninety years old, but could still look five years ahead. We have trouble keeping clients on point for a <u>one</u>-year horizon. And heaven help us if we have a bad quarter or two when a new client begins with us. While this shouldn't make any difference, we all know that first impressions count. Sometimes we will tell a prospective client about the need to have a ten year planning horizon, what we have done over the last twenty years, and how our consistently applied strategy will <u>probably</u> work over the next twenty years. After listening politely and nodding as if in agreement, the prospect then asks, "How'd you do last quarter?" At which point it is safe to assume that we have not communicated effectively.

Value Investing

We lean toward value rather than growth stocks. Of course, we want to buy companies with growing earnings. The problem with growth is that it is so easy to overpay for it. Most people are much more confident of their own ability to pick winners than they ought to be. This carries over to most everything in our lives. Nearly everyone suffers from an inflated view of his own abilities. No one will ever admit he is a below-average driver, but exactly one-half the driving population qualifies for that dubious distinction. While we may never be so overconfident as to enter a NASCAR race, many of us enter into the investment race just as under-qualified. A company that is growing its earnings rapidly year after year gradually develops a cult following of stockholders who are seduced by growth. They believe it can go on forever and that any price for the stock is cheap. Unfortunately, that is never the case.

Crowd Psychology

My introduction to crowd psychology had nothing to do with investing, but was a lesson never forgotten. It was a prime example of media influence and the tendency to assume that recent short-term trends will continue indefinitely. In 1954, I worked outside as a laborer. From July until mid-September, we never lost an hour of work from rain. Every day we crossed the Yadkin River bridge going to work. And we watched a sandbar slowly extend from the west river bank out into the water. Finally, that sandbar stretched over two-thirds of the way across the river, something that I haven't seen since in fifty years. The weather was miserably hot and dry. The newspaper reported that meteorologists said if the current trend continued, Piedmont North Carolina would become a Sahara Desert. (Thus, a classic case of taking a ninety-day trend and projecting it for centuries.)

What would we do without water? This potentially environment-threatening situation continued into early October. No rain. Then Friday October 15, Hurricane Hazel made landfall at Myrtle Beach and moved up the North Carolina coast. This devastating hurricane dropped six inches of rain on the Yadkin River valley that day. There was no more talk of drought or deserts. I learned that people, contrary to all their past experience and reason, will naturally believe that what is happening now will continue for a long time. And they will do silly things like spend good money to drill "reserve wells" that hadn't been needed for fifty thousand years, and to my knowledge haven't been needed since they were dug.

The Research Lab

The fool doth think he is wise, but the wise man knows himself to be a fool.
William Shakespeare, playwright and poet (1564-1616)

At RJR Nabisco, we ran what Tom Quinn describes as a "research laboratory" on money management. In the 1980s, we had $4 billion in RJR investment funds. That was big enough to attract hundreds of investment advisors, asking for our business. We were very inexperienced and we needed help. The consultant, Hamilton & Co., screened advisors and gave us an array of managers to select from. We got to meet many of the best in the country. As has been proven in recent years, this business isn't easy, and professional help is worth the price. We have talked with many people whose life savings would still be intact, rather than worth 30-50% of what it was in early 2000, if they had sought good advice. Even with $4 billion, and perhaps because of it, we sought help. As a result we got to hire and learn from some of the smartest investors in the world.

Learn From Others
Capital Guardian is one of the great investment companies. They manage mutual funds and institutional accounts. I met them in 1978. I visited their offices and then stayed in California for an investment seminar at Stanford University. The current CEO of Capital Guardian, Dave Fisher, was in my class. Bob Kirby, Capital Guardian's COO, spoke at that conference, with his usual charm and humor. Bob pointed out that his company had stuck with its fundamental investment principles over the years. At times, people had become impatient and dissatisfied with their returns – especially in highly speculative markets. Many clients fired Capital Guardian in 1972 because they would not buy the Nifty Fifty growth stocks, and one person in the class said "Capital Guardian is the best manager I ever fired, and I'm sorry I did it." Founded in the 1930s, Capital Guardian didn't get to be a major force in the investment world overnight. They grew by sticking to their principles. And they are one of the firms that Tom and I have used as a model for CornerCap.

The Oil Crisis
I always visited our investment managers when I was in their neighborhood. In November 1980 at the peak of the oil crisis, I walked into Capital Guardian's New York office on Park Avenue early one evening. To my surprise a portfolio manager, Vic Paricini from San Francisco was alone at a desk looking very concerned. I asked what he was doing in town. He said that he was in New York for a client meeting the next morning. He was sure the client was going to fire him - he didn't own any oil stocks.

To put in perspective the market environment at that moment, OPEC had raised oil prices since 1973 from $2.50 a barrel to $37 a barrel. There were gas lines in California and fears that they would spread across the entire country as they had in 1973. Everyone in the investment business was afraid not to own oil. It had begun to look as though oil might be the only thing worth owning. Oil stocks were 35% of the S&P 500 (the same level that technology stocks reached in early 2000). A few weeks earlier an officer of another highly respected investment firm had visited me.

His company was heavily weighted in energy. He was a former Assistant Secretary of Energy, and he had recently visited the Saudi Oil Minister Ahmed Zaki Yamani in Arabia. Sheikh Yamani, with the ability to set world oil prices, was at that moment possibly the most powerful person on earth. The investment officer said that Sheikh Yamani had assured him that oil would be $100 a barrel in April, five months hence. I have no doubt that the Oil Minister and the investment advisor believed this.

I don't know whether the client did fire Capital Guardian, but if they did it was extremely ill timed. I returned home and discussed the incident with Tom Quinn. At the time we were managing only the Carolina Equity Fund. We owned a number of energy and natural resource companies that were richly priced. Although we were very green at portfolio management, we were contrarians even then. We sold all our energy related stocks. They increased another 15-20% in about two weeks. Then they dropped for the next eighteen months as world oil prices plummeted. It was ten years before some of the major energy stocks regained their 1980 prices. Vic's concern that evening, for Capital Guardian's reputation and for the welfare of his client who was about to make a big mistake, was impressive.

Nothing Goes Up Forever – Not Even My Stocks

Some years later, another Capital Guardian portfolio manager, Edus Warren, gave us a lesson. In mid-1983, the popular market averages had been in the doldrums for a very long time. The S&P 500 and the Dow Jones Industrials had done well for the past year, but had made little progress over the last seven years. In contrast, small value stocks had been performing well, and our limited partnership had compounded at 27.5% a year over that seven years, including a spectacular 92% return for the last year. So we were on top of the world. Edus visited us and said, "I can see an extended period in which the Dow Jones Index will outperform everything else." And I thought, "But that is just foolish. Look at how well we have done – our small cap approach is great; it can go on forever." In retrospect, my thinking made no sense at all, but we were young and wanted so much to believe we would always be right. We had yet to learn just how humbling an investment career really is. So I dismissed Edus as out of touch with the times. Of course, it was I who was out of touch. Edus recognized an over-extended market. I did not. For the next seven and one-half years ending 1990, the Dow Jones Industrials did indeed outperform every other market yardstick. Our "hot" small cap value stocks gave a 3.7% return for that seven and a half years. Over the total fourteen and a half years, the return still was respectably above the averages, but not nearly so dramatic as we had hoped. Again, I was impressed with the market sense of the Capital Guardian people. As a footnote, we stuck to our approach, and over the fourteen years ending 2004, the fund had a 14.6% return. It pays to stay with what you know. It also pays to not get overconfident.

Coping With Success

Another firm that we admire is Pimco. This firm, with Bill Gross' extraordinary talent for bond investing, is unchallenged as the premier institutional fixed income investor. Bill is acknowledged as one of the ten most influential people in the financial world. He is believed to be paid over $20 million a year, and he may be one of the most underpaid people in America, given the extra return he delivers to Pimco investors. He has established a charitable foundation that has assets approaching a half billion dollars that he has donated.

These people and this firm haven't always been living legends. Not so long ago, at least not long ago to me, Pimco was just five guys trying to get a business off the ground. In 1979, our consultant Jim Hamilton took me to Newport Beach to visit a young group that Jim understood were "pretty good" bond managers. We were looking for some fixed income managers for a piece of the RJR pension fund. On a sunny, January morning we sat on their patio, had breakfast, and discussed what Pimco might do for us. These people were obviously bright, but to me they were painfully young, not much over thirty or so. How would I ever convince the finance committee of RJR that the Pimco people were mature enough to handle the money we would give them? But in a subsequent meeting, they made an equally good impression on my bosses, Joe Abely and John Dowdle, and RJR gave them a $10 million account.

At that time, Pimco had about $400 million under management. AT&T's pension fund had become their first institutional account and RJR was their second. So after a bit more than two decades, Pimco is now 1,000 times bigger than it was then. They have a $50 million account minimum. And yet they never forgot our early times together. I had not seen them in years until last March. I happened to be in Newport Beach, and my two little granddaughters and I stopped for a visit. Jim Muzzy, the first President of Pimco, is still there and he was gracious enough to spend some time with me. He said, "You hired us when we were so small that you probably shouldn't have." Not true, of course.[1]

Bill Gross was in meetings, but he sent me an autographed copy of his new biography. We got a tour of the fabled Pimco trading floor where my granddaughters, who are into computers, were duly impressed by all the hardware they saw. And they got Pimco sweatshirts. I explained that a visit to Pimco wouldn't mean much now, but later they could impress people by explaining that they had been guests on the Pimco trading floor. The Pimco people, despite their success, have remained generous with their money and their time. They have not forgotten people who were associated with them in their very early days. And I think it's safe to say, success has not spoiled them. We can all take a lesson from this when good fortune comes our way. The country lass at the square dance had it

---

[1] At January 2011, Pimco was three times its size in 2005 with $1.25 trillion in assets under management.

right when she said, "I always dance with the one who brung me."

CornerCap Investment Approach

CornerCap is usually considered a value investor. But this is something of a mischaracterization. We like companies with growing earnings and dividends. We just don't want to pay an excessive amount for that growth. Nor do we want to buy a stock that is selling at a low P/E ratio and not growing. That's not value – that's a loser.

The Problem With "Growth"

Our research segments companies by their earnings growth rates and compares that growth to their price/earnings ratio. In the long run this is the best way to make money in the market – by buying the best growth at a fair value. Stocks that have experienced recent rapid growth are often priced for perfection – the price reflects investor expectations that the company will continue to perform "perfectly". But this seldom happens, and when earnings perfection isn't delivered, the stock can suffer badly, and suddenly become a value stock. Coca-Cola, McDonalds, Home Depot, General Electric, Wal-Mart, Microsoft, and Cisco are stocks that have lost their growth status. However, it often takes years for such great companies to have their stock reflect the new reality. Investors are slow to change their perceptions of a company's prospects.

There is a long history of growth stocks that didn't grow. Xerox is a troubled company and Polaroid is gone. They were two of the Nifty Fifty technology-based glamour stocks of the 1960s. ("One decision" stocks that you could own forever, the experts told us.) LTV, the ultimate conglomerate when they were all the rage, closed its last operation in late 2001. It was the nation's fourth largest steel company. Before its life as a steel company it was the brainchild of Jimmy Ling who built an empire on acquired companies. LTV was Ling-Tempco-Vought at one time – with aerospace, sporting goods, pharmaceuticals, and much more. A story I heard in the late 1960s was that Jimmy Ling actually bought Jones & Laughlin Steel, his last big acquisition with no more analysis than looking at an S&P "yellow sheet" (a small two page summary published in a tear sheet book by S&P - not exactly detailed investment analysis). So much for the "One Decision Stocks" that you could buy and comfortably hold forever. There are no one-decision stocks. Today's similar stocks include E-bay and Amazon. Will they ever make enough money to justify their stock prices? No one knows for sure, and such stocks create big challenges for investors.

Is It A Good Time To Buy Stocks?

It is a capital mistake to theorize before one has data. Insensibly one begins to twist facts to suit theories, instead of theories to suit facts.

Arthur Conan Doyle, physician and writer (1859-1930)

Email to a Prospect who asked, "Is it a good time to jump into the market?" (January 2003):

You raise a good question about investing. I will answer you the way we have always answered this question, but I suspect that my answer won't give you much reassurance. Most people hesitate to invest because they want to be sure that the economy is in good shape before they buy. But markets lead the economy by about six months on average, and by the time it is obvious that the economy is better, the market is already higher. Then months later, everybody says, "Oh yeah! Now we see why stocks went up." But of course by then it's too late to buy.

My guess is that stocks have bounced back significantly because the economy is going to get better, but slowly. Stocks are still not cheap by historical measures, but inflation is low and that to some degree, justifies higher P/E ratios for stocks. I also suspect that this market will be like the market in 1976-82. We got an initial flurry that pushed the market higher for about a year and then the broad market did nothing for <u>six</u> years. Even in that period you could still make money by buying conservative stocks. If we are in such a period, stocks will probably deliver a 6-8% return over the next 10 years. This is far below what people have come to expect, but about average for periods of low inflation, and not a bad return after inflation, which is what really matters. There are always opportunities to profit even in a flat market.

You talk about "jumping in," but you should never jump into the market. Investing is something you do year in and year out. You pick a mix of stocks, bonds, and real estate that suits you, and you stay with that mix. It is pointless to try to guess when to move in and out of stocks.

I just wrote a message to one of our mutual fund investors who wanted to move from a conservative bond fund to our stock fund because it had done so well in the last five or six weeks. This is what I said, and it is good advice to anyone who wants to invest long term:

I want you to read a book on investing by Charles D. Ellis, "Winning the Losers Game." It will tell you more about what is important in investing than you will learn anywhere else, and you will be a lot richer in twenty years if you follow it.

You are watching too closely and worrying far too much about the market. What these funds have done over the last six weeks doesn't tell us a thing about what they are going to do over the next six weeks or six years. To answer your question about safety, <u>any</u> stock fund can move up or down a great deal in just a few weeks.

The best thing an investor can do is pick a good set of funds (or individual securities), including some stocks and bonds and divide the money among them. Then don't pay any attention to them except about every six months or year. Over fifteen years when the stock market was going up 11% a year, the average person investing in stock mutual funds made just 5% a year. This was because they constantly watched what the funds were doing and switched to those that had recently done well from those that hadn't done well, usually just in time to lose money.

If you look at your account, over the last seven years it has made 61%, or 7% a year. I kept a little less than half the money in the stock market. And during that time, the portfolio was down only one year; -5% in 1998. During those seven years if someone had stayed in the stock market all the time, they would have made less than 7% a year, and most people who constantly switched from one thing to another actually lost money for the seven years. You did so well because we set a course and then left things alone. I know it is hard not to "tinker" with your investments, but it will cost you a lot of money if you do."

The Carolina Equity Fund was our first investment vehicle. One lady reminded us recently that she had put money for her children in the CEF in 1979 and had left it alone. Over twenty-four years of compounding, there were good years and bad, but she ignored them all. And her benign neglect worked better than anything she could have done proactively.

As another example of patience, a friend of mine invested less than $20,000 in a portfolio for himself, his wife, and his sister in 1951. By buying sound stocks and being patient, their portfolios have grown to over $3 million. This didn't take any magic investing talent. His portfolio compounded at a bit over 9% a year, about in line with the long-term market results. Yet this modest investment has provided a fine retirement for his family.

I note that you said that your friend, our client, referred to me as a "miracle worker." In fact nothing could be further from the truth. Rather than work miracles, what we do at CornerCap is recognize that there are real limits to what anyone can know about the economy and market direction. We stick to a few basics that great investors like Warren Buffett and John Templeton tell us, but almost no one listens to - be conservative, don't try to time the market, and stay with it year in and year out. This is simple, but it isn't easy.

Diversify
Control Expenses - commissions, fees, trading costs
Be aware of taxes
Be a long-term investor – do not focus on the short term

Few people have the conviction to do this, and that is why there are so few successful investors.

Cynicism
Don't argue with an idiot, people watching may not be able to tell the difference.

Why would we be cynical about investors' judgment? Our cynicism comes from long observation of market participants and their irrational behavior. Bad decisions can only be the result of bad information or bad judgment. There are basic rules that are key to market success and professionals stress these fundamentals to investors again and again. Yet, people choose to behave otherwise even after they have repeatedly been told these basic rules. They simply lack judgment, and behave irrationally. For example:

As a pro bono project, an investor approached me in 1999 with a portfolio of extremely low cost basis stocks, mostly telecoms. The portfolio was worth $300,000. He wanted to give his daughter $10,000 and decided to sell that amount. A broker had said that he could sell the stock for $500, a 5% commission. I explained that at an on-line broker the commission would be $30 and if he really wanted to sell a few shares of AT&T, this was the best way. I also asked if the broker had discussed the tax implications, almost $2,500 in capital gains tax on the $10,000 sale. The broker had not.

I did not make any judgment about whether the holdings were "buys" or "sells." Nor was I asked to do so. But we did move the account to a discount broker, and I told him that if he ever wanted to sell, to let me know and I would help him do it on line. I heard no more from him for a few years. But in that interim, he sought advice from a friend who is totally unknowledgeable about investments. The mutual friend shared with me that the investor was making some "changes." I called to check and learned that he had decided that he couldn't stand to see his stocks go down any more and he sold all of them for a third of what they were selling for when we had our last conversation. He had moved the account back to a full service broker before selling. This broker was urging him to buy a "safe" investment, not a diversified portfolio, but a single energy company with lots of problems.

It's been said that man is a rational animal. All my life I have been searching for evidence that could support this.
Bertrand Russell

We are fans of Jonathan Clements, a *Wall Street Journal* writer. He cites that the last few years have been grim. – September 11, anthrax, California energy crisis, disputed presidential election, Enron, scandals. But people talk about the "bubble." He thinks this is wrong, that investors were not irrational in early 2000, but rather that a series of bad news knocked down the economy. He asks, "Can utter stupidity really explain the creation and subsequent destruction of trillions of dollars of stock-market value?" He thinks, No; I think, Yes. We may be dealing here in semantics as we debate the meaning of the words "bubble" and "stupidity".[1]

Everyone is entitled to be stupid, but some people abuse the privilege.
Unknown

A few years from now, people will say, 'any fool could have seen it was a market bottom and that you should have jumped into stocks', but today, it isn't obvious where the market bottom is. You really have to protect against your own overconfidence.
Meir Statman, finance professor at Santa Clara University

We have long followed Meir Statman's work on investor psychology, and we heartily endorse his statement. It is easy to become overconfident about your own ability. If the conditions he describes aren't a bubble, then I don't know what one would be. Actually, a few of the brightest, most seasoned people in the investment world were calling it a bubble in 1999.

Aside from valuations, economic outlook, or any other justification for the high market level, there was one thing investors should have realized from history - The world is not risk free, it is a dangerous place. Bad things happen. The 1990s are not representative of history, not even recent history. To believe that the world would continue to be so benign was naïve. I think Clement passes over this too lightly. Investors' limited historical perspective cost them dearly.

We at CornerCap stuck by our philosophy. On the point that no one knew when it would end, someone asked me if I ever doubted that we were correct in shunning technology stocks as they got higher and higher. My answer was that I never doubted that the bubble would burst and value would return to favor. However, I did doubt whether it would happen before the mania wrecked CornerCap as a firm. A few of our clients defected to the growth philosophy in late 1999 and early 2000. Tech stocks might have continued to soar for months. Once valuations reach "Absurdity," there is nothing to prevent them from going up to "2 X Absurdity." Had the market risen for another year, many more value investors would have lost faith, and more value firms would have been destroyed by massive client departures. A fair number were driven out of business as it was.

The question remains about investor "stupidity." Certainly investors are not stupid. Most are reasonably intelligent individuals. But the market thrives on crowd psychology. And the crowd is always wrong. In that sense investors are, as a group, always "stupid" at major turning points.

RESPONSIBILITY

Be responsible. Be informed. Question what you are told. You should constantly be asking – What are the credentials of the person who is advising me? What are his motives? Am I getting complete advice, or are parts being left out of the discussion? Is this advice common sense – or does it promise something just too good to be true?

Lemmings All

Lemmings are furry little animals that live in the far north. Contrary to popular belief, lemmings do not periodically hurl themselves off cliffs into the sea. But the term "lemming" is still very applicable to investor crowd behavior. Cyclical explosions in population do occasionally induce lemmings to attempt to migrate to areas of lesser population density. When such a migration occurs, some lemmings die by falling over cliffs or drowning in lakes or rivers. These deaths are not deliberate "suicides." They are accidental deaths resulting from the lemmings' venturing into unfamiliar territory and being crowded and pushed. When the competition for food, space, or mates becomes too intense, lemmings are much more likely to kill each other than to kill themselves.

Now doesn't that sound like mass hysteria in the market? The lemmings start out looking for something better, and in all the confusion many of them get trampled. When the competition gets too keen, they turn on their fellows.

Expectations

Two years after the bubble burst, polls showed that investors still harbored great stock market expectations. Nearly one-fourth still thought stock prices would rise 30-100% a year over the next twenty years. At the same time, conservative professionals were saying that people should be happy with 7-8% over the next ten years. Roger Ibbotson, who may have done more statistical work on the markets than any person in history, said that stocks would likely give 9.4% over the next ten years. [And even more unrealistic, the average investor was expecting bonds to earn 15% and money market funds to yield 16% over the next twenty years.][ii] Markets will not go up unless the public's inflated expectations are sharply reduced, probably by disappointing market results.

Investor Returns Lag Badly

From 1984 to 2000, the average mutual fund investor had an annual return of 5.3%. The S&P 500 returned 16.3% for the same period. How could the typical investor have earned 11% a year less than the market, when he could have done nothing and about equaled the market?

Several things account for this. First, trading costs probably take 1% a year. Mutual fund management fees take another 1%. But these two explain only a small part of the shortfall. Why the rest? Because rather than laying out a plan and sticking to it, most investors switched from one fund to another. There is no surer way to lose money than buying what has done well recently. (And that is why I get terribly frustrated when someone asks, "What have you done over the last quarter, or year, or even two years. The answer is totally irrelevant to anyone who is a serious investor.) Mutual fund owners switch funds about every two and a half years. They chase hot funds just as the game is ending. In March 2000, 85% of all mutual fund net inflows were directed to technology funds. Just in time to get wiped out.

If management fees cause underperformance, why have a manager? Because at some point, nearly everyone is tempted to follow the crowd. We at CornerCap earn our fee by keeping our clients focused on the straight path of disciplined investing. The point is – how much worse than our fee would the client do on his own? And the answer to that question is probably "Much worse!" We have seen the pattern over and over. People tell us that they have a long-term perspective and that they understand value investing. Yet often sooner rather than later, they see a tempting new idea and they want to switch styles, abandoning what they know intellectually is right, but just not being able to resist emotionally. That is why most people never make money in the market, and why they shouldn't do it themselves.

Aggressive Growth –It Didn't Work

Over a five-year period, one aggressive growth fund had a return of -33.5% a year, putting it in the bottom 4% of all funds. Remarkably, but not uncharacteristic of technology funds, this five years included one year (1999) when the return was +103%, an amazing result. Of course the performance for the other four years in total was terrible. The average shareholder who invested in the fund during that period had results that were very consistent with investor behavior. The typical investor put in more as the fund reached its peak and took money out as the fund got cheaper, and lost 87 cents out of every dollar invested. So the fund manager's stock-picking cost the client 67% of his money, but the client's own poor timing behavior cost himself another 20%.

Bad market timing is not unusual. Peter Lynch ran Fidelity Magellan, the top performing mutual fund for two decades. He estimated that two thirds of the people who invested in Magellan during that time lost money. Why? Because they waited until they had seen excellent short-term performance, and then they invested, just before the fund started to decline. At or near the bottom, they would take their money out and wait until the fund went up before buying again.[iii]

ETHICS

Perhaps people are not more unethical today than in the past. But the market crash has caused investors to demand that someone find and punish the "guilty." This has revealed a good deal that went on in the markets that is clearly not of the highest ethics.

Reputation is what people think you are; character is what God knows you are.
    Old Proverb

Accounting
The only number you can believe on an accounting statement is the date.
    Dr. Bern Beatty, Wake Forest University, Babcock   Graduate School of
    Management, September 10, 2003

A Class For Ethics?

Dr. Beatty and I discussed whether graduate business schools should teach an ethics course. I said, "Absolutely not. Ethics need to be taught in kindergarten." Somewhat to my surprise, he agreed.

We now have consultants to instruct business executives on ethics. We have MBA classes on ethics. This strikes me as an unfortunate commentary on morals and ethics in America today. If a student hasn't learned basic ethics before arriving at the graduate level, it is sad for our society. Ethics, the basics of right and wrong, should be learned from family, religious instructors, and grade school teachers. A graduate school course should be unnecessary. I am skeptical that a person can learn an ethic structure at that late date in life. In an MBA class, they would probably just learn ways to get around the rules.

Ethics need to be instilled during childhood. It isn't hard to spell out right from wrong – by word and example, you send the message: "Don't cheat, lie, or steal. Here are examples of that behavior, and if I see you doing any of these things you will be punished. Also, here are the benefits of doing the right thing." You can tell right from wrong, especially if you have been instructed at an early age.

In my early years I was often under the care of two wonderful grandmothers. They, and my parents, reinforced the concepts of right and wrong for me. They also taught me that there are negative consequences if you do bad things. Sometimes consequences are immediate and sometimes they are a long time coming. With my grandmothers, they were immediate. So by the age of six, I pretty well knew what was right. That doesn't mean I've always done right, but when I did something wrong, I knew that I shouldn't be doing it and that the consequences could be bad. Conscience doesn't keep you from doing wrong, it just keeps you from enjoying it.

Elders today actually defend their children's bad behavior. Of course these young people aren't going to know right from wrong. In schools, the teachers can't discipline for fear of lawsuits from parents. This is in such contrast to supportive parents who used to back up the discipline meted out by teachers.

A man has to live with himself, and he should see to it that he always has good company.
Charles Evans Hughes, jurist (1862-1948)

And even the recent market crises didn't give us much hope on better ethics, except by negative example. In my opinion, CEOs and politicians are generally interesting to watch. Moms and dads could point simultaneously to the disgraced CEOs and bleating, grandstanding members of Congress as two examples of the kind of adult that no child should grow up to be.[iv]

Are We In An Unprecedented Accounting Crisis?
Probably not. WorldCom, Enron, and other cases need to be put in historical perspective. The root of the accounting problem is that stock-market bubbles reward aggressive accounting. Increases in stock prices become paramount, conservative accountants and executives become discredited, and bending the rules becomes the standard.[v]

Investment Companies

The New York State Attorney General uncovered a scheme in which a hedge fund entered into an agreement with several major mutual funds companies that allowed the hedge fund, Canary Capital Partners, to buy the mutual funds at the price set at the close of business for up to another five hours, until 9:00 p.m. This late trading allowed Canary to capitalize on any information that might move the stocks in the mutual fund up or down the next morning. The scheme enhanced the return of the hedge fund. This was at the expense of all the other shareholders who owned the mutual funds. The percentage amount was very small on any given day, but over time it robbed the fund holders of millions of dollars.

Canary Capital is a black eye for the entire investment community. It is a cross that hedge funds and mutual funds will bear for some time. It shows how unpredictable the industry is, where the watchword is – anything can go wrong. I would not have believed that a group of major mutual funds would have entered into such an unethical relationship. And I would not have suspected that a fund like Canary would have resorted to such tactics to enhance return. The manager and his father are two of the wealthiest people in the U.S. I am at a loss to understand the motivation for the Canary manager's apparently unethical, and probably illegal, behavior. He has tarnished the image of his family, a family that conducted business on a national level for three generations. It is also unthinkable that four or more major mutual fund companies would enter an arrangement that penalizes their mass bread-and-butter retail market, and give an advantage to a selected big customer.

The mutual funds engaged in this for several reasons. They were willing to jeopardize their reputation for integrity and a fair deal for all their investors because they were under pressure to increase profits. In exchange for letting the hedge fund manager profit at others' expense, the fund companies received money from the hedge fund in the form of interest on loans and fees for other transactions. It is unclear that senior management at the fund companies knew about these schemes. But it is clear that they put pressure on their underlings to increase profits.

It is difficult to get a man to understand something when his salary depends upon his not understanding it.
Upton Sinclair, novelist and reformer (1878- 1968)

The Boss Sets the Ethical Standards

Ethics are set at the top – by example. If senior management is more interested in profits than how they are made, then junior people won't care how they deliver higher earnings. And management won't be inclined to ask how they got them, a dangerous situation. Nick Leeson bankrupted Barings Bank overnight with his risky trading schemes in Singapore. The year before, he was responsible for possibly a third of the bank's profit worldwide. Management might have asked,

"How can one trader be so successful; what is he doing?" Rather, they encouraged him to do more of the same risky, unsupervised trades. When the market ran against him, the bank was destroyed.

Drawing a parallel to CornerCap:

If we had one portfolio manager who performed well above his peers, we would want to know why. His results would not be consistent with our philosophy and we would need to know exactly how he was getting his results. The answer would likely be that he is taking much more risk than he should.

If we had a sales person who delivered many more new accounts than others in the firm, we would definitely need to know how. Is he better at making sales presentations and at closing prospects? Or is he attracting people to CornerCap by making outlandish claims about our past and future performance?

Corporations and Executives

To those who toiled in corporate America twenty years ago, the behavior of CEOs today looks completely out of control. The cases we read about may be extreme examples. Most CEOs are probably still hard working, conscientious people. But there is sufficient excess in their pay and perks to cause concern.

CEOs Behaving Badly

The Great Bubble Bull Market was taking off and lavish perks at the top didn't matter so much while everybody was getting rich. Even now, the cost of execs' extravagances pale against the losses suffered by shareholders of Tyco and GE. Since the beginning of the year [2002], Tyco's stock-market capitalization has shrunk by $84 billion to $30 billion, or some 74%. GE's market cap has shriveled about half as much in percentage terms, 34%, but more than half again as much in dollars, by $135 billion, to $263 billion. (September, 2002).[vi]

My Personal Favorite

My choice for high-flying CEO is the head of Westar, formerly a stodgy electric company in Kansas. David Wittig became famous for all the wrong reasons during the madness of the 1990s. At Kidder Peabody he evidently learned his spendthrift lifestyle from Martin Seigel who commuted to Manhattan from his estate by helicopter. Wittig became famous as an inside joke for a public-relations gaffe. In 1988 he was on the cover of *Fortune*. An article featured Mr. Wittig, then thirty-one years old, bragging about his $500,000 a year salary and plans to retire by the age of forty. He later joined Salomon Brothers, making more than $1 million a year. He bought a Ferrari, a sprawling apartment on Manhattan's Fifth Avenue and a beach house in New Jersey. Westar hired him to develop an acquisition strategy. He became CEO in 1998. The stock moved from $28 in 1996 to over $40. He made $2.5 million in 1998 and $8 million in 1999. "Seeing that bright, talented young guy up there gave us all a lot of confidence," said Richard D. Rogers, a federal judge in Topeka and a Westar shareholder.[vii]

Rogers' comment raises a question about how much judgment the judge had. We wonder what the judge, the stockholders, the board of directors, and the community were thinking to bring in this "talented young guy." What were his talents and his resume? Sufficient background information was available to question his credentials even before he got the job. For openers he had learned his craft from Martin Siegel at Kidder Peabody and Ivan Boesky at Drexel Burnham. Both men served prison time for their investment activities. He had been the joke of Wall Street, bragging about how overpaid he was. He had done far fewer deals than he claimed.

At Westar, he made a string of acquisitions, always a bad sign (see the M&A section). He ballooned the company's debt from nothing to $3.5 billion. The stock dropped 70%. He got a huge compensation package while supplying little information to the board of directors. They approved the pay anyway.

His lifestyle did not bespeak the hardworking, thrifty head of Kansas' biggest power company, with his Ferrari and perpetual tan. He added corporate jets for his personal trips. He bought a 17,000 square foot home and brought in a decorator from New York City. He bought a home in Southampton. He participated in real estate deals that hinted of fraud. In February, 2004 David Wittig was sentenced to more than four years in prison for his part in a federal loan-conspiracy case stemming from two transactions at a Topeka bank. This case was not directly related to his activities at Westar.

He faces a separate forty-count federal indictment accusing him and a former Westar executive of committing conspiracy, fraud and other crimes. Prosecutors allege Wittig tried to loot Westar, the state's largest electric utility. If his actions weren't looting, they certainly were in line with the life style he had enjoyed in New York before coming to Kansas. He spent millions on his home, furnishings and his new Ferrari. And he also wanted to maintain a similar style at work. He spent $6.5 million of company funds redecorating his office suite. Yet none of this should have come as a surprise; he had already telegraphed to the world his sense of values when he appeared years before on the cover of *Fortune*. Leopards don't change their spots, and the people who recruited him to Westar should have known better.

Pension Fund Accounting and Corporate Compensation

Pensions are a business that is dear to my heart, having worked for a decade in the corporate pension fund world. There has been a change in the relationship between corporate pension funds and executive compensation. When pension funds book a profit because the stock market goes up, these "earnings" are considered part of "operating profit" and are included in the calculation of CEO bonuses. Now pension assets are falling and the "losses" from those funds are being excluded from the bonus calculation for many CEOs. It seems that now pension losses are deemed to be a "special, unusual, and extraordinary item." And this is just in time to save the CEO's bonus.[viii]

Crooks In History

This has all happened before – corporate crooks are not new. For example:

Philip Musica - Behind the mask of Dr. F. Donald Coster M.D. Ph.D. the much admired CEO of McKesson and Robbins Pharmaceuticals, lurked Philip Musica, an Italian immigrant, convicted felon, bootlegger, government snitch, and swindler. Coster had acquired the venerable drug company during the 1930s. While the kindly Dr. Coster was courted for the U.S. presidency, he was living a secret life and bleeding McKesson and Robbins for millions of dollars. Musica claimed inventory in Canada that didn't exist. At the time, there was no requirement for auditors to even confirm the existence of inventory, but this case changed all that. His true identity (and the fact that he had simply invented millions of dollars of revenue) was revealed. The morning the police were coming to arrest him, he went home to his Connecticut mansion and shot himself.

Charles Ponzi - Few other people have enjoyed the distinction of having a crime named for them. But Charles Ponzi, who arrived from Italy with $2.50 in his pocket, pursued the title with a diabolical fervor. In the summer of 1920, he conned thousands of working people out of $20 million. Booted from America, Ponzi next offered his services to Benito Mussolini. Forever after, such pyramid frauds have been known as "Ponzi schemes."

Cassie Chadwick – She was born in 1857 in Canada. Cassie at sixteen stole money from her mother to help her pose as a debutante on holiday from Europe. She worked as a fortune-teller and clairvoyant. In Canada, she was arrested for theft and forgery. She arrived in Cleveland in 1882. Using her maiden name, Elizabeth Bigley, she married Dr. Wallace S. Springsteen. However, the marriage ended after eleven days when her husband learned that she had been charged for forgery in Canada. She went to prison for this, and after jail, she returned to Cleveland in 1897 and married Dr. Leroy Chadwick.

Cassie scammed Cleveland banks out of untold amounts of money in the late 1890s. She said she was Andrew Carnegie's illegitimate daughter (showing great understanding of human nature, she let it slip to one or two Clevelanders, swore them to secrecy, and let gossip do its work). Everyone knew that Cassie was good for her debts. For years no one mentioned the matter to the religious Carnegie. Claiming to bankers that the strength behind her borrowing power was her $5 million worth of bonds signed by Andrew Carnegie (which no one had ever seen), she assumed an additional $1 million in debt, which she spent on lavish gifts for herself and her friends. Bankers in Cleveland, Pittsburgh and New York City flung their doors wide open for Cassie, loaning this "simple, naïve" woman big money at outrageous rates of interest. They believed she would inherit Carnegie's $400 million. The poor souls were unaware they were trying to bilk "the most notorious woman of her time."

Eventually, however, Cassie's house of cards fell apart. When the authorities were closing in on her, she said: "Public clamor has made me a sacrifice. Here I am, an innocent woman hounded into jail, while a score of businessmen in Cleveland would leave town tomorrow if I told all I knew. Yes I borrowed money, but what of it." Over the years she made up a trainload of aliases and borrowed millions to finance a lifestyle she hadn't earned. And the men (mostly men, of course) who were defrauded by Cassie blamed her hypnotic eyes. After being caught by suspicious bankers, she was sentenced to fourteen years and fined $70,000 for conspiracy to defraud the government and an Oberlin bank. Mrs. Chadwick died a year after being put behind bars in an Ohio prison in 1907 at age fifty.

Ivar Kreuger - Around 1900, Swedish-born "Match King" Ivar Kreuger inherited a small match factory from his father. Within thirty years, he'd parlayed the business into an international monopoly controlling four-fifths of the entire world's production of matches. He did it through bribery, intimidation, and blatant fraud. Indeed, Kreuger created the tale (totally untrue) that it was bad luck to light three cigarettes on one match. According to legend, when the Doughboys of World War I were in the trenches, lighting two cigarettes at night would give the enemy enough time to aim its weapons. And when the match was then passed to the third soldier, "bang!" he was shot dead. An interesting story, but it was concocted by Kreuger for the sole purpose of selling more matches. Kreuger was just as loose with the facts when it came to his company's finances. And although the accounting standards at the time were lax, Kreuger took "creative accounting" to a new level (threatening to fire his auditors if they didn't accept his bogus figures). But a business built on weak and shifting sand can't stand bad weather; Kreuger was done in by the 1929 stock market crash. When it became apparent that Kreuger would be vilified, he killed himself.

Stanley Goldblum - In the 1960s, insurance salesman Stanley Goldblum acquired Equity Funding, which he would use for massive fraud. By the mid-seventies, Goldblum and his lieutenants had managed to add $800 million in phony profits and 65,000 phony policyholders to its books. The fraud was so large that nearly 150 people in the company participated in making up phony documents, creating non-existing policyholders (and even "killing off" a few of the phonies to look legitimate), and obscuring the truth from auditors. A disgruntled former employee revealed the scheme to authorities, Equity Funding went broke, and Stanley Goldblum drew a five-year jail sentence.[2]

These schemes would not have worked without greedy people who were "taken." It is especially hard to feel sympathy for the bankers who loaned Cassie Chadwick money at ridiculously high rates. She could never have succeeded if they had been honest themselves.

Keylon Furniture (The name has been changed to protect the Guilty)

A leather chair has been in my office for over thirty years. There is nothing remarkable about the chair, but there was something remarkable about the company

---

[2] This was a great scandal in my early investing days. Equity Funding was a very high-flying stock for a while.

that made it. In the late 1960s, Judy and I visited a small furniture manufacturer and bought two chairs. A few years later, I returned to order another chair, the one I still use. Sadly, the young owner we had met before had been killed in a traffic accident and his brother was now president. He agreed to make my chair. But the president's assistant never seemed to get the order right; there were numerous scheduling delays. The company operations were clearly not in good order. Also, my final bill was wrong. I suspected that this was because of a botched attempt by the company to avoid income tax.

Fifteen years later, a bizarre story unfolded about that company president and his assistant. They had hatched a scheme to defraud a New York bank of $30 million. They and a few other corporate officials created counterfeit purchase orders, on stationary from major furniture retailers. Using only these counterfeit orders for collateral, they drew on a line of credit with a bank that sent them as much as $.5 million a day. The bank did not discover the fraud. Nor did the furniture company's outside auditors. When someone else finally uncovered the fraud, millions of dollars were about to be transferred to Hong Kong. The president and his assistant were preparing to flee the U.S. themselves.

The assistant U.S. District Attorney who prosecuted the case is a friend. His mother and father are both CornerCap clients. Now in private practice, he shared some thoughts on this case:

- The New York bank had few controls on the young loan officer who loaned so much money.
- The auditors could easily have discovered the fraud if they had insisted on seeing the actual work-in-process at the furniture factory. Management always claimed that the work was being done in another building, or the finished goods were stored elsewhere.
- A number of side issues arose around this case. An earlier lending bank may have discovered the fraud, but rather than reporting it, allowed a second bank to take over the account. The first bank recouped its funds, but perhaps acted unethically in not reporting its suspicions about the furniture company's wrongdoing

In the end, this small business had several scandals relating to its cash management practices. A multitude of lawsuits was filed by Keylon management, a conglomerate that acquired Keylon, its major accounting firm, and several financial institutions that loaned money to Keylon. Some lawsuits have been settled while others are still pending even after all these years. In 1990, Keylon's president and other officers were found guilty of fraud and sentenced to maximum prison terms.

Analysis is sometimes a matter of a few sensible rules. Some people have "yardsticks" to measure performance in their own industry, and can quickly spot a fraud. (We are fairly capable of listening to an investment management story and gauging whether it makes sense as an investment strategy or as an investment business. If you are going to work in an industry, you had better be well enough versed in it not to be taken by frauds.) We had a client who was a very successful competitor of Keylon in the leather furniture market. He was quite familiar with the Keylon story. He said, "Everyone in the industry saw the sales figures that Keylon reported and thought they were a joke. We never believed that anyone would take the reported sales volumes seriously." This Keylon competitor said that either of two simple tests would have identified the fraud – First, ride by the small factory and count the cars in the parking lot. It would be impossible to produce the amount of furniture being reported with the limited work force that could arrive in such a small number of cars. Second, go to Marshall Field's in Chicago and walk through their furniture department. There was not a single piece of furniture produced by Keylon on the floor, despite all the reported sales to Marshall Field. Such an easy analysis would have saved the bank $30 million and great embarrassment.

CEOs and Common Sense

Revelations at Sprint about two top executives, their personal tax shelters, and the company's relationship with their auditor have raised some very interesting points that deserve a critique. Among them:

- Conflict for an accounting firm doing the personal taxes of executives while it is auditing the company.
- Advice of the accounting firms on very unusual tax shelter programs.
- Willingness of executives to enter into tax deferral or avoidance schemes suggested by those accounting firms in ways that put their entire wealth at risk.

This is not just another case of corporate misconduct, executive ego or greed. In many ways, these two executives who have been dismissed from top jobs at Sprint tried to do the honorable thing for their companies. They did not sell any stock. They took advice from one of the most highly regarded public accounting firms in the country. They laid their case before the IRS when they realized that their actions were questionable. And to date they have not been accused of doing anything "wrong" – whatever that means anymore. So if these two men are honorable, what is the issue here, and what might have been done differently?

On the first question – I see nothing wrong with the company's auditor doing the personal taxes of its executives. Maybe I'm naïve, but these two accounting functions just seem so far removed from each other that, under ordinary circumstances, a sensible person has to reach to find a conflict.

But what happened here was not ordinary. We move to point number two, the tax shelter programs. A couple years ago, a major accounting firm presented me the outline of a tax reduction proposal. It involved a complex group of offshore trusts and partnerships. The bottom line was that if the tax shelter program were done properly, the IRS would not see anything worth examining. This is a fairly poor defense of the entire proposal – "we're hiding things from the IRS where they aren't likely to look." Such programs were set up to defer or avoid taxes, and they seemed far outside the mainstream of preparing 1040s or auditing a company. The accounting firms themselves were enticed by the enormous fees these strategies would generate for them. They would not touch a deal with less than a $5 million dollar tax issue, and they would take something like 40% of the tax savings. So the accounting firms were preparing a study for the client, and realizing a minimum $2 million in consulting fees.

One tip-off about the validity of these deals was that the accounting firm made every prospect sign a confidentiality agreement so they could not share details with others. The accounting firm said this was to limit the number of users of such programs, because if they became widely used the IRS would shut them down. Not a very comforting thought.

Once again, a little common sense should have warned the two executives that they were in a dangerous area. They were not getting a guarantee from the accounting firm that what they were doing would be okay.

And finally, the executives violated two cardinal rules of sound investing – (1) diversify and (2) don't put your lifestyle at risk. While it is admirable to be loyal to your company and its stock, such action in this case violated these rules. To have so much net worth in a single stock, especially the company you work for, makes no more sense for the CEO than it did for the worker bees at Enron. If the two executives had exercised the options, and liquidated enough Sprint stock to pay their tax bill, they would not be in trouble today. Any shareholder can understand the need for company executives to sell stock, no matter how sacred, to pay the IRS. Even if they had entered the program to avoid taxes, they would have been wise to sell enough stock for reserves, in case the tax bill needed to be paid later.

A deal, similar to Sprint's, by Tyco executives gives a little more specifics about how the maneuver worked. As we said in a CornerCap newsletter, the problem is really with the boards of directors in granting this level of option incentives in the first place. $100+ million will tempt most people to pump up the stock price, bend/break the accounting rules, avoid/defer the tax, commit fraud, or whatever.

Should Management Defend the Price of the Company's Stock?

While I do not consider Warren Buffett a perfect role model, he never ceases to amaze me with his clear thinking and his behavior. I don't always agree with his tax policy ideas, but he has never given a reason to question his integrity.

As an example, he took a negative view on the price of his stock. Time and again we have seen CEOs issue press releases that tout their company's great future and attempt to justify the stock price, no matter what ridiculous heights a manic public has driven it to. Often these justifications don't make any business sense. But they do feed the appetite of stock buyers and send the stock to even higher prices.

In contrast, Warren Buffett ignores the price of his stock. Instead he focuses on what he refers to as the change in "intrinsic value" of Berkshire Hathaway, how much value has been added to the business enterprise. He considers that a much better measure of management performance than the stock price. Doesn't that make sense? He is measuring something over which he and his management team have considerable control and should be accountable for. They can't do much about the stock price.

The only pronouncement that I remember Buffett making about the stock was that it was too high, based on the underlying business value, and he wouldn't be a buyer. How refreshing! And what a model for other CEOs. Much shareholder anger and grief could be avoided if more executives would say something like this, "Look, we are a fine business with a great outlook for profit growth for several years ahead, but let's face it, our business model only supports growth of 15% a year, and our stock shouldn't be selling at its current multiple." Such statements might cause the stock, perhaps selling at a P/E of 35, to drop back to a P/E of 30 rather than climb to a 60 P/E on unrealistic expectations. But isn't that better than going up to a 60 P/E and then dropping back to 30 later? It's a lot easier on shareholders to take a 14% hit than a 50% hit, and a lot easier on management too. But you don't often hear managements talk that way.

Of course, advice from me, who has never even been close to being a CEO, sounds naïve. But there's one problem with that argument. Warren Buffett has done it – and the company didn't collapse, the stock didn't really suffer, and shareholders didn't complain.

Government

We – you and I, and our government – must avoid plundering for our own ease and convenience, the precious resources of tomorrow. We cannot mortgage the material assets of our grandchildren without risking the loss also of their political and spiritual heritage. We want democracy to survive for all ages to come.

President Dwight D. Eisenhower, March, 1961

Politicians Have a Hard Job

I can't be very hard on politicians. After all, they must tell at least 51% of us what we want to hear, or they will have to find another job. But it's hard not to find fault with the ethics of those in political power. And it doesn't really matter which party, Republican, Democrat, Whig, or Socialist, they all act about the same.

It is amusing to see the "scapegoat du jour" appearing before a congressional committee. The poor slob who got caught stealing hundreds of millions of dollars is sitting there declaring his innocence. To add insult to injury he is being lectured (for the benefit of the television cameras) by people who have cheated on college exams, have promoted special interests for their own benefit, have covered up their own misdeeds, and who daily make false statements about laws and taxes that would put ordinary citizens in prison.

Consider Social Security.[3] If any company in America reported its pension fund or its corporate profits the way the government reports Social Security, the

---

[3] See section on Social Security.

corporate officers would be imprisoned for fraud. In fact, corporate executives have recently been sent to prison for much, much less. Social Security and medical care are two of the major issues facing America in the next twenty years, yet in the Presidential campaign both candidates spent a great deal of time talking about what they did in a war thirty years ago, and very little time on these issues of major concern to all of us.

Another example is the great debate about American jobs going "offshore." The truth is that politicians, nor anyone else, can do much to stem this tide. We live in a world of open communications and free exchange of information. People in Asia will work for a lot less and they are going to find the jobs where they can compete. This is not a one-way street. In fact, America has had a net gain in jobs thanks to the foreign countries that have opened plants and offices here. But you don't hear much about that. It is the displaced workers in textiles, furniture, and the like who get all the press attention.

Typical of the rhetoric that politicians must give us was a recent speech by an Assistant Secretary of Commerce. She spoke at a local Economics Club luncheon. Being in the center of southern textiles, naturally in the Q&A session following her comments, someone asked, "What is the government doing about all the textile jobs we are losing?" The answer was something like this. "I have come here to visit Gastonia and Kannapolis (textile mill centers) and to see first-hand the problems. This administration is keenly aware of the plight of these workers, and concerned that their jobs have been sent overseas. In fact, we are so concerned that the President has authorized a $30 million study to help."

What is this about? The bottom line is that the government is going to spend $30 million of taxpayers' hard-earned money so that unemployed workers can be reassured that "something" is being done. And will hopefully vote for the people who are "helping" them. The Department of Commerce knows that there is nothing that will be done to bring these jobs back to America. What they should say, if they could speak honestly, is: "There are three points here: 1. These jobs are gone. 2. They are not coming back. 3. Your government will buy you a one-way bus ticket to anywhere you want to go to get another job." $30 million dollars will buy lots of bus tickets, and unlike a study, it might accomplish something.

All political parties die at last of swallowing their own lies.
    John Arbuthnot, writer and physician (1667-1735)

Globalization
Holding back the tide of global trade is a near-impossible task. And no politician can stuff that genie back in the bottle. Anyway, who has the moral authority to tell half the world's population – those living in China, India, Southeast Asia, Russia, and Eastern Europe – they can't participate in the great adventure of capitalism and trade?.[ix]

We get the government we want. It is so easy to criticize, to belittle, professional politicians. But do we really want "amateur" politicians? When the "everyman" goes into politics to teach the pros how to do it right, when the businessman goes into government to apply business principles to government, the failures greatly outnumber the successes. Why? Because the everyman and the businessman discover that, they are in a game with a different set of rules. A democratic government needs professional politicians – compromisers, arbitrators, negotiators. The qualities that we criticize – craftiness, waffling, misinformation, double-talk are the very skills needed to bring about the consensus that makes a democratic society work.

BUREAUCRACY

A committee is a cul-de-sac down which ideas are lured and then quietly strangled.
    Barnett Cocks

Company Policy

Company policy exists in any organization because every group needs a set of rules. As an organization expands, its purpose gradually becomes, not to innovate, but to perpetuate itself.

The world in general doesn't know what to make of originality; it is startled out of its comfortable habits of thought, and its first reaction is one of anger.
    W. Somerset Maugham, writer

The Monkeys

Start with a cage containing five monkeys. Inside the cage, hang a banana on a string and place a set of stairs under it. Before long, a monkey will go to the stairs and start to climb toward the banana. As soon as he touches the stairs, spray all of the other monkeys with cold water. After a while, another monkey will make an attempt with the same result - all the other monkeys are sprayed with cold water. Pretty soon, when a monkey tries to climb the stairs, the other monkeys will try to prevent it.

Now, put away the cold water. Remove one monkey from the cage and replace it with a new one. The new monkey sees the banana and wants to climb the stairs. To his surprise and horror, the other monkeys attack him. After another attempt and attack, he knows that if he tries to climb the stairs, he will be assaulted. Next, remove another of the original five monkeys and replace it with a new one. The newcomer goes to the stairs and is attacked. The previous newcomer takes part in the punishment with enthusiasm! Likewise, replace a third original monkey with a new one, then a fourth, then the fifth.

Every time the newest monkey takes to the stairs, he is attacked. Most of the monkeys that are beating him have no idea why they were not permitted to climb the stairs or why they are participating in the beating of the newest monkey. After replacing all the original monkeys, none of the remaining monkeys has ever been sprayed with cold water. Nevertheless, no monkey ever again approaches the stairs to try for the banana.

Why not? *Because as far as they know that's the way it's always been done around here.*

And that, my friends, is how company policy begins.

The Forms Control Specialist

When I worked as a cost analyst, I needed a form for a routine procedure that my department performed. It took about thirty minutes for me to lay it out and then I asked if we could get it printed. The person I asked in the print area (where our only Xerox machine was closely guarded) told me that he couldn't do it without approval from the parent company. I drove downtown to the headquarters building and met with the "Forms Control Specialist." He told me, "Boy, it's a good thing they stopped you before you printed this form on your own, or you would have been in a lot of trouble. We can't have people going off and making their own forms. It wouldn't meet the specs of print type, border, block layout, etc. And most important of all, it wouldn't have an assigned Corporate Forms Control number. That's my job – to design the form properly, assign it a number, and record that form in the official Forms Control Log."

Why did we do all that for a simple form? *Because as far as they know that's the way it's always been done around here.*

Sark and the French Invasion

Sark (one of the Channel Islands only a few miles off the coast of Normandy) is within sight of the island of Guernsey. When Queen Elizabeth I visited Guernsey, she looked at Sark and asked, "What's over there?" She was told, "An empty island." She said, "The French could claim that island at any time. Let's get someone to live over there and be sure it stays in British hands. Sark was divided into twelve parts and each part was given to a family to homestead. It would remain theirs free, so long as they maintained a cannon facing the sea to fend off the French fleet, should it arrive. Those cannons are still maintained today.

Why are those cannons still there? *Because as far as they know that's the way it's always been done around here.*

The Coffee Break

I once visited a corporate office where I worked on a project with some of their staff. At a coffee break, I went into the canteen area and got a cup of coffee. I took it back to my desk, and my host politely told me that coffee must be drunk only in the canteen. He said that the rule was supposedly made by the former officer who controlled all administrative functions at the company for many years. Despite the fact that she had been gone six years, the coffee rule was still in force.

Why must coffee be confined to one room? *Because as far as they know that's the way it's always been done around here.*

The Meeting Planner

Everyone thinks of himself as an essential part of the bureaucratic machinery. At the meeting planning section of a large company, one team member told me, "I am certain that my job is secure. My department plans three hundred meetings a year." He thought that each of those meetings was important. There was more than one meeting per business day, and each included airline tickets, hotel rooms, meals, and many other expenses. He might well have asked himself, "Are these meetings adding to the profits of my company? Or are they important because they give me something to do?" But instead he obviously took for granted that his work was essential. That's how a bureaucracy works. His job was to promote more meetings so that his department had more to do. And a rich company can afford that kind of thinking. It is much easier to tolerate it than to fire people. But when a new management took over the company, strapped for cash and loaded with debt, guess who was eliminated. The company discovered that it could survive with far fewer meetings and without many other formerly "essential" services as well.

Why did they have a meeting planning function? *Because as far as they know that's the way it's always been done around here.*

Innovation in a Bureaucracy

It isn't easy to create change in a bureaucracy. The entire system is built to resist change and preserve the status quo. Understanding the concepts of how organizations are structured for survival and how they resist change are useful skills. Tom Quinn and I were able to create RJR Investment Management within R. J. Reynolds Industries in 1983. We needed all the help we could get to bring about this change. Jim Hamilton, our outside consultant, helped tremendously in convincing our management that an in-house investment venture was worth the effort.[4]

CLIENT SERVICE

Happy Clients Are Critical

Being involved every day in client service, I've become keenly aware of the service level when I am a customer. It is amazing how many people are not trained to help customers. Time after time, I've seen the waiter or the hotel clerk or the retail sales person just putting in hours. They don't connect satisfied customers with their continued employment. They seem to think, "This would be a good place to work if we didn't have all these customers bothering us." Most of them don't seem to understand that they need to make customers happy. And management

---

[4] See Appendix One

should do a better job teaching them.

As an example of excellent service, I recently had a meal at Ruby Tuesday, a place that my granddaughters love. It was quick in-and-out, and it is understandable that they would not ordinarily get the highest quality waiting staff. To our surprise, the waitress was excellent. She was always nearby without being intrusive. When our little granddaughters needed more mustard for the hamburgers, she was there. She anticipated anything we wanted. She was polite and friendly, and not just at "tip" time. It wasn't big bucks, but I thanked her and gave her an extra large tip. She had earned it.

As for poor service, a few days later, Judy and I were guests at a new upscale restaurant. The owner was onsite and talked with us. It's always impressive when the restaurant owner is managing by what I call "just walking around." It's a fair bet that this restaurant will be a big success. However, there was a problem with our waiter. In a place like this, you would expect the help to be a notch above Ruby Tuesday's. Our waiter was competent, but he had no social skills for dealing with his customers. Our host ordered a glass of wine, and to my dismay the waiter told him that he had made a very bad choice in selecting a blush wine. In fact, the waiter said, he didn't consider blush wines to be wines at all. They were really soda pop. Our host, always the gentleman, simply said politely, "Well maybe I can learn something, what wine do you recommend?" The waiter had no idea how condescending he sounded. He made an extremely poor impression. And to make matters worse for the restaurant, he had no idea who he was lecturing on wines. His customer was the building owner and his landlord who had brought us to dinner to introduce us to the new restaurant. This man was in a position to recommend the restaurant to countless customers, and instead of royal treatment, he got a short lecture on his lack of wine knowledge.

If The Service Is Bad, Tell Them So

Businesses can't take customer service and satisfaction for granted. You ignore it at the absolute risk of your business. We at CornerCap understand customer service. We can't control stock markets. However we can manage the way we view our clients, our relationship with them and the service we deliver. As a customer, I won't tolerate shoddy service from people I pay my hard-earned money, and we don't expect our clients to tolerate it either.

The Airline from Hades

Following is an exchange of letters and emails with an airline, the result of a call to their customer service '800' number from an airport:

Letter to Gene Hoots
From Gigantic Global Airlines Customer Care Manager
Dear Mr. Hoots,

Thank you for taking the time to let us know about your travel experience. We appreciate the feedback, and regret learning of your disappointment in our performance. Your comments will be communicated to the appropriate area of Flight Operations and used for future coaching and training.

I truly understand the value of your decision to fly with Gigantic Global Airlines. We will make every effort to leave you with a better impression when we have the privilege of serving you again. Thank you again for sharing your comments. Your continued patronage is genuinely appreciated.

To Gigantic Global Airlines Customer Care Manager
From Gene Hoots

I received your letter thanking me for taking time to let you know about my travel experience. It was more than an experience. But a brief letter letting me know that you received a phone call from me and that my comments will be communicated to Flight Operations isn't very reassuring. Dealing with your personnel at Newark showed that they do not reflect your stated philosophy of customer care.

Friday May 28, our flight from Charlotte to Newark was delayed by thunderstorms in the Newark area. Our connecting flight was scheduled to depart at 6:30 pm. When we arrived at Newark there were understandable delays, though the weather had cleared. What was not acceptable was that our plane waited by the jet way for about 10 minutes. The pilot apologized saying that he had called three times for someone to connect the jet way so he could open the door and let us off.

My wife exited the plane and went immediately to a Gigantic Global employee at the gate and asked about the flight to Paris. The lady employee checked her computer and told my wife that our flight to Paris had gone and that we needed to get in the customer service line - an hour long at that point. While I was in line, my wife checked the departure board and saw that our flight had not yet gone. We hurried to the gate, thirty minutes late. As we arrived our flight was pulling away. The ticket agent knew immediately who I was and said that they had held the flight as long as they could.

We then went back to the customer service line for an hour wait to see an agent. During our wait there was an incident that did not involve us, but it gave a bad impression of your customer service personnel. Lines were long, and tempers were short on both sides of your service counter, understandably. I know that Gigantic Global does not control thunderstorms and that delays happen. However, a customer took a picture of the long line waiting for service. One of your employees over-reacted. He came from behind the counter and demanded that the customer give him the camera. This was not a good way to handle the situation. It made Gigantic Global Airlines look a bit like the Gestapo. The customer, in a loud voice, said, "This is still a free country, and no one is going to take my camera and no one is going to arrest me." Your employee withdrew, but it was not Gigantic Global's finest hour - to have a customer service person physically threaten a customer in front of 150 or so customers waiting in line, people who at that moment weren't thinking favorably about you anyway.

When I reached a customer service representative, the really indifferent attitude of your representatives became apparent. The lady curtly told us we could get a night at Howard Johnson and a meal in the airport. Since our flight did not leave until the next evening, I asked about any meals on Saturday, the next day. She said I would have to come back and see her again tomorrow for that. (This may be true but it's bad policy.) She explained that our bags would be held in Newark and we should go to the baggage claim area and retrieve them at carousel 4 (We figured out that it was actually carousel 8).

In the baggage area, after a thirty-minute wait, we talked to one of the three employees in the baggage room. (The other two were talking to each other about how their workday was over and they weren't staying past 10:30 pm., an option I would have liked for myself, as it turned out.) This lady assured us that our bags were at the airport and that they would retrieve them for us. We waited three and a half hours, and then the lady talked with us again. When she examined the situation carefully, she checked and then told us our bags had gone on the flight to Paris. So we had now waited at the airport for four and a half hours for bags that weren't there. The lady in the baggage room gave us a sincere apology, the only sign of real customer service I saw all evening - An "I'm sorry" goes a long way toward building customer relations, but you don't hear it often.

So we returned the next evening for our flight. To add insult to injury this flight was delayed an hour because two people had checked bags and did not show for the flight. Those bags were finally off-loaded. Just the opposite of what happened to us. I have gotten conflicting information, but it is my understanding that under today's security rules, bags will not be taken on a flight unless the owner is matched and on board. Even if taking the bags without the passenger is not a security problem, Gigantic Global certainly appeared inconsistent in allowing one flight to leave, and yet holding another flight for over an hour.

I talked to the chief flight attendant on our flight. She was very courteous and explained that she was the one who delayed this evening's flight, and that while my circumstances the evening before weren't exactly the same, it should have been handled differently. Perhaps she was just overly cautious, and I can't fault her for that, but again if Gigantic Global has a policy it was applied inconsistently.

On our return two weeks later through Newark, I again saw the same poor attitude. I was trying to see a departure board in an area. One of your employees had it roped off and I couldn't read the flight gate. I asked about this and she pointed vaguely toward another part of the terminal and told me to go there and look at a board. In general, this just reinforced the impression that your employees will direct a customer "anywhere, just so you will go away and become somebody else's problem." I waited, and in about two minutes the area cleared; I walked to the board and read my gate. A tiny bit of assistance from that lady would have made a very favorable impression.

It is disappointing to read in your in-flight magazine's letter to customers, which is pretty standard these days for every CEO - We want your business. You're very important. All our people are here to serve you. And then to compare that to reality. "You can pretend you care, but you can't pretend you're there."

At Newark your people were indifferent at best, and downright hostile at worst. A few simple changes in the way they performed could have gotten us on our flight. At the least, some attention to detail would have meant that we could have gone to our hotel without an unnecessary three-hour wait for luggage that wasn't there.

I must add that on our flight to Paris, the crew were very helpful, friendly, and did a fine job.

I write this to you because I am in the business of providing personal service to clients, and I'm very aware of service quality. I know that the airlines today are facing difficult times. But it doesn't help matters if your front line people have a bad attitude. In his letter the CEO also says that your employees think Gigantic Global is a great place to work. Even if that is true, in the final analysis, it won't matter what they think. It will only matter what your customers think.

As a final note, to make the point that customer perception is important, I would like you to know something about my wife. She is suffering from a very difficult disease. She was hardly physically able to make a long trip, but she did it because it was something that she believed she needed to do as a duty to someone else. She made no complaints about her personal discomfort or the inconvenience your people caused her. But she will not forget it. And when the name Gigantic Global comes up, her negative comments can offset an enormous number of your advertising dollars. I suspect that if she travels again, it will be very hard to persuade her to fly Gigantic Global.

I would appreciate a response to this letter. In sheer frustration, I called your complaint department while I was in Newark airport that evening. I received your letter to my home noting that you had registered my call. The letter did not say anything specific about my complaint or even that I had made a complaint. That alone doesn't inspire much confidence about what Gigantic Global might do as a result of my comments to make things better for your passengers.

Let's be very clear. I didn't call that evening to let you know about my "travel experience." I called to let you know what a really bad job Gigantic Global Airlines was doing in serving your customers.

Email to Gene Hoots
From Gigantic Global Airlines Customer Services

Your letter has been forwarded to my attention for research and a reply. I was deeply concerned after reading your letter to Gigantic Global Airlines Customer Care department. I truly felt your disappointment in our service and I want to extend to you and your wife a sincere apology. I cannot begin to express how disturbed I was after reading the series of events you described in your letter.

It is true, weather is a situation outside of our control, but the way we respond in that situation is what our customers will remember. Our representatives are to provide you, our valued customer, with a caring and professional attitude at all times. Reliable and accurate information is important in the jobs that we perform. Unprofessional service and indifference towards our customers is just not acceptable. I regret the negative impression this experience has given you of Gigantic Global Airlines and I want you to know how sorry I am that we did not meet your expectations.

Please know that we do care about our customers and your concerns are important to us. This information is documented in our Corporate Customer Care report for internal review by our senior management as well as the other departments where service concerns are listed.

As a show of my concern, I would like to send you and your wife a tangible gesture of good will, which you will receive by U.S. mail. I appreciate you taking the time to share your concerns with us and I hope you and your wife will allow us another opportunity to extend to you the quality customer service you deserve and we expect.

Thank you for allowing me the opportunity to address your concerns. Thank you for contacting Gigantic Global Airlines.

Email to Gigantic Global Airlines
From Gene Hoots

Thank you for your response. It makes a great deal of difference, a positive impression, when a customer just gets an acknowledgement that says - "Hey, we messed up, we know it, we apologize, and we'll do better."

Not to make a continuing issue of this for you, but if you want to talk with me about my impressions first hand, I would be happy to do so.

Email to Tom Quinn
From Gene Hoots

You might want to share this email with others at CornerCap. I was making a point here that, especially with old codgers like me, such bad service is just not going to be tolerated. This bunch in Newark couldn't have been much more rude if they had pulled out billy clubs and beat the customers.

I called their customer service line from the airport, and they sent me a form letter that brushed me off. It "thanked me for sharing my 'travel experience,' with them," as though I had written them a 6th grade essay about my summer vacation.

I am always telling people how proud I am of our entire team in Atlanta. But as I say in the letter about the chairman of Gigantic Global - It doesn't matter what we say or think about how great CornerCap is; all that matters is what the customers think.[5]

---

[5] See Letter to Hospital in Section 6: Key Issues in the Future – Crisis in Health Care.

DUTY

What Happened To "Duty"?

That word 'duty' isn't popular anymore. I never hear anyone say, "I did it because it was my duty." We do something because it's nurturing or fulfilling or enriching or fun or exciting or good for our health or helps us reach our potential. Duty has been out of style ever since the 60's. Reflection these days deals more with what we are owed, rather than what we owe. If we were brought into this world, shouldn't somebody be taking care of us? Shouldn't we be given good health, and good jobs, and maybe a Lexus or a Mercedes? And if we aren't receiving these things, then why not?

Rev. Neal Sadler, St. Matthew United Church of Christ, Wheaton, Illinois, 10/20/2002

Paul Tibbets

In his book, *Duty*, Bob Greene recounts his interviews with his father who served in the army in Italy through World War II and with Paul Tibbets, the pilot of the Enola Gay, the bomber that dropped the first atomic bomb on Hiroshima. Greene says that the biggest response from readers was about a statement by Paul Tibbets. "I cannot communicate with people who are less than sixty years old... We speak different languages." This also struck me as significant, perhaps because I was sixty the year he made the statement. I've thought about why he felt that way.

I've decided that a great barrier separates those of us born before World War II from those born after (only a very few were born "during".) Tibbets keeps coming back to the word "Duty." As Tom Brokaw pointed out in his book on *The Greatest Generation*, these people's lives were tempered as teenagers in the Great Depression of the 1930s. Their opportunities were limited – most had never traveled outside their home state and few had a chance to go to college. Then in their late teens or early twenties, a World War forced life and death options on them. They grew up quickly; they learned to set priorities about what was and wasn't important.

Paul Tibbets, probably the best bomber pilot in World War II, managed and trained eighteen hundred men for a life-and-death mission to drop the atomic bomb. He was twenty-eight years old. He said, "By that time I had the maturity of a man of forty. Where I was, you either grew up very fast at twenty-one or you didn't live to be twenty-two." That's the kind of work that tends to focus the mind.

It is surprising what a man can do when he has to, and how little most men will do when they don't have to.

Walter Linn

He said you were given a job and you did it. So when he speaks today, nobody under sixty understands him. His value system is completely different. For a generation born after 1945, with the exception of those who served in Viet Nam, the Gulf Wars, or a few other jobs, life has been pretty easy. Bob Kirby of Capital Guardian Trust, a man and a company I much admire, wrote in *Institutional Investor* in 1979, the 50th anniversary of the great stock market crash, that he was concerned about the future because of our easy life. He said, "Ease does not build character; adversity builds character." If Bob was concerned then, I wonder what he thinks twenty-five years later, because that quarter century has been pretty much a time of ease for America.

The Lifestyle Bubble
In the 1990's we experienced another bubble that probably had close parallels to the market bubble. However, the market bubble was easy to spot; I never recognized the second bubble, created by economic prosperity and the end of the Cold War.

A False Sense of Security
That bubble was a false sense of physical and emotional security. Looking back, we ask how we could have been so naïve when we saw the rest of the world suffering from terrorist attacks. We knew that countries were developing weapons – chemical, biological, nuclear. And Americans were at the head of their enemies list. Yet we couldn't make the connection that these people might use them on us. Of course, as things turned out, it was a far simpler matter to attack America than we ever thought. It didn't take nuclear capability or biological weapons. All it took was a few well-financed men who were willing to die. Like most revolutionary concepts, this one seems quite simple once someone else shows how to do it.

My son and daughter-in-law have lived in Paris for fourteen years. She is from Yemen, and they travel to the Middle East frequently. They are quite familiar with how the rest of the world lives, and they have pointed out that we in the U.S. have lived in a cocoon. We must begin to understand what the rest of the world thinks of us.

The message again is contrarian. Many of the rules we have used in investing also apply to other parts of our lives. First, we must be responsible for ourselves. Our government agencies will of course do their best. They too were weakened during the 1990s. I was appalled at an FBI report issued a few weeks before the bombing. It admitted that FBI agents had actually lost several hundred of their own weapons, including their personal side arms. Some of these had later been used in robberies. A number of computers were missing, including some with very sensitive data. Good heavens! If the individuals in a government investigative agency can't keep up with their own weapons and equipment, doesn't that raise a red flag about whether they're competent to protect us?

A General Decline

In fairness, through our complacency and "feel good" attitude, many agencies, along with the military, had their morale destroyed by a government that reflected the will of the American people. Yes, in a democracy we get the government we want. And in the 1990s we wanted a government to "entertain" us. It was great fun to learn about the President's latest misadventure or what kind of underwear he wore. Those were about the most important things we let our minds focus on. I confess that reading the news isn't as much fun anymore. Whatever else we thought about President Clinton, he certainly was a spellbinder, and he <u>was</u> entertaining. Bill Clinton was Wily Coyote. Every day I read the news about his official, and unofficial, activities as President. And nearly every week it seemed like he had just run off a cliff and was clawing the air to get a foothold. Then he would plummet down a few thousand feet and seem to crash. I would say to myself, "Well, that's the end of his career." And in the next scene there he was doing it all again, and always surviving. A truly amazing man! We have not seen a more consummate politician since FDR. I confess that his politics and mine differ, but I have an idea that if we met face to face, he would have me charmed and converted into a "friend of Bill" in less than five minutes.

We Wore Rose Colored Glasses

And with our easy lives, we tended to play, and our character- building suffered. I marvel at those we have chosen as our national heroes and role models. Athletes whose only credential is that they can play a sport better than most of us. Entertainers whose only credential is that they can act or sing or dance better than most of us. Yet we want to know every detail of their lives. We hang on to their every pronouncement on subjects that they are less qualified to speak about than we ourselves are.

Life for people of my age and circumstances has meant – 1. Work – That ethic was important. I started working in a lumberyard at fourteen. 2. Saving – There just might not be enough at some point, and no one ever knew when that was. It isn't always onward and upward – not in the stock market, not in the job market, not in relationships, and not in world progress. Lasting good comes only with hard work and thrift.

The economists who explain that "the best thing we could do for America is get out and spend" are amusing. As though throwing your money away is somehow going to save the world. I need look no farther than our client base to see the fallacy in that argument. Usually our clients are people who have saved all their lives. They have built a substantial asset base by saving and investing, and this gives them an independence that most people do not have. It allows them to take care of themselves, and in many cases, others less fortunate – either by gifts to family members or charitable organizations. They did not get in this enviable financial position by spending.

The same principle will apply in the future. Saving, not spending, is the route to prosperity. General George Patton said to his troops in World War II, "The object is not to die for your country; the object is to get the other dumb SOB to die for his country." A parallel holds in personal finance –"The object is not to spend excessively for the economy; the object is to get the other dumb people to spend for the economy."

In the market, we looked at valuation levels and said, "It can't last." Others said, "We don't see anything that's going to stop it." To which we replied, "Of course you don't see anything. The market goes to extreme heights because <u>most</u> people can't see anything that will stop it. But the higher the market goes, the more vulnerable it is to any disappointment, even one that might be shrugged off by investors if prices were at more reasonable valuations." Or as someone said, drawing a parallel to the beginning of World War I, "When the troops are massed, there's always an archduke somewhere ready to take a bullet." We never know who, or what, will "take the bullet" that sets off a bear market until after the fact.

A new generation, in fact several generations, are learning tough lessons. And they will adapt. Our lives have changed. We are suddenly looking to our President to give answers to some very tough questions. If there is anything good that comes from 9-11, it may be that we return to building character in our people again. That means growing up quickly.

I share Paul Tibbets' view. I see a diminished sense of duty almost everywhere. No one has patience. On the highway, self- absorbed drivers don't even have common courtesy. It is as though they own the road. In parking lots, they feel it is their god given right to park in two spaces, ignoring the inconvenience it causes others. In public places we talk loudly on our cell phones. We don't consider that others around us are not interested in what we have to say, and might want to have their own conversation or sit quietly without distraction. It is as though we feel that the rules don't apply to us, that we're special.

Too Much, Too Easy, Too Soon" – Way Too Much

The lack of responsibility can be explained by "Too much, too easy, too soon." So many of us have thought, "I'm entitled to it." People must learn that the universe does not revolve around them. Maybe there is still hope that young investors have learned something that will benefit them. A young man of thirty-four said that so many of his peers had become arrogant in the late, great Bubble. And why shouldn't they. They were thirty years old and had seen nothing but a rising market and rising economy since they were twenty years old – in other words they had seen the best of times all their adult lives. They were sure they had everything figured out – it was easy to make money, easy to get a job, and easy to retire at forty. Now they are a more subdued group. Perhaps they have paid a relatively small tuition to get educated in the school of hard knocks. It could have been much worse. The economy will muddle on, they will have decent incomes, and they will make money in the market during their lifetime if they have learned from this experience.

Children Forever

We have an entire generation that has never grown up. I see them preoccupied with the trivial and the superficial. Their lives center around "my needs" and "me." In a recent news story such people talk about the death of their parents – and even here, they focus on what this is doing to <u>me</u>! They describe themselves as very dependent on those elderly parents, and how the passing of the parents will make it very hard on <u>them</u>.

Their parents are the "greatest generation.", but I'm afraid that in raising the next generation, they tried too hard to shelter their young from the deprivations that they suffered. And again, "ease doesn't build character." When I die, I hope my children are sufficiently independent to get on with their lives. My advice to them will be, "I'm dead, get over it."

To avoid poverty, do three things: finish high school, marry before having a child, and produce the child after you are 20 years old. Only 8% of people who do all three will be poor; of those who fail to do them, 79% will be poor.[x]
William Gaston, assistant to President Clinton

Why Can't Gene Understand His Clients?

Like Paul Tibbets, I have trouble talking to people under sixty. This generation gap is painfully obvious when I'm discussing investments with the clients that I refer to as "second generation." But it is important to understand each other, and we continue to work hard at communicating.

In late 1998 we had poor results. One client had made a few million dollars on a technology startup and his CornerCap portfolio had done poorly for three months. He called us and demanded, in best "executive" mode - I want your specific plan on how you are going to recover in the next six months this major loss that we have suffered! I had no answer. No answer I could give would have been acceptable. He wanted CornerCap to correct his performance - solve this problem immediately. But what he demanded just isn't relevant to the market. We all take what the market gives us for any six months, maybe any six years. We do not control the market; it doesn't respond to our wishes. The client terminated us and moved heavily into technology stocks in late 1998. I don't know what happened to him, but I'll bet he has less money now. And six years later, he's probably discovered the futility of "planning" what you're going to make in the stock market. If he stayed with the small, risky technology stocks he told me he was investing in, he's going to need a twenty-five year plan to recover his losses.

While we were dealing with this client, we also discovered that many of our younger clients had made money in just one or two stocks, usually technology stocks. In more than one case, their gains had been spectacular; their undiversified portfolio had outperformed any portfolio CornerCap would have constructed during the time they had been investing (the time usually being some portion of the 1990s).

Here again, we could not communicate. When I used words like risk and value and bear market, I may as well have been speaking a foreign language. In fact I <u>was</u> speaking a foreign language. Their investing history was too short for any of those terms to have meaning. That has all changed now, and they and I have far more meaningful conversations.

Perhaps Americans Are Growing Up

Everything is not all right, it never was, it never will be…I remembered something my father once told my sister…when she walked into the dark room in which he was sitting and asked, 'Is everything all right, Father?' He answered her in a way that was humorous, succinct, and cosmically truthful. 'The last time everything was all right was August 15th, 1945.[xi]

The Mile High Club, Kinky Friedman

Most of you are too young to know anything about August 15, 1945, but the day is one of my earliest memories. It was my sixth birthday, but that's not why I remember it. [A few days before, my mother told me that America had dropped an atom bomb on Japan. I asked her what that was, and she said it was a "big bomb." That's about all anyone knew at the time.] On my birthday, we walked the three blocks from the apartment where we lived, and I stood at Fourth and Spruce Streets in Winston-Salem and watched a parade. My parents told me that World War II was over.

At that moment, the United States was the only world power, and as powerful as it was going to be until maybe the Berlin Wall collapsed forty-five years later – and maybe as powerful as it would ever be. That was a <u>big</u> day. And many of that generation feel they have watched the benefits of their hard-earned victory taken for granted and frittered away by the next three generations.

I was born at a dividing line. I was too young to know the Great Depression first-hand and just old enough to remember the last two years of World War II. And while I wasn't one then, I actually knew grownups. Not just people who got to be forty years old, but people who had become real adults at forty, or much younger. Those <u>real</u> grownups had struggled for twelve years to have a job and put food on the table in the 1930s (25% unemployment, not the 6% that the politicians now declare a "disaster"). Then they spent four more years sacrificing their lives to defeat an enemy that would have made our world a nightmare for only Heaven knows how many generations.

In the 21st Century, we are perhaps collectively growing up. The world isn't as simple or as much fun anymore. I am amazed at the number of people who looked at the world through rose-colored glasses, especially reflected in stock prices in the late 1990s. They thought the economy would grow forever, that peace was like fresh air – that it is there to enjoy and that the world is a benign place. But we're learning how naïve we were. My daughter who lives in Charlotte said to her brother after 9/11, "We must now be concerned with people killing us. It's awful!" Charles lives in France and has traveled extensively to such troubled spots as Yemen, Pakistan, Afghanistan, and much of Eastern Europe. His response to his sister was, "Get used to it. It's the way the rest of the world has always lived." Not only have we latter-day Americans been naïve, we've been hopelessly sheltered.

Just because I sound like an old crab does not mean that I think America is headed downhill forever. Like anyone now looking across a forty year age gap, naturally I'm a little puzzled by the actions of young people today, but that's only normal. In ancient Europe the elder generation thought kids were going to hell. And civilization has managed to survive for a long time since then. I think our attitude problems are certainly correctable. We've had a bad attitude for only thirty-five years, and that's a pretty small slice of history.

I believe our country is headed perhaps toward a new maturity. The United States is growing up. Not that we didn't have grown-ups anyway. It's just that all the real grown-ups are dying. World War II vets are dying at the rate of over 4,000 a week. We need a new generation whose mettle is tested by real adversity. For more than thirty years, many of this nation's best and brightest – in academia, media and politics – have devoted lifetimes to "concerns." The conceit was that we were so smart and capable that we could simply assign an agency to "eliminate risk in the workplace," rearrange college sports to achieve numerically perfect "gender equality," conquer cancer by declaring every enclosed space "smoke-free," eradicate a rampaging killer virus by engaging in "safe sex" or banish the existence of hurt feelings with the creation of speech codes.[xii]

Normandy
People sleep peaceably in their beds only because rough men stand ready to do violence on their behalf.
George Orwell

I was two weeks old when Hitler invaded Poland and my earliest remembrance of World War II comes from 1944-45. I recall seeing an endless stream of planes and gliders fly over our farm in Piedmont North Carolina. My guess is that they were on their way east to Fort Bragg. There the 82nd Airborne was preparing to meet destiny on the coast of France at a little town called Sainte Mere Eglise, a place nobody had ever heard of. Probably some months after those planes flew over, I watched my grandfather's grim face as we listened to the evening news with Gabriel Heatter – "Ah! There's good news tonight!" We got the latest war update.

At that time I got one more brief War memory. During much of the War, my grandparents, my Uncle Ken and his wife Ila, and I lived on a very isolated farm. Aunt Ila had an older brother, Everett, whom I saw only a few times. He was in the 82nd Airborne, Glider Group. He was killed at Normandy, and I remember attending his memorial service although the significance was lost on a four year old. Decades later, Ken told me about his last meeting with his brother-in-law Everett. It was shortly before the invasion forces left for England. Everett came to visit his sister and he took Ken aside and said, "I just want to tell you goodbye because I won't be coming back." Ken asked, "How can you be so sure?" And Everett said, "I'm thirty years old, and us old men are all expendable. They've put us in the gliders." The glider troops had almost no expectation of survival. This fine young man had considerable conviction that he would die, yet he volunteered anyway. Like millions of others, he left the farm or the factory or the school and did what he saw as his DUTY.

It was fifty years before those terrible, dark days came to mean much to me. Judy and I attended the fiftieth anniversary of D-Day in 1994. It was so impressive that last June, we had our son again drive us to Normandy from Paris. It was a few days after D-Day and there were no crowds, no celebrations. We walked on Omaha Beach and through the cemetery at Colleville sur Mer. I wanted to pay respect to the nine thousand American boys who are still there on French soil after sixty years. It is important that our children and grandchildren do not forget the sacrifices that these troops made when they did their duty on "The Longest Day." We are all beneficiaries of that. One World War II soldier said, "Tell them we gave all our tomorrows, so that they might have theirs." I want to take my granddaughters to Omaha Beach someday. They need to understand the price that somebody else paid for them.

2: PLAYERS

It doesn't matter whether you win or lose; what matters is whether I win or lose.
    Darrin Weinberg

The term "playing the stock market" never appealed to me. Investing is serious business, and while probability is involved, it is definitely <u>not</u> the same as a trip to Las Vegas. In Las Vegas the cards are stacked in favor of the house; the only player who wins long-term is the casino. This is true despite all the stories your friends tell about how much they made on that gambling weekend. By contrast, the stock market has been a winner for those who invested patiently and controlled their emotions.

Granted, investing is an extremely competitive "game." And in the game there are definitely "players." Sadly, in the wake of the bursting Bubble, we have learned that many of those players had stacked the deck in favor of <u>their</u> house. We have known for years about some of the unfair advantages that "the house" has had, but even cynics like us weren't prepared for all that has been uncovered in the last four years.

SECURITY ANALYSTS

Since the Bubble, analysts have fallen into ill repute. For years, we have understood the nature of analysts. At RJR Investment Management, Tom Quinn managed six hundred million dollars. Every day he received, unsolicited, a stack of analysts' reports several inches high. Tom knew that analysts' recommendations were badly flawed. He contacted each brokerage firm and requested that they take him off their mailing list. These reports were worse than useless. We had to pay someone to open the stuff just to be sure there wasn't something important (non-research information) in one of those envelopes. We developed our own research, which we still use today. (If you want to see the results of our research, ask us and we will share with you more detail than you will likely want.) Analysts are very useful in giving background information on a company or an industry, and if used properly, their information can be valuable. Just don't put faith in their rankings because they are influenced by many outside forces, not the least of which are the investment banking relationships with companies they are analyzing.

We were also aware that published financial data, not interviews with corporate management, are the best source of information. Many analysts seemed to enjoy their relationship with top corporate executives for ego-satisfaction. Still, every corporate executive is limited in what he can share with an analyst, without revealing inside information. If he is dishonest enough to engage in the practice, then he is also probably dishonest enough to lie to the analyst about the company's prospects. As in other areas of life, integrity counts a great deal in the long run, but frequently not much in the short run.

An examination of analysts' earnings forecasts for Enron between 1984 and October 2000 shows an uncanny ability to accurately predict almost $1 billion in profits that, in the end, never existed. Although only the analysts themselves can fully explain how they arrived at their estimates, the statistical examination suggests that Enron was adept not only at cooking its books but also at manipulating those who covered the company.[xiii]

Once I was talking to an Assistant Treasurer of RJR about an analyst/investment management firm that I was thinking of hiring. His only reaction was, "Didn't they write a negative report on RJR recently?" That comment spoke volumes about how he felt about my giving them our business. RJR did not prevent my doing business with the firm, but that is not the point. The point is that there is a natural animosity between corporate managements, especially those in the finance area, and analysts who are negative on the stock. That Assistant Treasurer had one major assignment – to assure that RJR maintained its AA bond rating in order to minimize borrowing costs. Losing that AA rating could cost this man his job. He had a personal vested interest in anyone or anything that was negative on the Company's finances, including a negative stock research report.

Firing Low, Hiring High

At one major fund, a veteran portfolio manager who had the misfortune to stick with his value stocks simply quit. He called technology stocks "tulip stocks" referring to the tulip mania of the 17th century. He retired in February 2000 after twenty years of sound investing and was replaced by two young portfolio managers who bought technology. Over the next sixteen months the holdings they placed in the portfolio declined 20%. If they had left the portfolio alone, it would have been up 22%.

Investment bankers who were taking companies public determined how much some analysts were paid, based on the analyst's ability to drum up IPO business. Some firms sold stocks even as they were placing "buy" recommendations on those stocks. Henry Blodget's pay was $2 million in 1999, $5 million in 2000, and then unbelievably $12 million in 2001 even after his recommendations had been destroyed in the market for twenty months. He was a major contributor to his company's bottom line. He was a regular on television business news. (In June 2001, he no longer appeared on TV because of an arbitration suit against him.)

For me, Blodget's major problem was his age. That probably speaks more about my age. I thought that he was much too young to know what he was talking about. Not that he wasn't bright and hard working. Just that he hadn't lived long enough to put his experiences into historical context. When I looked at seasoned veterans like Buffett, Templeton, and Jeremy Grantham, I saw men with scars from lost battles and bear markets. I knew they had enough experience to be worth listening to. But that doesn't explain why so many people did listen to "King Henry." They listened because he had a message that they wanted to hear. That's what a bubble is about – suspending disbelief – telling yourself that it really is true when you know that it doesn't make any sense.

First Call is a company that analyzes and tracks the forecasts of companies and analysts. Their spokesman has been Chuck Hill who appeared frequently on television business news. He has done extensive research on analysts' forecasts and results. He provided data for a *Financial Times* article, and the result is not good news for the analysts. Over an eleven month period, the analysts "strong buys" (and there were many) did only slightly better than the market.

From September 2000 - August 2001	
16 'Sell' Recommendations	4.00%
New 'Strong Buy' Recommendations	-19.00%
S&P 500 Index	-19.60%

In contrast, the few "sell" recommendations, a very small percentage of the total, outperformed the market by more than 23%. This is not an atypical scorecard for the analysts' forecasting ability.

Who Is Really At Fault?

The outrage has brought many revelations about analysts: Analysts tend to be bullish, especially about companies that give investment-banking business to their firms. Analysts are fuzzy about how they arrive at their recommendations and even fuzzier about how they arrive at their price targets. Analysts lick the hand that feeds them. Those in the forefront of the current stampede to heap scorn on analysts were, until quite recently, the analysts' biggest cheerleaders. When an analyst predicted a $50 stock would go to $500., why did the boob on the tube interviewing him not venture to be so rude as to question the basis for this forecast?

The news that analysts are subservient to the needs of investment banking, while investment banking is the source of their grossly inflated pay, has finally reached Washington. Eager to soothe Washington, Wall Street has formulated a code of behavior for analysts, "Best Practices for Research." It contains some truly novel notions: like the customer comes first, and it commands analysts not to lie, steal, cheat or consort with investment bankers. But the analysts merely provided the entertainment at the greatest party ever thrown. The folks really whooping it up were … just about everybody.[xiv]

Solution To The Problem

The bottom line is, like everything in life, that it's your personal responsibility to know what you are doing. It is so much less complicated if you don't lose your money in the first place rather than having to sue your brokerage firm to try to recover what "they" have lost. Investors should take responsibility for their own mistakes. No investor in Enron could make the case he couldn't know what he owned. The data were there. Investors must pick up the slack, do their own work, and take the heat when they mess up. Things just go wrong. Murphy's Law has not been repealed, although for two years, before March 2000, it seemed to have been suspended. The stock market is risky. Get used to it.[xv]

Analysts' Objectivity

Jack Grubman, the analyst, was negative on AT&T. His top boss, Sandy Weill, was on the AT&T board. Grubman's investment banking associates were not participating in a lucrative underwriting that AT&T was doing. He changed his rating to a buy, the investment bankers participated and got $44.5 million in fees, and then he dropped his buy rating. Was this coincidence?

The official story is that the AT&T chairman felt Grubman should take another look at the company, that he had misjudged its prospects. Weill requested Grubman to do so and AT&T did a "dog and pony" show for him. Weill said he never told Grubman what to write.[xvi]

At one point, Grubman suggested that he had upgraded AT&T because his boss had agreed to help get Grubman's twins into a prestigious private school. Serious analysts did things like that. This shows how little they cared about what such work was doing to their retail customers. When Weill asked Grubman to "take another look at AT&T", what did that mean? Anyone who has ever worked in a large organization knows that pressure from a boss can be subtle. Only the hopelessly naïve will ignore a boss's "suggestion." It looks as though Grubman agreed to up his ranking long enough for his company's investment banking division to get a consulting contract from AT&T. He then lowered his ranking. It also looks as though he agreed to do this provided his boss would use influence to get Grubman's five-year-old children into the private school. His company made a $1 million donation to the school, but said there was no connection to Grubman.

And so it went in the 1990s. The only ones who suffered were the millions of investors. Come on! How stupid do these people think we are? If my CEO and the CEO of a major customer (on whose board my boss sat) made a request of me, I wouldn't take it as a "request". Only an idiot would see it as anything but an order, if he valued his job. Once the Chairman of RJR called me to a meeting. He was an alumnus of the University of North Carolina –Chapel Hill. When I walked into the conference room he was there with three UNC Vice-Chancellors who had driven over from Chapel Hill. Seeing me as the investment guru of RJR (among the blind, the one-eyed is king), the Chairman said, "Gene, would you have some spare time to help UNC evaluate their endowment investments and work with them in hiring money managers?" What was I supposed to say, "Sorry, Mr. Stokes, I'm just too busy."? I actually did the job, and enjoyed it. But that is not the point. This was not a request; it was an order.

The Real Value Of Analysts

Analysts know a great deal about the businesses they cover, but their stock ratings (whether the stock will go up or down) are useless. They have a biased opinion; they do not want to give a negative ranking and displease the company that might use the broker's investment banking services.

This desire to please varies from analyst to analyst. Mostly it depends on whether they are a buy-side or sell-side analyst. These two terms are used rather loosely in the investment business, but basically: Buy side analysts work for money management firms, banks, insurance companies - firms that invest their money in the stocks. Sell side analysts work for the investment bankers and brokerage houses that make commissions when they get people to trade the stocks.

Every institutional person knows these research recommendations are worthless. But there are millions of individuals who believe that what they read and see on television is objective. The average buyer of stocks in the 1990s truly believed that the analysts knew what they were doing. After all, the stocks they recommended went up day after day. But everything was going up in that insane period.

Getting To Know Management

People often ask us – Do you talk with company managements and get to know them? We believe this is a useless exercise. We get all the factual information we need about the company from the data that others have gathered. And management opinions about where their stock is going are as useless as those of everyone else. Over the years, I have had only two discussions with management about their company's stock, and I remember both of them vividly.

One was with a tobacco company CFO who was a friend of mine. In a phone conversation about something else, I asked him about the prospects for his company's stock which had been going down, or at best sideways, for a couple of years. He said, "Nobody here (meaning the management) sees any reason for it to go up." It doubled in the next year.

The second incident was even more discouraging. I remember exactly where it took place. Judy and I were in the lobby of the Brown Palace Hotel in Denver on a Saturday afternoon in 1986. We happened to meet the president of a NYSE listed company whom we had known casually for years. He had left North Carolina and moved to another state. His company was having operational and financial problems. I casually mentioned that I followed his stock, but I said nothing about their problems, not wanting to embarrass him. Without being prompted, he said, "Yes, our stock has been down (from 25 to 6) and we are very concerned about it. We are working to turn things around and to restore shareholder value." He said all the right stuff. But in a year or so, the company went under. He and the CEO had been looting it. Their behavior bordered on criminal. I never talked with him again. But to show that some people never learn, a few years later I read that a company in their industry had hired this ex-CEO as a consultant. And in no time at all he had that company teetering on bankruptcy and threatening to sue him.

So there you have the benefit of my only experience with corporate management as a source of investment information. If they have bad news they probably won't tell you, and if they deliver good news you probably can't trust it. So look at the numbers yourself and draw your own conclusion.

Living In The Past

In most cases, your broker today "isn't your father's broker anymore." Some investors have dealt with their retail broker for decades. They still call their broker and ask for the "rank" on a stock that interests them, despite the fact that the rankings are worthless. Such a customer usually thinks of himself as a very successful long-term investor (if you buy and hold Exxon, for example, for forty years your gains will look enormous). He has no idea how much of his large gain is attributable to simply being patient with the market for forty years and how little is due to his broker's "research."

The analysts are all very bright people. In 1999-2000, they knew that millions of people trusted them even though their recommendations were wrong. There are stories that these analysts swapped emails with each other about how bad their recommended stocks were.

The analysts ranking nomenclature should have been a clue to how the system worked - "strong buy", "buy", and "hold". The proper ranking should have been "buy", "hold," "sell." But they never used the "sell" word. If a stock got so bad that they absolutely could not tell people to hold it then they simply "dropped coverage" - meaning they discontinued writing about it rather than tell people they should sell it.

The Conservative Analyst

One very conservative brokerage firm serves small communities. Its brokers tend to recommend local conservative stocks. For instance in my geographic area, the firm might recommend Wachovia Bank and Carolina Power. In Montana their analyst recommended Montana Power at $45 a share. But staid Montana Power entered the telecom business and lost a lot of money. The broker's analyst kept a "buy" recommendation on it until it hit $12 and then she put out a "sell" recommendation, explaining that she had just "missed" the business downturn. But she was at least right on her second recommendation; the stock is now $.26 per share. And so it goes with analysts.

The High Flyer

As a final example, let's examine a company that has been something of a Wall Street darling in the last few years. It was a successful IPO, one of very few in the last four years, and it soared to a P/E ratio approaching 100. This was largely based on a very high earning growth rate early on and analysts' projections that annual growth could be sustained at 30% for years to come. But for quick-and-dirty stock analysis, I look at the company's return on book value and its debt level. Based on that, the company could sustain a growth of just 13%. The only way it could increase growth was to borrow much more heavily (leverage up) or greatly increase its profitability on the assets employed. Neither seemed very likely, especially a big increase in profitability. Competition doesn't allow that to happen very often. As this became apparent, along with some other bad news, the stock dropped 75%, approaching its IPO price. This has been a major disappointment to investors, but a confirmation of the conservative, value approach to picking stocks. At some price, this stock will be a good investment. But we'd rather own it when others become disillusioned rather than when they are enthusiastic about great future profits.

Final Thoughts

As the punishment of the "creators" of the Bubble draws to a close, we should keep in mind that there are no easy remedies for this sorry episode. The proposed $1.4 billion settlement between major brokers and various agencies will not solve the problem. The analysts probably were not guilty of criminal behavior. The internal emails they wrote were likely more absurd office politics than real opinion. Even more ridiculous is the intent to physically separate equity research from investment banking. Questions arise immediately. How far should they be separated? With email and phones it is impossible to keep people from communicating if they work for the same firm.

I am amazed at the number of people who still call the brokerage firm to get their "rating" on a stock – despite the publicity that shows these broker ratings and asset allocation models are no better than throwing darts or flipping a coin.[xvii] For a few hundred dollars a year, you can get all the research you need from the *Value Line Investment Survey*. It gives historical data and projections for 1700 companies. It has been a building block in our research process at CornerCap. Even this research is no better than the underlying numbers supplied by the companies themselves. And that has become something of a problem, with rogues like Enron and WorldCom around. We think that the bad numbers have come from only a few companies and that the process will be corrected.

INVESTMENT MANAGERS

A man who has never gone to school may steal from a freight car; but if he has a university education, he may steal the whole railroad.

   Theodore Roosevelt

A Preventable Fraud

Prominent money manager Alan Bond, who appeared regularly on the television show "Wall Street Week," was convicted of fraud for cheating pension funds out of millions of dollars. Bond, a Dartmouth College and Harvard Business School graduate, is now indigent.

Bond was arrested and accused of defrauding clients by sending unprofitable securities trades to their accounts while directing most of the profitable ones to himself. Authorities said Bond made $6.3 million from the cherry-picking scheme while his clients lost more than $56 million.

Bond had an opulent lifestyle - dozens of cars, a large home, a beachfront condominium, and frequent shopping sprees. His American Express bills ranged from $200,000 to $470,000 a month. "Mr. Bond said he acted in pursuit of dreams," the U.S. District Judge said. "Dreams is a euphemism for what I characterize as greed and ego."

He did this while out on bail awaiting trial on previous charges of taking more than $6 million in kickbacks from brokerage firms. Bond had already been sentenced to twelve and a half years in prison for cheating clients and ordered to pay $6.6 million in restitution.

He would wait until the market closed before deciding whether to allocate trade proceeds to his account or his clients. Of 605 profitable trades he made over fifteen months, Bond credited 562 to his account, authorities said. Ninety-six percent of the 1,186 losers went to his clients.

Personal Responsibility For Picking Your Advisor

Alan Bond is one of the most dramatic examples of unscrupulous investment advisors. But this could not have happened if the clients who chose his firm had exercised even minimal due diligence. All the signs were there that this business was out of control.

The key in picking an investment advisor is to know the person who is handling your money. Character is far more important than investment philosophy or past performance. If you don't have the right people, the other things don't matter. In the case of Mr. Bond, minimal investigation would have shown that there was something seriously wrong. Anyone even casually acquainted with the investment management business would know that on the $600 million Bond had under management, it would be impossible to honestly generate enough income to support his lavish lifestyle. The signs might not have been obvious to a private client, but any person in the investment business or any consultant who screens investment advisors should have seen the problems.[xviii]

BROKER ADVISORS

An account executive at a brokerage firm telephoned a client who had purchased his first stock - Proctor & Gamble. The broker said that he had just heard they were going to split. "Oh! What a shame," the client lamented. "I'm so sorry to hear that. And, they've been together for so long, too."

A broker called his elderly client and told her that he had sold her Hewlett-Packard. She said, "That's ok. I never liked their cars anyhow."

There are good brokers and bad brokers. Some are very good at taking care of their clients. You must sympathize with their lot. They have to be educators, confessors, psychologists, and cheerleaders. It isn't easy playing all those roles. It involves hours on the phone trying to solve clients' problems, and endlessly listening to their fears and complaints.

But if you seek a broker to give investment advice and manage your funds, as well as custody them, it is your job to know the kind of broker you are choosing. A word of caution – as with money managers, too many people are in the brokerage business who don't belong there. In 1987 a fellow worker in New York, and a very fine analyst/portfolio manager, said that only about one third of the people in our business know what they are doing. And after years of observation, I agree. Two thirds are not competent money managers. Oh, they make a good impression and use all the current buzzwords in a presentation, but they really don't know how to manage money competently. And when you set out to find help, you had better be able to separate the sheep from the goats.

Brokers, like investment managers, tend to follow the crowd, but the herd instinct is very prevalent among brokers. They are part of a large organization, and to varying degrees, depending on the individual brokerage firm, they must stick to the corporate "story." You want a broker with maximum freedom to give you objective advice.

Don't take a butcher's advice on how to cook meat. If he knew, he'd be a chef.
Andy Rooney

Brokers Aren't Always the Villains

Our criticism was not of individual brokers during the bubble. Many of them did not sign on to the new economy and technology stocks. Rather, we complained that the brokerage firms sent a message that customers wanted to hear – the new economy was real and technology stocks would be big winners for years to come.

There is an effort to paint the wacky bubble as a conspiracy. One couple lost millions while they were receiving advice from Morgan Stanley. Yet, the couple rejected repeated advice to protect their huge stake in Microsoft with a hedging technique that would have prevented a large loss, but at the cost of missing any large gains on the upside. Their decision amounted to a big bet that Microsoft would continue to go up. That is not unreasonable, but they also decided to finance other investments with borrowed money. They borrowed to pay taxes and other expenses and they also borrowed to make other unsolicited purchases of other tech shares. With their margin calls during the collapse, their $11 million shrank to $1.6 million in seven months.

Unless you make a career of it, stock picking is a fool's entertainment. The marketplace offers plenty of nifty products that allow investors to sleep at night. It's hard to feel sorry for investors who thought they were entitled to year after year of implausible, unprecedented returns on their life savings.[xix]

A Broker's Lament
Grubman has made a fortune for himself and for the investment-banking division. However, his investment recommendations have impoverished the portfolio of my clients and I have had to spend endless hours with my clients discussing the losses Grubman has caused them.
Retail Broker, *Wall Street Journal*, May 2, 2003.

So Grubman cost his clients lots of money and the broker had to explain it to them. What about the broker himself? Didn't he know any better? Was he just sending out the buy recommendations of the firm? Do this test – If your broker/advisor was telling you to switch into technology in late 1999, then you had better find another advisor. The one you have doesn't have the analytical resources to recognize a decent investment, or he doesn't have the will to stick with what makes sense. Either will cost you a great deal of money over time.

Rating a Broker
Below are ten comments that are red flags in dealing with a broker. [Our opinions are in the brackets at the end of each paragraph]. The right answers don't change because the market is up or down. Sound investing principles stand the tests of bull and bear markets. Many investors are misguided by ignorant or unethical people in our business, and a comparison might be helpful.

After getting battered by the stock-market, many folks are turning to brokers and financial planners for help. The problem: As you look for top-notch advisors, none of the usual tests help much. Sure, your friends might rave about a particular advisor. But if your friends are financially unsophisticated, how can they judge the quality of advice they have received? Similarly, an advisor might have a spotless record with securities regulators. However, because an advisor hasn't ripped off clients isn't a good endorsement. So what should you do? Consider the list below... If you hear any of these ten lines, you should grab your money and run very fast in the opposite direction:

"We need to completely reposition your portfolio." Your advisor might revamp your investment mix when you first sign on. However, if he wants to overhaul your portfolio again, either the initial advice was bad or he is looking to collect commissions. [CIC – We will examine your portfolio and make as few changes as possible for your long term objectives. Trading is expensive, and the less change the better. It will likely be necessary to make some changes, but the costs of change should be explained, as well as the expected benefits from the changes.]

"What you really need is cash-value life insurance." Policies which combine life insurance with investments occasionally make sense, especially for estate planning. But cash-value life insurance is a big money maker for advisors, so be wary of anyone who pitches it as a universal financial solution. [CIC – An advisor should present insurance as part of a financial and estate plan. Cash-value insurance may make sense, but compare it to the much less expensive term insurance. CornerCap does not represent any insurance products. We prefer to refer clients to experts in the field, and to analyze the insurance proposals for clients as an objective resource.]

"With B and C shares, you avoid the high cost of load funds." If you purchase the A shares, you may dodge the initial sales commission. But one way or another, advisors will get their cut, either from the fund or through some sort of asset-management fee. [CIC – For larger individual clients, CornerCap does not use mutual funds, except for very special "niche" products where the fund offers a specific expertise that CornerCap cannot provide directly. CornerCap does offer smaller investors a family of mutual funds. These are mostly our own internally managed funds that carry no loads and no 12b-1 fees. We are careful to spell out the expense ratios for these funds.]

"This variable annuity is perfect for your IRA." An individual retirement account gives you tax-deferred growth. Why put a tax-deferred annuity inside it? Advisors will talk up the annuity's usually useless insurance feature because annuities generate lucrative commissions for the advisor. [CIC –Annuities carry large costs. The client is paying these costs to defer taxes on the earnings from assets placed in an annuity. However, an IRA already defers taxes, so the client is paying for an advantage that is useless. Sales commissions are very high on these products, and they are sold aggressively.]

"It's a safe way to earn 8%." Treasury bills, those short-term government securities that currently yield just above 2%, are considered risk-free. Anything that promises a higher return involves higher risk. Avoid advisors who tout performance without mentioning the risks and costs involved. [CIC – There is no free lunch. When a return is higher than the risk free treasury rate, there is always some risk. We are careful to describe the risk that goes with the potential rewards for any investment.]

"It's a great opportunity, but you need to act quickly." If you invest for goals that are years or decades away, you should never have to make a snap decision. [CIC – We urge clients to never make hasty decisions on any investment. An investor should take time to feel comfortable with his decisions.]

"I've got a great record." Unless an advisor has a verified performance history, you can't assess such claims. However, most investors lag behind the stock-market average. Avoid advisors who assure you they can do better. [CIC –Ashland Partners verifies our compliance with GIPS on a firm-wide basis. Verifications provide additional assurance that the firm's policies and procedures are designed to calculate and present performance results in compliance with GIPS. The data are accurate and calculated to supply meaningful information about our past performance. Past performance is not a guide to future results for any investment firm. Much more important, the client must be comfortable with our philosophy and long-term approach.]

"You need to save $379 every month to pay for your daughter's college education." Such precision has an air of authority, but it doesn't do justice to all the financial uncertainty involved, including what returns you will earn, what will happen with your tax rates and how much your investment goals will ultimately cost. [CIC – We give broad indicators for saving, and spending, for our clients' planning purposes. However, many variables affect future investment results. Projections are only a guideline. Pinpoint detail in numbers shows mathematical accuracy; not necessarily more useful projections.]

"Let's be conservative and assume a 12% rate of return." With pie-in-the-sky return assumptions, any investment plan and the most expensive financial product can look good. Be suspicious of any advisor who confidently predicts double-digit annual returns. [CIC – We try to avoid making <u>any</u> projection about future returns, but for long-range planning, assumptions are necessary. We use the historical returns for stocks and bonds – about 9% for stocks and 6% for bonds. We also include a much lower, "worst case" scenario. Currently, after a long period of high returns in the 1990s, for the next several years, the markets could easily provide a sub-historical return. That should be a caution to those who expect immediate positive results from stocks.]

"You can spend 10% of your retirement portfolio each year." If you are saving for retirement and your returns don't match your advisor's promises, you will be disappointed, but you can always compensate by saving more. However, if you are retired, the consequences could be devastating. If you spend too much, you could quickly deplete your portfolio. Today, prudent advisors generally suggest 65-year-olds withdraw only 4.5% or 5% of a portfolio each year. If an advisor tries to entice you with a withdrawal rate above 6%, it's time to lace up your running shoes and edge toward the door. [CIC – The percent that you can take from your retirement portfolio depends on many factors including life expectancy and future return on investment. With an expected return of 7% for a long-term retirement portfolio, if you draw down more than 4% a year, the income may not keep pace with inflation. Older retirees may feel comfortable drawing down more, but they must realize they are invading principal, and their total portfolio will most likely shrink in the coming years.][xx]

Strategists – Model Portfolios

All major brokers publish a model portfolio. Of twelve firms' model portfolios over a five-year period, the best portfolio outperformed the market by almost 3%, a good record but far less than the brokers suggest they can do in their promotional materials. The average underperformed the market by 1.6% a year, and only two of the twelve brokers outperformed the market.

Brokerage strategists who lay out a suggested asset mix of stocks, bonds, and cash each year are equally disappointing. As a group, the brokerage firms get this wrong too. Year after year, customers would fare better by just picking a single strategy and sticking with it rather than altering their mix based on the brokers' advice.

Oversight Or Tunnel Vision?

A lack of supervision and willingness to overlook bad behavior contribute to the brokerage firms' problems. A lady was a star at one major firm and another firm hired her with a $1 million signing bonus. She was given no training, no compliance supervision, yet she was handling $165 million in client assets. She found new clients in 1999 and criticized them for holding conservative municipal bonds. She showed them "results" that indicated she had made 50-70% a year for her clients, but the new clients apparently did not ask her how she did this, or for how many years. Sounds like greed, doesn't it? They subsequently lost 85% of their nest egg. She also lost money for seventeen relatives. Her brokerage firm settled with six of them for over $660,000. This probably makes for fairly icy conversation at family get-togethers. No one in her firm questioned what she was doing until the portfolios declined. In one instance, she is said to have promised a widow that she would take $500,000 and invest in stable assets that would produce $4,000 a month in income. That should have been a tip-off. $48,000 a year on $500 thousand is 9.6% cash yield. In 1999, a conservative portfolio might have yielded a third of that amount. If this promise was made, it couldn't possibly be kept.

And in another case, this same brokerage firm wooed a couple for their business. The couple had a single stock worth $48 million and the broker's top executives met with them to explain all their services. The couple claims they told the broker to sell their shares but the trade was never done. Yet the couple never seemed to demand an answer about why the trade wasn't made. There was a question about the ability to sell the shares because they were restricted shares, apparently purchased in a private transaction. In this case, the couple won an arbitration award of $7.7 million, a small fraction of the assets they started with. Who was actually at fault? The brokerage firm could probably have done a better job of protecting its clients' interests and in educating them. But weren't the clients also responsible for what was happening to their investments? A diligent investor would not watch $48 million disappear without raising some serious questions.[xxi]

In yet a third case, a broker treated his clients to a wild ride during the bubble. He became a broker just as the technology boom was beginning. He and his clients rode the market up and back down. So, many of his clients are hardly poorer than at the beginning, but they are bitter now. By late 2002, the firm had paid out $1.5 million in four cases against the broker. The broker says he maintained many conservative accounts for clients, but some pressured him to go entirely into technology stocks. In an atmosphere of continuing litigation and animosity, clients are asking themselves who they should blame – the broker, his firm, the analysts, themselves? There is plenty of blame for everyone, but guess who is out the money? The clients. And if they had done due diligence, they wouldn't need to recover their money.

A final example is another broker who changed firms. He had no compliance. He generated commissions of $6 million on about $100 million of client assets. A more appropriate commission level would probably have been $200-350,000. But his managers never asked why the firm was paid so many commissions. Against the rules, he was allowed to keep a personal computer in his office. And with this computer he did what the rules were intended to prevent – he falsified the clients' accounts. So while they thought they had huge gains, their funds disappeared and they were left mostly broke. It would be almost impossible for one person to carry out such a scheme, to create and mail false statements, if <u>anyone</u> in his office had been questioning his activities.

Brokers aren't going to change. They will always give the suckers what they want to buy. Right now the mood is gloomy, so of course they are touting safety, preservation of principal, and income. Where were they with that advice when you needed it? They were touting what you wanted to hear then, and what you want to hear now. As investors sink into despair, there will be more reassurances that brokers are the people you need. And just when you need someone to tell you that stocks are cheap and should be bought, there won't be anyone there to do it – because the broker knows that message will be unpopular and who wants to deliver an unpopular message. That only gets the messenger shot.[xxii]

Supporting The Syndicate Bid – A History

I got my first investment banking lesson in the 1970s as Malcolm McLean, the largest shareholder in R. J. Reynolds, sold large blocks of his stock in secondary offerings. Mr. McLean had engineered the sale of his company Sea-Land, the containerized shipping pioneer, to RJR in 1969. (See Mergers & Acquisitions section) Like most entrepreneurs, he was unhappy in a bureaucratic organization, and so he set about selling huge blocks of his RJR convertible preferred stock to raise cash for new personal ventures. These secondary stock offerings generally were for about $20 million, large in that day. A broker syndicate would agree on a price with him for his shares. Then the syndicate, usually several brokerage firms, would sell the shares to the public. It worked this way:

The army of retail brokers would call their customers and explain that on a given day (probably in a few weeks) shares of RJR stock would be offered at <u>no commission</u>. At that time, commissions were not insignificant and this was a big selling point. The brokers would also explain the merits of owning RJR stock, fundamentally a good thing. The customer would agree to buy the stock at the closing price on the designated day.

Let's say the syndicate had 500,000 shares to sell for Mr. McLean. Using their huge sales force, their objective was to sell every share of the stock, and if possible, to sell an over-subscription. Let's suppose that they got customers to commit to a total of 540,000 shares. Now the syndicate had to move 500,000 shares for Mr. McLean at a fixed price. If the issue was oversubscribed, then the syndicate had purchased 500,000 shares and had agreed to sell 540,000 shares. It was therefore "short" 40,000 shares. How would they get those shares? On the afternoon of the offering, the syndicate would begin to buy the shares needed to cover their short position, and usually the stock would rise as they bought this large block. This had the effect of raising the closing price by perhaps as much as $1 per share. But that made no difference to the syndicate since their customers had agreed to take all the shares the syndicate held at that day's closing price. So the syndicate paid Mr. McLean his agreed price for his shares, and pocketed the difference, a spread the syndicate had created by over-selling the issue.

This spread would represent a handsome profit to the syndicate brokerage firms. Was this illegal? No. Was the syndicate within ethical bounds to do deals this way? It can be argued that they were because they clearly took risk. If they could not sell all the shares, then they still had to buy Mr. McLean's shares, and they might be stuck with them in their inventory, perhaps eventually selling them at a loss. But it didn't usually work that way. For a few hours the next morning after the deal closed, the price of the stock would stay steady and then it would drop more than normally. Why? The stock was no longer being supported by the syndicate bid – meaning that the syndicate had covered its short position and wasn't buying any more stock.

Customers did get the stock without paying a commission. And with RJR, they were well served by being urged to buy the stock. It was a great investment over the next fifteen years. But it still seemed a bit shoddy to have the customers buy shares in a deal that was set up to extract top dollar from them with the likelihood that in the short term the stock would probably fall to a price that would be cheaper than the price they paid.

Advertisements – What's Wrong With This Picture?

This ad from a major business magazine suggests a sense of urgency in investing. It implies that the professionals have an advantage that you can get too. In fact real professionals use no such tools. Warren Buffett doesn't even have a calculator, let alone a quote machine or real-time information. Such immediate information is mostly for entertainment value. As for getting to listen in on the corporate analysts, these are the same people who told us to buy technology stocks. The sad truth is that all these so called "tools" to give the investor an

> **"The .com Real-Time Streaming Stock Portfolio"**
> **- Capitalism in Real Time.**
> **Now you can invest like the pros.**
> Access a powerful suite of real-time investment tools
> Create a real-time watch list
> Get real-time news
> Listen in on corporate analyst conference calls
> Select market-moving variables
> Track your portfolio with alerts on news, analyst comments, and prices
> Discover a host of trading tools unavailable anywhere else

advantage will give no advantage at all. There is no immediacy about the investment process; it can be carried out deliberately and without haste. A serious financial publication should be ashamed to run an ad like this.

The following ad from a major broker is sound advice. But who is the ad talking about? It suggests that the client hasn't done these basic things to avoid the bear market, but that brokerage firms have.

> **There are two times when people forget their investment principles. At the top of the market and at the bottom.**
>
> It wasn't easy sticking to long-term principles when it seemed like everybody else was getting rich in the short term. It's even tougher now, when the tide has turned and you see the investments you've counted on for your future begin to shrink before your eyes. But the fact is, basic investment principles are most important precisely at the times when they seem most irrelevant. There have been 30 bear markets in the last 100 years – each one followed by a recovery. The people who have weathered the storms and reached their goals have been the people who have had the courage of their convictions. So stay the course. Focus on your long term goals. And work closely with a financial advisor. The principles of investing aren't exciting or easy. All they are is true.

Nothing could be further from the truth. Brokerage firms misled, misguided and mis-sold their customers during the bull market. They were as guilty of violating these rules as the clients were. They didn't stick to long-term principles, because they had no long-term principles except to get the client to generate a commission immediately. We saw brokers place clients' IRAs into annuities that the clients didn't need, and the brokers got large commissions for doing so.

The brokerage industry had a miraculous conversion to "old time, value-oriented, balanced portfolio, conservative religion". But it came three years too late to help the customers. And it came because their survival depends on convincing the customer that this is what they believed all along.

Never mind that their previous ads and actions demonstrated otherwise. Facts should never get in the way of a good sales pitch. So what can the customer expect? Just what he's always gotten. Promises that the broker knows the true path to success – which still means whatever is popular at the moment. Just now, what happens to be popular also happens to be right, but both the customers and the brokers will quickly forget this. At some point, when it is again a very "good time" to buy stocks, these customers and brokers will be putting all their money into something else – bonds, money market funds, real estate, or hedge funds.

> **The way to approach an uncertain market isn't uncertain at all.**
>
> As an investor you're concerned about the market volatility. But by continuing to take a disciplined approach to investing, your Financial Advisor can help guide you through the current market uncertainties. The first step is to ask your Financial Advisor about the latest research from our award winning team of analysts worldwide. This perspective will help you make decisions as you and your Financial Advisor review your financial plan. (November 5, 2001)

The average person should not buy stocks on his own. Nearly everyone will follow the crowd. It takes a strong will to think for yourself, especially in an area that most people don't take time to understand. Very few people can do it. That is why they need an advisor who knows what to do and will do it, even when it is unpopular. The ad certainly tells the truth. What it doesn't tell you is that almost none can, or will, follow the basic principles.

This ad also has excellent advice. But where was this ad when it was needed in 1999 and early 2000? Then, only one of their analysts was being touted. He was a king of technology stocks, urging the customers to buy more, even as many of these stocks were about to begin a decline to oblivion. As for this "award winning team," has anyone ever actually seen a track record of the recommendations of these "award winning" teams? No! The truth is their advice is pretty much useless over time, and frequently worse than useless. It can be downright dangerous to your financial health. As to the notion of re-evaluating your financial goals, evaluation

> **Lately, you've been hearing a lot about us.**
>
> **Now you're going to hear from us.**
> There has never been a more critical time for straight talk and commitment from the financial services industry....
> Leaders respond constructively to criticism...
> We're raising the bar at every level of our firm on what were already the highest ethical standards in the industry....
> We've linked our analysts' compensation more directly with the performance of the stocks they cover....
> We're continuing our leadership in Wealth Management.....Wealth Management builds balanced portfolios....research informs asset allocation models and sophisticated diversification strategies that can help manage risk. (July 8,2002)

should be a constant on-going exercise. You should not need to re-evaluate them. No one at the broker was talking about evaluating goals in 1999 and early 2000. All long-term goals were forgotten; people were urged to get in on the opportunity of a lifetime – technology stocks.

A fresh look at your risk tolerance? How about the same old look you should have had all the time? Nobody at these firms talked about risk when it was greatest. At that point, they promoted the idea that the only risk was not being in the market. In short, they said there was no risk. Risk is the possibility of not having your money when you need it most. People needed to be reminded of that when the market was pushing to unsustainable P/E ratios. But few people were talking about losing money at that point. Rebalance now? Rebalancing should be continuous to keep your portfolio on its long-term asset mix. This means regularly cutting back on the winning class of assets and adding to classes that have underperformed. Such a systematic approach would have gotten many investors out of the overpriced technology stocks and into bonds or cash as the market

> **Re-Evaluate Your Financial Goals**
> You and your Financial Advisor should re-evaluate your objectives in light of the current economic conditions, while keeping in mind that markets have historically withstood the test of time. With a sound financial plan; there should be no wholesale changes in your long-term strategy. However, in the short term, your Financial Advisor may recommend ways to make your cash work harder while reducing risk and keeping an eye on an eventual recovery.
>
> **Reassess Your Risk**
> You may also want to take a fresh look at your tolerance for risk in this climate. It's important to consider your short – and long-term goals, and adjust your portfolio according to your time horizons. Your Financial Advisor can take you through the nine questions that will help reassess your risk-tolerance profile. After which, you and your Financial Advisor will have a guide for selecting appropriate investment vehicles, and the proper way to allocate them.
>
> **Rebalance Your Assets**
> As always, review your portfolio with your Financial Advisor on a regular basis. Take this opportunity to discuss your asset allocations and diversification strategy. Your Financial Advisor may suggest reallocating some equity positions, diversifying your bond portfolio between taxable and tax-free issues and taking a defensive position in cash equivalents like CDs, T-bills and money funds. Together, you can decide which course of action will best help achieve your financial goals.

rose dramatically. Again, nobody was talking about rebalancing.

Now, with all the stock values evaporated, these experts are suggesting that you rebalance. You might ask, "Rebalance what, the 5% of my money I have left following your advice so far?"

And you should review your portfolio with your advisor on a regular basis? Only one problem – when the market got rough, many people couldn't get their broker to return their phone calls because it isn't much fun talking to angry clients. Your best course is to take the advice offered in the ad and continue to use it – not just now, but from now on. And when this bear market ends, these experts will be urging you to get in on the action again. As a broker told me years ago – you have to generate commissions when the buyers want to trade. In other words, you have to give the suckers what they want. P. T. Barnum at his best!

These ads contrast sharply with what had been going on in the brokerage industry. Analysts were hyping stocks to get the investment banking business, even though they knew the reports and ratings they were issuing were at worst false, and at best very optimistic. Retail brokers were generating business based on the reputation of these analysts, leading clients more and more to technology stocks as the market rose. But – Why were clients listening to them, given the brokers' historic inability to forecast anything. That's what a bubble is about – "Let's have fun. We're making money, and I don't care why. It can surely go on forever, or at least I don't want to think about it ever stopping."

EXECUTIVE BEHAVIOR

By 1988, I'd seen enough self-important people in the corporate world to last a lifetime; then Tom Quinn and I started our own business. Ever since, I've had to answer to my clients, Tom, and Judy (and not always in that order.) I was privileged to work for a great company for many years. It was ranked nineteenth worldwide in profits, but as one executive described it, RJR was the biggest little company in the world. People knew each other from top to bottom, and while it was far from perfect, with the usual office politics, it was a company mostly without executive egos. As is always the case, the CEO set the tone. And during many of those years RJR was run by low key CEOs. In fact when Colin Stokes retired, the CFO said that he had never known anyone with as much power as Mr. Stokes who was so little affected by it.

Then the "Barbarians" seized control of RJR and changed the management style. It will be debated for years in Winston-Salem whether that was good or bad. But everyone can agree that it <u>was</u> a major change. Little did we know that RJR was just a warm up for what was to happen fourteen years later in much of corporate America.

Compensation

Executive compensation has moved way out of line. The ratio of CEO pay to average worker pay soared over the last ten years. And the CEOs generally continue to receive pay increases despite bad times for their employees, lower profits, and lower stock prices. There is an air of unreality about the situation, and I suspect it is because the CEO, more than ever, sits atop a bureaucracy that shields him from the "real" world. No one, not even the board, will step forward and tell the emperor that he has no clothes on.

Over the last few years, the pay and perks for these executives moved beyond justification. It was not always this way. I cite an example from twenty-five years ago. Our CEO was involved in volunteer work for his church. This required him to travel with his church committee to a distant city on a Sunday. He opted to use one of his corporate jets for a quick trip. Now no one would have challenged the CEO's use of the company plane for that personal use. But he asked the corporate aircraft department to send him a bill for the miles traveled at the mileage rate for the jet, and he personally paid that bill. That is character – doing the right thing when you don't have to.

Stock Options

Stock options are a cost that has not been accounted for, in some cases a very expensive cost. In examining the proposals for correcting the accounting problem, no solution has struck me as appropriate. It is a complex issue and not easily solved.

Business Week's latest survey shows that in 2001, after years of anemic growth and falling stock prices, more than 200 boards of directors decided to reward CEOs for their desultory performance by swapping out-of-the-money, high-priced options for lower-priced ones. Options for executives now account for a staggering 15% of all shares outstanding.

The most serious criticism is that options inflate earnings. The Fed believes that by not expensing options, corporations were able to add three percentage points to their average annual earnings gain from 1995 to 2000. Operating earnings would have grown an average of 5% during this period, not 8.3%. At a time when investors are demanding quality earnings, this is serious. There is no way of measuring the true worth of options when they are issued. Putting a high price on them would deliver a serious hit to the bottom line and lead companies to stop issuing options. A better alternative would be to expense options over time as they are exercised. This brings tax law and accounting rules into alignment and smoothes out the impact on earnings.[xxiii]

Misplaced Motives

"Buyer beware" is always good advice, whether you're buying a stereo or a stock. The CEOs of Oracle, AOL-Time Warner, Cisco, Dell, Disney, JDS Uniphase and Siebel Systems all received well over $100 million each from exercising company stock options.   These CEOs are probably highly motivated to sell their companies to the Wall Street research analysts and anyone else who might create more buyer interest.   These companies' stocks have all declined 50% to 95% in value from their peak. Why do corporate boards choose to reward failure?

Over 80% of the billions of dollars realized from employee stock options went to senior executives, primarily those with the larger, S&P 500 companies. According to the *New York Times*, last year 47 executives in the 100 worst performing companies in the S&P 500 took home at least $5 million each by selling company stock or options that were given to them as incentive compensation.   Are these boards motivating their managers to create long term value for their shareholders or to promote their company's stock to the investing public in order to reach some target price?

In the late 1990s, executive compensation practices evolved to a winner-take-all lottery. It began with the idea that issuing stock options would allow executives to walk in the same shoes as other shareholders. It ended with an infectious greed that contaminated good judgment. Instead of motivating hard work to build long-term value for the company, it encouraged excessive risk, creative accounting, and, sometimes fraud.

And worst of all, the get-rich-quick scheme worked – and it's legal. Many executives oversold their companies to the investing public. Investors bought, temporarily pushing the stock prices up to the option exercise prices, and the executives cashed out. The investors owned a piece of paper worth less than half of what they paid for it, and the executives quietly took the investors' cash to their local bank. Even with all that has been written, we do not believe that the average investor understands what he was sold or knows what he funded with his hard earned cash.

This is not a problem about a bubble that has come and gone. This has still not been fixed. Haven't we learned our lesson? How much of a "commission" do we want these senior management salesmen to be paid for temporarily getting their stock price up?

We believe that most corporate executives are quality, talented people.   But when there are no controls and executives can bestow unimaginable wealth on themselves, they will again, maybe with better camouflage next time. We should not assume that self-interest dictates prudence. We should not again assume that equity ownership through the leverage of stock options aligns management and shareholders' interests. We believe that the responsibility for righting these wrongs is with the board of directors. (CornerCap newsletter, January 2003)

Corporate Charitable Giving

In the Mergers & Acquisitions section we will discuss the shortcomings of corporate management in their acquisition programs. The same applies to their corporate charity activities. In a recent speech, the director of charitable giving for a major bank said that his company distributed $50 million each year to various charitable causes. This would best be left to the shareholders. If we invest in an enterprise to make money, then that is what we should expect. Giving away millions of dollars each year may be justified by the intangible benefits of more business, but it is doubtful.

Still, it would have been surprising if the director of giving had not said that the gifts are worthwhile. After all, his is a great job that certainly creates lots of friends. Anyone giving away $50 million a year is going to meet many people who tell you how great you are. (As noted before, I've been there.) But what really disturbed me was the speaker's criticism of Milton Friedman who said that businesses should be run to make profits and not for charity. Friedman's ideas on free enterprise have worked very well when given the opportunity, which isn't often. It has been said that Hong Kong is the perfect laboratory for Friedman's economic theories. Since 1949, Hong Kong, a world-class city, has been built on a rock that has absolutely no natural resources except people who have sought freedom and have been willing to work very hard. They have accomplished this with virtually no welfare safety net or corporate charity.

Investment Fund Boards

One problem that afflicts every investment oversight board is its investment time horizon. In theory a pension fund or a university endowment invests with some assurance that the fund will have a life of fifty years or more. But the investment policy actually reflects the board's, not the fund's, time horizon. It is human nature to want to be deemed successful in our efforts, and just so with board members. They do not want to exit their position and have it said that the fund did poorly on their watch. The typical board member has a tenure of five years. So the investment time horizon will be a compromise somewhere between eternity and five years, and usually closer to five years. Such a short time horizon can lead to bad decisions – either excess caution - fear of losing in the short run, or high risk - trying to make too much money in the short run.

Most boards opt for caution. Although board members have prestigious titles and resumes, they still behave like the typical investor. One experience comes to mind. During the oil bubble in the late 1970s, I had my annual "show and tell" for the finance committee of the board. Oil stocks were booming. In my presentation, I reflected the view of Capital Guardian (cited before) that oil was not necessarily the place to be. This seemed to me to be a non-threatening, cautionary comment, duly hedged so that no one would be offended. (Rule One – Don't offend the Board of Directors. Your boss might not appreciate it.) But it was obvious as soon as the words were out of my mouth that they were offended. One director interrupted to ask, "Excuse me, but did you say oil stocks are going to go down?" Now that is not what I said, but that is what he heard. And the whole committee was quick to agree that I didn't know what I was talking about. They, like everyone else, probably owned lots of energy stocks, and they didn't like my message. These were men who weren't accustomed to being told things they didn't want to hear, and they weren't shy about letting the messenger know it,. But they <u>were</u> wrong. In a few months oil stocks dropped sharply.

MERGERS AND ACQUISITIONS

A retired business executive, a senior manager at a major U.S. company, recently spoke to me openly and critically about the performance of corporate acquisitions. His perspective was up close and personal. He talked about the companies he had worked for, one in the telecom industry and the billions of dollars that industry had wasted to acquire foreign companies. He chalked most of this up to management arrogance – their unswerving belief that they could make a success where everyone else had failed. Research data suggest that his criticism is right on the money.

Rationale For Mergers And Acquisitions

If the company can't grow internally, then management says they owe it to the stockholders to grow by acquiring other companies. An acquisition philosophy does not recognize that the stockholder is managing a portfolio of his own, and if given the cash he will diversify for himself. He doesn't need a corporate management to do that for him. Managers are arrogant to think that their tenth-best idea for capital expenditure is better than their shareholders' first-best idea.

Unfortunately, management is paid by the size of the company, not by its profitability. I am convinced that many managers rationalize their acquisition programs as good for the shareholders, despite historical evidence to the contrary. Managers of public companies squander profits on empire-building projects that fail to earn a decent return. Investors would be better off if the earnings were distributed as dividends or used to repurchase company stock.

Of course managers take action in their own self-interest. Who doesn't? They are only human. While I had nothing to do with the acquisition program at RJR after I began managing the company's pension assets, the acquisition program was still of tremendous interest to me. Each time the company announced an acquisition, I did <u>not</u> focus on its projected profitability for the shareholder. Instead I focused on how the acquisition might expand my personal "empire." The *Money Market Directory* is a big green book that lists every significant pension plan in the U.S. When RJR announced an acquisition, I ran for the *MMD* to see how big the new pension plan was. Every acquired company had a pension plan of its own, and that plan would be combined under my direction. And the assets I managed grew from only $220 million in 1977 to $4 billion in twenty-seven countries by 1986. Part of this was the result of new 401k plans, increased contributions of cash, and market appreciation, but perhaps half of the twenty-fold increase came directly from acquisitions. So while acquisitions <u>might</u> benefit the shareholders, my real interest was in how much the acquisition would benefit <u>me</u>. I can't believe that most other people are any less motivated by self-interest.

Why Mergers And Acquisitions Fail

It's not hard to make a list of reasons that acquisitions fail. Most financial types focus on paying too much; if you do, it's hard to offset that mistake later. But even if the price seems like a bargain, there is still plenty that can ruin even the best-laid merger plans. At the top of the list is "cultural differences" - intangible, but

Reasons Mergers Fail
Cultural Difference
Did not understand the business
Over estimated the "synergies" Paid too much, poor negotiations
Lack of clear leadership
Customers ignored

extremely important. When people have worked a certain way for years, sometimes decades, they develop a culture that is hard to change.

Managements should give much more thought to acquisitions before they make them. They should realize that the chances of a successful merger are slim at best; the odds are no better than one in three. Investment bankers play a big role in promoting acquisitions. And why not? The fees that they derive from a merger can be enormous. And company management might be better advised to examine the bankers' motives when they are being urged to acquire or merge.

What bankers contribute is a bill.
Warren Buffett

Management invests time and ego in screening for an acquisition candidate, massaging the numbers to see if it makes sense, and negotiating with the seller. To say that the price is too high and then walk away is extremely difficult. It is tempting for management to rationalize the high price – "we'll really get more growth, more cost savings, more synergies than we've budgeted, and besides this deal just needs to get done. If we overpay a little, who will ever know?"

How To Value An Acquisition

Stern Stewart is a consulting firm founded by Joel Stern. I met Joel in 1969 when he headed a consulting group at the Chase Manhattan Bank. Joel was a disciple of Milton Friedman at the University of Chicago. I learned much about basic financial analysis and discounted cash flow valuation from the seminars he taught to the RJR finance people. Joel has moved on to Stern Stewart and the EVA approach to management. Much of EVA is the old material from 1969, but it is still excellent. Stern Stewart lays out the correct way to value an acquisition, describing what I have always vaguely thought about acquirers, but could never articulate. If I ever sold a business, I would hope to find a buyer who had never heard of Stern Stewart.

Approximately 70% of M&A deals destroy shareholder value for acquiring companies. To understand what has to happen for a deal to add value for the acquiring company's shareholders, the acquisition price needs to be segregated into three pieces.

The first piece of the purchase-price puzzle is the value of the target company's current operations. This is the company's value assuming no growth in earnings or cash flows, and it can be estimated by capitalizing current operating profit after tax (i.e., valuing those profits as a perpetuity by dividing them by the cost of capital for the company.)

The second piece to the puzzle is relatively easy to determine once the current operations value is estimated. Take the market capitalization of the target company just before the acquisition announcement and subtract the current operations value from that market cap. We are left with the value of expected growth. The target company often will have growth expectations embedded in its valuation, which set a high hurdle for the acquiring company to clear. But assume the amount being paid for the future growth value is reasonable and that the acquiring company's management team can achieve that growth simply by maintaining the status quo.

The third and final piece of the puzzle is the control premium. It is the excess over pre-acquisition announcement market capitalization that is being paid to make the deal occur. Control premiums have averaged approximately 30% over the last two decades. If near-term synergies cannot be achieved to justify the control premium, then the deal will destroy shareholder value for the acquiring company. Why do the synergies need to be near term? First, if the synergies necessary to justify the control premium are not realized within twenty-four to thirty-six months of the takeover, they never will be realized. Second, the time value of money, as synergies are realized in later years they must be even greater in order to justify the premium on a present-value basis. After three years, it is impossible for them to become large enough.

There are two types of synergies – hard and soft. Hard synergies are things such as cost savings that can likely be realized - closing overlapping branches, retrenching senior executives, etc. Soft synergies are things such as revenue enhancements due to bundling of products, cross-selling, etc. The track record for companies achieving soft synergies is very poor, and if management is justifying a significant part of the control premium with them, it will likely destroy shareholder value.

Finally, look at what the senior executives have at stake in the acquiring company, and in particular, the pay packages for those individuals. More than any single variable, pay packages for senior executives are based on the size of the firm they are managing. That has not escaped their notice. There is a powerful incentive for senior executives to increase the size of their business in order to boost their pay, even if shareholder value is destroyed. Understanding the pay packages of the senior executives can give critical insights into their likely behavior and willingness to overpay when the next deal comes along.[xxiv]

AOL-Time Warner: Dinosaurs Mating

AOL-Time Warner dramatically drives home the point about the culture clash in acquisitions. (Surprise – Ted Turner didn't like working for a bunch of "kids".). This merger had an ill-conceived business plan that projected far too many "synergies" from the combined companies, and the result has been disappointed shareholders and a tanking stock.

This was no small deal. The outcome was about the same as the 70% of mergers that fail, but it was gigantic in size. The declining stock has wiped out $200 billion in market value in the past two years. The merger was so big that the wags are now saying it required not just one, but four scapegoats! All four of the top AOL executives at the time of the deal are now gone. Time Warner people are now in control, and they are talking about spinning off AOL – returning to what they were three years ago before the merger took place – except that the Time Warner shareholders are probably poorer because they traded the world's biggest media company for a piece of what was really a dot-com stock. And the AOL shareholders are probably a bit better off because they traded some of their fairly worthless pieces of paper that were selling at an astronomical price for ownership of that gigantic media company.[xxv]

And The List Goes On

Other examples of a less than stellar job in merging and acquiring can be added to this list:

Cisco

It is hard not to pick on Cisco. Over a year after the bubble burst, in May 2001, Cisco management was addressing the business, not the stock. The outlook was revealing. The company swallowed $1 billion in restructuring, wrote off $2.5 billion in worthless inventory. The company promised to return to its fabulous year-over-year growth. But how? The growth was really an acquisition binge. Cisco spent $34 billion to buy seventy-one firms including $10.3 billion in two years for companies with little assets or prospects. Another case of combinations not working out.[xxvi]

Tyco

And by mid 2002, the news got worse for acquirers. Tyco was in deep trouble. Tyco had bought 700 companies in the last three years alone, at prices from a few hundred thousand dollars to $9.5 billion. Annual growth was 20%. Then the real value of some of those big acquisitions became more evident when Tyco needed cash and tried to sell them. Bidders were only willing to pay much lower prices than Tyco had recently paid.

WorldCom

And of course this one was perhaps the worst disaster of all. WorldCom had seventy acquisitions before it collapsed in scandal and bankruptcy.

RJR Tobacco – An M&A History

Reynolds Tobacco would be a great research study on corporate acquisitions. Lay aside, if you can, the current moral dilemma of the tobacco industry (which we'll discuss in a following section) and think of R. J. Reynolds Tobacco Company in the early 1960s. It was extremely profitable, as were all the cigarette companies. But the nature of its product meant that there would be an ongoing threat to its ability to grow. (Ironically the real limits to industry growth did not come for almost another forty years, but no one could know that in 1960.)

The company grew from a domestic U.S. cigarette manufacturer into a giant, worldwide company with interests in scores of foreign countries and, at various times, in food, alcohol, aluminum, packaging, shipping, and oil. Now, after events that have been well chronicled, the company is once again a U.S. cigarette manufacturer much as it was forty years ago. Only a recent merger with its former rival Brown & Williamson Tobacco keeps it close to what it was four decades ago.

RJR's acquisitions succeeded in varying degrees. They all exhibited elements of the reasons mergers fail. Some were very poor and a few were extremely profitable, but on average the shareholders of the original tobacco company would probably have fared better if management had used the enormous cash flow to either retire outstanding stock or pay dividends to shareholders. To analyze all the RJR acquisitions would be a major study which we will not attempt here.

It was finally RJR's acquisition of Nabisco Brands and the resulting clash of two very different corporate cultures that was the company's undoing. The irony of all this was that RJR shareholders finally got taken out at a fantastic price in 1989. Those shareholders are many times better off today than if they had kept their stock, given the fortunes of the cigarette industry over the following sixteen years. Most deals do not have such a happy ending for shareholders. Even in this case, there were other stakeholders who did not fare so well – employees and the community at large.

In contrast to RJR, major rival Philip Morris always maintained an abiding faith in the future of tobacco. They expanded internationally and capitalized on their Marlboro brand. The proof of their success is their share of the U.S. cigarette market. In the early 1960s, RJR dominated the industry with a 35% market share compared to tiny Philip Morris' 5% or so. Over the years, that has reversed. Now RJR has a 25% share and Philip Morris has a giant 50% share. Philip Morris' Marlboro success abroad has been even more impressive.

But even Philip Morris couldn't resist the siren song of acquisition and diversification. They bought Miller Brewing and a number of food companies – notably Oscar Mayer and General Foods. And finally after the implosion of RJR, Philip Morris bought much of the old Nabisco. However, the Philip Morris management apparently has recognized the "culture clash" between tobacco people and food people, and they have spun off their food business into a separate company.

A Couple of "Tobacco" Guys Sitting Around Emailing

The following is e-mail correspondence with a former RJR employee and client who, like me, has spent most of his life in or around the tobacco industry from growing tobacco on the farm to working for a major cigarette company. "Andy" and I got into an e-mail discussion about what happened to RJR over the years. Following are reflections on RJR in no particular order.

To Gene Hoots:

Sad to see a once great company with all its rich one hundred year plus southern heritage being reduced to this. I may be wrong, but I believe the dynamics of its demise were set in motion years ago when the management shifted from tobacco men to outsiders. From then on the company, it seems, has been used and abused by its various holding company management for personal gain and glory with all their chest pounding adventures funded from the tobacco money they were publicly embarrassed to identify with, not to mention being associated with a "bucolic" Winston-Salem based company which they no doubt felt had to be rescued from its slow talking southern culture and fashioned into something more sophisticated, something more worthy of their esteemed personal image and their wives' social status back home at their Long Island country club.

To "Andy":

A further comment. Bill Lybrook, the RJR Corporate Secretary (his grandmother was RJR's older sister) told me in 1971 that he remembered distinctly the moment that began R. J. Reynolds Tobacco Company's downfall. He said in the early 1960s at a meeting, the board discussed what to do about the health threat to tobacco. He said that Reynolds management decided to diversify by acquisition into new products that they could sell in their existing markets in the U.S. At the same time, Philip Morris made the decision to combat the health and smoking threat by taking tobacco products abroad to new markets. And he said that was the beginning of the end. If his memory was correct, then the key decision was made at least a decade or so before outside management arrived.

The acquisitions began shortly after that fateful meeting – a program with limited financial successes: gift wrapping paper, Pacific Hawaiian (Hawaiian Punch), Penick & Ford corn starch, Filmco plastic film, Patio frozen Mexican foods, Chun King oriental food, Sea-Land containerized shipping, Aminoil international oil production and trading, Burmah Oil production, Del Monte fruits and vegetables, Hublein wines and spirits, and finally Nabisco Brands with its array of grocery products.

Along the way we also considered Hartz Mountain Bird Seed, Myrtle Beach (yes, almost all of Myrtle Beach could have been bought about thirty years ago), the Figgie Company (predecessor to Tyco), and Occidental Petroleum (Armand Hammer would have been an interesting RJR board member in contrast to the traditional local tobacco men who already had to contend with an entrepreneur in

Malcolm McLean), and more.

We were a company that hadn't decided what it wanted to be. I remember standing on the deck of the Queen Mary in Long Beach one evening in 1981 and listening to a senior company executive address a gathering of prominent tobacco analysts. He said, "RJR Industries is a major marketer of consumer goods worldwide, with strategic interests in shipping and oil." All the analysts looked at each other and said, "Huh?" Joe Abely, the CFO, was more accurate when he privately said, "We are a cigarette company with a few expensive hobbies."

And most accurate was an old friend and client who worked in RJR research until he was drummed out of the corps for his "radical" views. He defined RJR's mission as providing "Nicotine Delivery Systems." This was a phrase that every major tobacco company wanted to avoid. But our friend was writing research reports on this, as early as 1973. And I first heard him use the term in 1975. Well, it's interesting, but it's only history.

To Gene Hoots:

Thanks for the background Gene. Nostalgic to hear all those old names of people and companies. Those were heady halcyon days to be sure. (How on earth do you remember all that?). I remember now, we were a company with a mission, zeal, plenty of money and the most expensive hired brains in the west. We were young and we were unstoppable, making history with the largest acquisitions in corporate history. Feels good to recall it, especially the being young and ambitious part. Yes, it was great to be a part of it all. Felt important you know. Who would have guessed that twenty-five to thirty years later this is what we would be reading about our old alma mater.

Thanks for the tour. They were good memories and I am forever in debt to RJR for the opportunity to have lived some of it.

To "Andy":

Not to belabor all this, but you have set me thinking about stuff I haven't focused on in years and since I have a few quiet moments this early morning, I'll jot them down. In the early to mid '70s we had an acquisition flirtation with a couple other businesses that I remember:

Roberts Farms - probably the largest farm in the U.S. It was 200,000 acres near Bakersfield, California. It grew English walnuts, vegetables, and, most important, grapes. Roberts approached RJR about going into the wine business and buying him out. I suspect Hollis Roberts, the owner, was over-leveraged. I heard that he later went broke after getting involved with Aronholt Smith, the S&L villain in southern California.

My uncle Kenneth Hoots was a farmer with a fifth grade education. He was a friend of Bill Lybrook. One day he asked me, "Why does Reynolds pay so much money for these little food companies when you could start the same thing for a fraction of the purchase price? Reynolds has smart people; it's all a trick to save taxes isn't it?" I didn't have the heart to disillusion him that it was no "trick", we just didn't know what we were doing. We had paid Gino Palucci about $68 million for Chun King in Duluth, Minnesota. I later learned from my pension fund peer at General Mills in Minneapolis that Gino had offered Chun King to them for $28 million, and they turned it down. But what could a milling company in Minnesota know about Chinese food that a cigarette company in North Carolina didn't know, right? We made Gino the Chairman of RJR Foods, in New York City at the time. He promptly opened his new company in Duluth, Gino's Pizza Rolls. He cut deals to have his pizza rolls contract packed in the Chun King plants. I asked why we allowed this conflict of interest and I was told (a) Pizza rolls don't really compete with Chinese egg rolls. Yea, right! and (b) Gino is such a food marketing genius that it is worth letting him do this, a good tradeoff for all the expertise he brings to RJR. I don't recall anything he ever did for RJR but sell us a company at an inflated price.

In the farming industry, Malcolm McLean tried hard to get Ty Wilson, CEO of RJR Foods at the time, to buy Malcolm's huge 120,000 acre farm in eastern NC, but Ty had already seen enough of Malcolm's "good deals" by observing Sea-Land. That farm apparently has been a real loser. I was down there last New Year and not much is going on even now. Kenneth Hoots was acquainted with First Colony Farm, Malcolm's property. He knew the problems with trying to farm on that large a scale in the swampy areas of eastern NC. He said Malcolm's sales strategy should be to get it all planted in corn, and then in the late spring when it looked really great, "Give it a damn good selling to somebody who don't know nothing about farming." That's what Malcolm tried to do with Ty, but it didn't work.

A winery operated by Rodney Strong (not Rodney Strong Winery, that came later). Rodney, a former ballet dancer in San Francisco, had moved to the wine country and had started a winery. The owners tried to sell it to RJR for about $5MM as I recall. But by that time a slight bit of sanity prevailed in these acquisitions. I figured that based on its cash flow, the owners should pay RJR $1 million to assume their debt. Later Rodney Strong created his own very fine line of wines. I see them in upscale restaurants today.

Aromatics International - A flavoring company in Atlanta that supposedly had some technology that RJR Tobacco thought was great. The guy who owned it, Lonnie Pope, a true entrepreneur, sold it to RJR for about $5 million. (Most big companies are not very successful when negotiating with entrepreneurs. Malcolm McLean of Sea-Land proved that time after time.) It turned out to be worthless. We sold the inventory for $150,000 and closed it. It wasn't a "fit" for a large company like RJR. RJR sent a man from Winston-Salem down to Atlanta to run Aromatics. He told me that he once was in a meeting with his biggest customer in San Francisco trying desperately to close a sales contract for the coming year. He was called out of the meeting. Somebody in Winston-Salem in the controller/budgeting area was phoning to ask why he hadn't submitted his five year plan. The corporate five year plan couldn't be consolidated without his input (about

$2 million in sales added to the rest of the company's $5 billion in sales, or something like that). He explained, "There is no five year plan for Aromatics. Don't you understand, there is no five day plan for the company unless I close this sale. Without it we're out of business." Twenty years later, in talking with the daughter of Aromatics' second in command, she mentioned that her father had not been very happy in the short time that he was a part of the RJR family. Once again a clash of cultures.

Myrtle Beach – In 1971 RJR had an opportunity to make an enormous investment in Myrtle Beach. It's not generally known but one family controlled thousands of acres there including prime ocean-front land. RJR considered the investment primarily because it would generate long-term capital gains and RJR had accumulated several million dollars in capital loss carry forwards that it needed to offset. In retrospect, the resort development business would not have been a good fit for RJR, but it was an exciting project. I stayed from Labor Day until Thanksgiving in Myrtle Beach getting real estate appraisals. And as we look back today, the numbers are staggering. The appraisals came in at about $65 million for the property. The family that owned it was considering selling the stock of their real estate company to RJR in a stock-swap merger for $25 million in RJR stock. Thankfully for them, RJR decided not to go forward. Doubtless, the RJR stock would have appreciated greatly, but the property they own must be worth at least $3 billion today.

And finally, one of my favorites - the Marx Toy Company. In the early 1970s we had a flirtation with Louis Marx, owner of Marx Toys. They made the Big Wheel, the Duncan Yoyo, and other toys. Marx was a bigger than life character. He had been on the cover of *Time*. His company was highly visible but marginally profitable. He wanted to unload it on RJR for $30 million. I was assigned to go to NYC and work with him for a few days. He was apparently under the mistaken impression that I could actually make a decision on this, so he wined and dined me. For about three days, this was our schedule:

In the morning I would arrive at his office in the Toy Center at 23rd Street and Broadway. I would go over numbers until lunch. Then, he would have his assistant summons "the car." His assistant was retired Air Force General and World War II hero, Rosie O'Donnell (That was his real name. The television star came later.) The car was a Rolls Royce, a dark green four-door convertible. There were only three like it in the world. When Queen Elizabeth visited Bermuda, Buckingham Palace asked Mr. Marx if he would lend it to her for a few days. There was no other suitable transportation for her in the Western hemisphere. He flew it to Bermuda for her.

Anyway, we rode uptown to 21 Club each day with the top down, General O'Donnell up front with the driver, and Mr. Marx and me in back. Louis Marx had his own table and he was treated like royalty. Here I was, not often out of Winston-Salem in my whole life, and he acted as though it was the most natural thing in the world to introduce this bumpkin to his friends at "21." We first went to the bar where he introduced me to Phil Cochran. (Cochran ran a trucking business in upstate NY. But Mr. Marx said that Phil was a pilot in Burma in World War II, and was the inspiration for the comic strip "Terry and the Pirates" by Milton Caniff. A few years ago the television actress, Betty White, wrote that she dated Cochran when she lived in New York.) At our table, Mr. Marx introduced me to the guy who ate at the next table every day, the CEO of American Home Products. (I met his son in Charlotte recently. He remembered that his dad ate there every day.) Then a lady stopped by and Louis Marx introduced me to her. She was "HoneyBear" Warren. Of course she had to be really impressed by my white bucks and double-knit slacks in "21". I had seen her picture on the cover of *Life* magazine, one of Chief Justice Earl Warren's three daughters and married to John Charles Daley the television star of the time. Then Craig Stevens, "Peter Gunn" the television star, stopped to visit with us. And so it went, heady stuff for a country boy.

Marx had an interesting personal life. He raised two separate families. With his first wife, he had a son and a daughter. The son worked for Donaldson, Lufkin, Jenrette. The daughter was married, and Marx spent a good deal of our lunch telling me how he hated his son-in-law. The first Mrs. Marx had died, and Louis married a Billy Rose showgirl. They had four sons. Marx was a military buff, a friend of Dwight Eisenhower and other generals. His four sons had names like Bradley McArthur Marx and Eisenhower Patton Marx. Some months later I learned the reason for the low opinion of his son-in-law. He was Daniel Ellsberg of Ellsberg Pentagon Papers fame, the archenemy of Nixon's Vietnam policies. Oh, by the way, we didn't buy Marx Toy. A British company did, and it went bankrupt.

The Odd Couple – R. J. Reynolds Tobacco And Sea-Land

Of the acquisitions RJR made, this one was the strangest to me. Most of the others had at least a common thread of consumer non-durable products running through them. Even the later oil play had some logic because it appeared to be such a bargain, if not a long-term fit for a corporate strategy. But Sea-Land was a merger of a high return, low capital consumer goods company and a low return, capital intensive, very complicated business. The theory was that the enormous cash flow of the tobacco company could be used to build up the shipping company into a great, profitable enterprise- and that was the reason for the acquisition.

Why Did They Merge?

The story I heard may not be totally accurate, but it is probably closer to the rationale for the purchase of Sea-Land than the theoretical explanation: In the late 1960s, conglomerates were all the rage on Wall Street. Companies specialized in buying other companies in diverse industries, hence the name "conglomerate." A conglomerate liked to find a company that sold at a low price/earnings ratio, necessarily lower than the conglomerate's p/e. Then the acquiring conglomerate could exchange its stock for that of the target acquisition company, and the result would be higher earnings per share for the conglomerate. Which in turn led to a higher price and higher p/e and more acquisitions. This was really a Ponzi scheme, but no one saw it at the time. In this environment, RJR was a perfect target, a cash rich company with no debt and great earning power. In the summer of 1968, RJR stock began to move up on heavy trading volume and with a peculiar pattern. The volume increase would begin on Wednesday afternoon and last through Friday. The RJR executive committee was very worried, fearing that the company was the target of a conglomerate. And it may have been, but we'll never know. Management's answer to the issue was to look for a company that had heavy debt and needed capital. Such a combination with tobacco would scare away any would-be acquirer. (Of course management might have asked themselves, "And exactly what will we do with such a company after we get it? And, if it would make RJR unattractive as an acquisition, why wouldn't it also be unattractive for existing shareholders?" But those were probably secondary concerns at that moment.)

The Man with the Answer Arrives

Anyway, at this opportune time, enter Malcolm McLean. Malcolm was not unknown to the RJR people. He had come to Winston-Salem as a young man and, along with his brother Jim and sister Clara, had built McLean Trucking. Then when he was thirty-five, Malcolm developed the idea for containerized shipping. Gambler that he was, he sold his trucking interest and formed McLean Industries which created Sea-Land. He revolutionized world shipping. But shipping is a capital intensive, competitive industry and Sea-Land was always strapped for cash, and Malcolm badly needed a buyer. He was undoubtedly one of the world's great entrepreneurs and negotiators.

The gentlemanly RJR tobacco men never had a chance. They badly wanted to make an acquisition and he sold them on the idea that he could solve their problem as a potential takeover target. As things turned out, Malcolm sold RJR a business that was never very profitable. Each succeeding management recognized that it had limited potential, but I think each new management believed that they would be the one who would turn it around. Once again experience proved that Warren Buffett's observation was correct, "When a great management meets a bad industry, I'll bet on the industry."

For this less than stellar company, Malcolm personally received 3.65 million shares of a convertible preferred stock that paid a $2.25 annual dividend and converted into common at the unusual conversion rate of 1.5 shares of RJR common for one share of preferred plus $16 cash. So there was great leverage in the preferred stock. Above $32 per share, the preferred moved up $1.50 a share for each $1.00 the common rose. So in exchange for his shipping company Malcolm received 10% ownership of one of the greatest cash generating machines of modern history.

The Most Amazing Entrepreneur I Ever Met

As already noted, Malcolm couldn't stand the structure of a large company; at heart he was an entrepreneur and would never be anything else. He sold all his RJR stock in secondary offerings and reinvested in many enterprises. Finally, he bought U.S. Lines, another major shipper that borrowed heavily, and it went bankrupt in the mid-1980s, costing him much of his personal fortune. History is filled with 'ifs', but if he had kept his RJR stock and collected his dividend of $22,500 a day, the stock would have made him several billion dollars when the buyout came in 1989. But with Malcolm McLean, it was never about money, it was all about building something that was exciting, taking a risk, doing what no one else was bold enough to do.

Even when he was running the trucking company in Winston-Salem, he operated on a financial shoestring, and was proud of it. A White Truck dealer once told me that he sold Malcolm several trucks in the early 1950s. He said, "I financed Malcolm for ninety percent of the purchase. Then Malcolm and I went to Charlotte and met with my district manager, and the truth is I just lied and said Malcolm had given me the ten percent down payment, but he didn't." That was Malcolm. He was nothing if not persuasive.

His attitude was, "If you borrow enough money, you own the creditors, they don't own you. They can't afford to let you fail." But even with that philosophy, he needed to stay ahead of his creditors. He said that his work day sometimes consisted of going to the Old Town Club and sitting in the sun in a chair beside the golf pro's shop and reading the *Wall Street Journal*. He would tell the golf staff that if anyone called, he wasn't there. He left the care and feeding of creditors to his CFO, M. C. "Red" Benton who later became the mayor of Winston-Salem. Malcolm said that this was when he was most productive; he could think quietly and avoid creditors at the same time. You had to admire his style.

A Very Bright Young Banker

And a second historical note related to Sea-Land. As I mentioned, the preferred stock, known as RJR Preferred B, was unusual in its conversion feature. In 1977 I was at a luncheon in New York hosted by Salomon Brothers. Some of their young traders were there and one of them saw my nametag identifying me as an RJR type. He walked over and said, "Oh, RJR, you've got the convertible stock with the funny $32 thing." Now this was a very obscure feature of an obscure stock. Yet this young man obviously knew it from memory, very impressive to me. I noted his name and never forgot it - Robert Rubin. A name that was to become much more widely known in the next twenty years as he rose to head Salomon Brothers and then served as Secretary of the Treasury in the Clinton administration.

An Acquisition "Success"

RJR made one acquisition that was very profitable - the purchase of the Burmah Oil properties in mid-1976. I worked fourteen months on the analysis, but can take absolutely no credit for its success. This deal was interesting because, Burmah Oil itself was a corporate diversification disaster. Burmah was a U.K. company that had been a conservative holding company for nearly a hundred years. It was considered "a widows' and orphans' stock" because it was so safe. It owned a major percentage of British Petroleum. Then, about 1973 the management decided that being a passive holding company wasn't "exciting" enough, so they set out to diversify. They acquired, among other things, Castrol Motor Oil, the U. S. producing oil fields of the Signal Oil and Gas Company of Los Angeles, and various oil properties in the offshore Gulf Coast. The market for oil tankers was heating up due to the energy crisis in 1973, and Burmah decided to build and operate a fleet of very large crude carriers (VLCCs), giant oil tankers. Burmah management was warned that their shipping partner had a checkered background at best, but management was confident that they had picked the right partner. They began to build their fleet. However, in the midst of the project to build ships that could economically carry great quantities of oil from the Middle East around the tip of Africa to European markets, the Suez Canal reopened, allowing a much shorter route to market for the crude oil. The huge ships were no longer competitive with the small ships that could go through Suez. The giant ships were obsolete even before they left the shipyards, and some of them made their maiden voyage straight to the scrap yards in the Philippines, never carrying one load of oil. Burmah declared bankruptcy on the last day of 1974, just a year after it began its shipping venture. The fallout was so severe that the Bank of England had to guarantee loans for Burmah while they worked out their financial problems. Burmah sold assets to survive, and like any enterprise in distress, it had to sell its best assets first – and at bargain prices.

RJR had made an investment in oil, buying Aminoil (American Independent Oil), a New York based company that operated an oil field in the Kuwaiti portion of the Neutral Zone between Saudi Arabia and Kuwait. (Getty Oil operated the Saudi portion.) With the energy crisis, an investment in oil looked promising in early 1975. Burmah was offering to sell all its U. S. oil properties, and RJR, through Aminoil, decided to bid. After fourteen months of on-again off-again negotiations, RJR bought the properties for $522 million in cash. Unbelievable now, but at June 30, 1976, this purchase was the largest cash acquisition that had ever been made, and the second largest ever. (Only the Mobil Oil acquisition of Montgomery Ward for stock had been larger – another great failure by the way: what every oil company needs, a chain of retail stores and consumer catalogue operations.)

The Burmah acquisition proved to be a winner. The oil fields in the U.S., mostly offshore Texas and Louisiana and the Huntington Beach, California fields produced millions of dollars in oil profits each year, and in 1984 RJR sold the properties to Phillips Petroleum for $1.7 billion, more than three times the purchase price. This acquisition had worked out well, largely owing to the steady rise in the price of oil. Ironically, a year later the properties were estimated to be worth only about $1 billion as oil prices fell.

This was a really big deal to me personally because it was an opportunity to learn so much. I am indebted to RJR to this day. Among the lessons from this work:

The cutthroat world of investment banking. At the first meeting on the Burmah project on a Monday morning in May, 1975 in New York, two of us came from RJR. Attendees were primarily Aminoil people and the investment bankers representing Burmah. Burmah had taken the unusual step of engaging two investment bankers to represent them. One of them hosted a lunch at their Wall Street offices. They presented us a data book that included their asking price, $700 million. This was the biggest price ever asked for an acquisition at that time, so the meeting was unquestionably important, especially to the bankers. Yet before the lunch was over, one of Burmah's investment bankers from the second firm whose office was in mid-town, pointedly excused himself from the lunch, explaining that he had something "very important" to attend to back up town. This seemed to be his way of letting us know that we really weren't very important to him, although it's hard to imagine what could have been more important than the biggest deal ever. This banker went on to make a big name for himself in the world of mergers. A huge ego is critical in this business.

The necessity of keeping a business liquid and not being forced into asset sales. In order to secure the loan guarantees from the Bank of England, Burmah had to relinquish ownership of its BP stock, virtually at the bottom of the bear market in 1974. If Burmah could have held the BP stock, in six years BP alone would have generated enough value to have saved Burmah from financial distress.

The importance of the energy industry and Middle East oil. It was a learning experience to report for fourteen months to Jack Sunderland's organization and to learn first-hand about the energy business, the most vital business in the world at that time. Jack was a no-nonsense, capable executive. He had integrity and prided himself on delivering on his word. Years later the respect that Jack had earned with the Kuwaitis benefited RJR with a $179 million settlement when the Kuwait government nationalized Aminoil's interests there. I greatly respected Jack. I never met a tougher, more determined executive, and yet he had to deal with someone who was more than his match. I was in his office one day when he got a phone call. He excused himself and said that he had to take the call. He had a brief conversation. Jack hung up the phone, turned to me and said, "That was J. Paul Getty. I've had a thousand arguments with that man, and I've lost every one." Over the years since, I've continued some contact with Jack. His knowledge of the Middle East has been helpful to me in my own dealings with Saudis, Yemenis, and others from that part of the world.

The unique skills of the entrepreneur. This was my first exposure to Malcolm McLean, the founder of Sea-Land. He had a strong interest in this project and favored buying the oil properties. (Knowing Malcolm was a once-in-a-lifetime experience to meet a genuine entrepreneurial genius. He deserves special comment. See the end of this section.)

A clear vision of what the business should be is critical. Over the years, I've come to believe that Burmah was a billion dollar tactical success, but part of a large strategic failure for RJR. This was not at all apparent to me at the time, because I had no sense of corporate strategy. On one of my periodic trips back to Winston-Salem from Aminoil in New York, I had a conversation with CFO Dave Peoples and Treasurer John Dowdle. They both quizzed me at length about just why RJR should be in the oil business. Of course I gave them the best answer I could – it was a bargain, it was diversification, energy was a growing market. But it was obvious that my arguments weren't convincing. They didn't have to justify their position to me, but I left that meeting thinking that these guys just weren't very open-minded and couldn't accept this great opportunity for RJR at face value. Fourteen years later, I began to appreciate what they were thinking. That we were a cigarette company and any acquisition would be hard to fit in a corporate strategy because anything we bought diluted the profitability of the company. Their long-term vision was the right one, regardless of whether Burmah was a good deal.

And finally learning that we don't always know what is good for us. The energy business was definitely the place to be in the 1970s. I had my heart set on moving to Houston and working in this dynamic industry. But after fourteen months working on the project, away from my family for much of that time, on the day the acquisition was announced Jack Sunderland thanked me for my help, but also said that with the merger of Aminoil and Burmah there would be no place for me in Houston. So I had to abandon my dreams of becoming a Texas "oil man." I caught a train in New York City and headed back to Winston-Salem for a job that had essentially ended. I was disappointed, and it was a long, sad trip.

Once back home, there was little work to be done on mergers since RJR would be some time digesting this major purchase. I busied myself with routine tasks in the business planning department, but the truth was that I didn't really have a job. Today, a company would promptly fire someone in a position like that. But RJR was paternalistic in those days, and they kept me around. On my own time, I began to actively manage the fund that later became the Carolina Equity Fund LP. Quite coincidentally, in a few months John Dowdle asked me if I would manage the RJR pension fund. An offer that I accepted, thinking it would be a short-term assignment. The pension officer wasn't a very big job in those days.

The oil business peaked three years later in 1980. A job in Houston would have been a disaster. Energy companies were firing employees by the thousands. Only now, twenty-seven years later is energy again gaining prominence as a growth sector of the economy. In contrast, pensions and investing grew exponentially over that same period. Due to market appreciation, acquisitions, cash contributions, and 401k plans, the assets at RJR expanded from $200 million in the U.S. to $4 billion in 27 countries between 1977 and 1986 when I left the company.   Chance placed me in one of the great growth industries of the last thirty years. And it is fortunate indeed that I didn't get what I wanted - a career in the oil business.   That lucky break led me to a job that has been thoroughly enjoyable for nearly three decades.[6]

Malcolm McLean

Certainly Malcolm wasn't perfect, and in the end he had less than stellar business success and a company that went bankrupt. But he was always fascinating. He called himself a "builder, not a runner." He meant he was an entrepreneur not a professional manager. And indeed that was true. Every day for Malcolm was an adventure, dreaming up some new business scheme – he would throw off a hundred ideas a day, and most of them made no sense at all as you listened to them. But he thought in terms so large that the average person couldn't follow his reasoning. Like most successful entrepreneurs I've met, he had a great deal of trouble verbalizing his thoughts in a logical, organized way – a trait that often made his proposals sound downright crazy. But of course they weren't all crazy.

He created containerized shipping. He is little known today for having done this, but he changed the way everything in the world is shipped. He had this vision to revolutionize shipping when he was in his thirties, and he had the tenacity to build a giant containerized-shipping company from scratch, risking his personal fortune and reputation on something all the "experts" told him could not be done. He talked to the best marine architects in the world about his idea for a container ship. They said, "If you build a ship like that, it will turn upside down when you put the boxes on it."

A Questionable Residence

One anecdote about Malcolm involved his residence. The story goes that when Malcolm moved to New York City, he went to the voter registration office to register. The clerk in the office looked over Malcolm's application and said, "You don't have a high school diploma. You will need to take a literacy test." And as if to make the point, the clerk said, "See, on your application you have listed your 'residence' as the Pierre Hotel. Now obviously you work at the Pierre Hotel, you do not live at the Pierre Hotel." "No," Malcolm said, "I live at the Pierre Hotel."

And the clerk decided that Malcolm really didn't need to take a literacy test.

A Head For Numbers

Malcolm carried in his head a set of valuation rules that let him put a price on

---

[6] I originally wrote this material in early 2005. In mid-2005 I got a call from Rosemary Sunderland. She told me that Jack had died a few weeks earlier after a long illness. She wanted me to know that one of the last things he did was read my book and my comments meant a great deal to him. Probably not so much as my opportunity to know Jack meant to me.

virtually anything from a huge company to painting a house. His unique ability to do this was legendary, and he enjoyed doing it as though it were a parlor game. This convinced me that a corporate giant has little chance of winning negotiations with such a crafty entrepreneur. The following, written by Floyd Rogers in 1989 in the *Winston-Salem Journal* describes my experience with Malcolm:

Gene Hoots was at his desk in Aminoil's Rockefeller Center headquarters in New York City one spring morning in 1976 when Malcolm McLean called from his home in The Pierre Hotel and said that he wanted to come by to see Hoots. Hoots was a manager in the mergers and acquisitions department at R. J. Reynolds Industries. McLean, having merged his Sea-Land Corp. into Reynolds seven years earlier, owned about 10 percent of Reynolds and sat on the board. McLean was a powerful man, and brilliant. "I stood a bit in awe of him," Hoots said.

Reynolds was interested in expanding its oil holdings by buying the major U.S. subsidiaries of Burmah Oil Co., and Hoots had spent almost the last year and a half doing a detailed study of their value. When McLean got to the office that morning, he wanted to talk about Burmah. And he wanted to know what Hoots' analysis showed its subsidiaries' value to be.

"Before he asked me to come to the final number," Hoots said, "he took a sheet of paper and wrote a number on it, and then he turned it upside down. And he asked me to give the value that I had come up with, and I had come up with something like $580 million...something in excess of what we paid for it. I gave him my number, and he turned his paper over and said, 'That's my value.' I looked at his number and we were about 3% apart.

"And I said, 'Well, where did you get that number?'"

"He said, 'At the house [He always referred to his suite in the Pierre Hotel as "the house."] this morning before I walked down here, I read that little brochure that the bankers gave us... And I had time to think about it walking down here, and that's the value I came up with.'"

Hoots said he felt that he had wasted fourteen months coming to a conclusion that McLean had reached while walking ten blocks or so from The Pierre to the Aminoil offices at Rockefeller Center.

"That's exactly what I said, and do you know what he said? He said, 'You have to use your methods, and I use mine,'" Hoots said. "And what he knew was that, even as powerful as he was, you couldn't go into the board of directors of Reynolds, to the eighteen or so people in the room, and simply say this is what it's worth and I know it, without any supporting facts."[xxxvii]

Two other examples illustrate Malcolm's unbelievable ability to value almost any type business transaction from the smallest to the largest:

Malcolm had come to visit Jack Sunderland late one afternoon, and Jack told Malcolm that in the evening a painter was coming to give Jack a quote on painting his house. Malcolm immediately began his game: "I'll tell you how much he'll charge you." Malcolm got out his famous pencil and paper; he used scratch pads constantly. (I used to joke that the scratch pads were magic, but Frank Power, my friend at Aminoil, reminded me that the magic was in the user not the pad.) He asked Jack, "How big is your house? How many stories? How many doors and windows?" Then Malcolm told Jack the bid would be $1,280. Jack said the painter charged him $1,250.

Years later I was in New York on business with a man from Winston-Salem who worked for an actuarial firm there. He and I were in the Ritz Carlton lounge, a few blocks from Malcolm's home in the Pierre. Malcolm was there with Mrs. McLean and another couple. But he could not resist any opportunity to talk business. He had long since disassociated himself from RJR, and he probably wanted to pump me for information since he was back in the shipping business as a competitor. This despite the fact that I knew nothing of value to him. Anyway, he sent Mrs. McLean and his guests home, and he joined us. When he learned the company my friend worked for, he started his parlor game. He knew the founder of the company from his Winston-Salem days and he also knew that it was a private company that did not reveal its financials. "I'll tell you how much profit you made last year." he said. "How many professionals work there? How many secretaries and staff people?" My friend told him and he said, "Your profits were $___.

I don't remember the number, but my friend got a startled look and exclaimed, "Who told you that?"

Malcolm was obviously very close to the right number. He laughed and said, "Nobody told me. It's easy. In a professional service firm like yours, the rule of thumb is X (again I don't remember the number) dollars of profit per professional employee and Y dollars for each supporting staff person. It was so simple when he explained it. The amazing thing was that he could keep all these details stored in his head and pull them out at will.

Beach Property

The only time I ever attended a full RJR board meeting was for was a discussion of the Burmah purchase. Malcolm was very much in favor of buying the oil company and sometimes made his point with a quip or comment that didn't always sit well with the more formal directors. He commented that he knew a great deal about the oil business because he had run a service station in Red Springs (in eastern NC where he grew up). Now that comment from anyone else would have been absurd. Pumping gas at a service station forty years earlier does not generally qualify a person for an informed opinion on a half billion dollar oil deal. But knowing Malcolm, it's a fairly safe bet that he absorbed more knowledge about the oil business from a year or so in a rural service station than the average person does in a twenty year career with Exxon-Mobil.

At the same meeting, there was a discussion about one of the energy fields RJR would be buying in northern California near a major geological fault line. Another director spoke up and said that an earthquake might split the site and drop half of it in the Pacific. Malcolm's comeback was, "Good, then we'll own beachfront property!"

"Nothing's Going To Change"

Of all the comments made by acquirers, this one makes the least sense to me. If you aren't going to change anything, then why the heck would you pay that enormous premium for control? The negative result of mergers seems to be the same no matter the size of the company or the industry involved. I recently talked with a man who had resigned as a director at a funeral home. I asked him how his company had fared after they sold out to a big national firm. His answer was what I expected. He said that the day the sale was announced (a very well kept secret) the funeral home owner called all the staff together and said, "We're selling, but nothing is going to change." This is what management says after every acquisition. The ex-funeral director said that every mortuary scans the obituaries daily to calculate their market share. When the buyout took place, his funeral home had twice the market share of their big local competitor. Now that competitor has three times the market share of his old company.

Yet another lesson in M&A on how deals don't work.

Acquisitions – The Quest For The Elusive "Growth"

There is no such thing as a "growth" company, and investors are unwise to pay top dollar for growth that probably won't last.

Mega-mergers are as likely to destroy shareholder wealth as to create it. In most cases, the cost of integration overwhelms the expected economies. Customers lose out and market share declines. A big merger deal may temporarily distract shareholders from a company's otherwise lackluster performance, but it doesn't do anything to make a company more dynamic. You don't get a gazelle by breeding dinosaurs.

Corporate managements seem easily seduced by the out-sized deal. Why? A major acquisition is the fastest way to compensate for a company's failure to grow internally. Shareholders should always look skeptically at acquisitions. A company that expands via acquisition grows not because it is good (although it may be), but because its investment bankers are good.

But shareholders are as much culprits as they are victims. Their expectations induce CEOs into poor deal making. It's a fair bet that nearly every CEO feels he is expected to deliver above-average growth in revenue and earnings. Any CEO of a large company who's still tempted to shoot the moon should consider that without relatively unique circumstances, a bold growth strategy is likely to end in tears. Growing internally isn't as enticing as a big deal, but it's a much safer bet for shareholders.[xxviii]

Another word of caution about putting a high value on growth stocks. Stock market profits don't keep up with the economy. Since 1871 reported earnings per share have had about 1.4% real growth per year. This is less than the 3% growth of the economy or the 1.6% growth in per capita gross domestic product. This was long a puzzle - why didn't reported earnings grow as fast as the economy? The reason is that many of the fastest growing companies are privately owned. They don't report their earnings and public investors can't own their stock. Once such companies become public via an Initial Public Offering, they usually grow much slower.[xxix]

MEDIA

The world is not nearly so bad as the popular media tell us. We must remember that there is no good news. Good things generally aren't news. News reports never begin with the statement, "Today there were no murders, no robberies, no traffic fatalities. There were no tornados or blizzards and none are in sight. The economy is okay, and the stock market didn't do much of anything. Details at 11."

More and more, the media hype everything possible to get our attention. Charlotte, NC has had exactly one major hurricane in its recorded history - Hurricane Hugo passed through Charleston and moved across South and North Carolina causing severe damage in 1989. But this is still ingrained in everyone's memory and there are obviously deep-seated fears that it could happen again. So anytime there is a hurricane in the Bahamas or closer, no matter what direction it is headed, the news begins something like this, "Could we be in store for another devastating hurricane? Hurricane Cassandra may be headed this way. Stay tuned for our expert weather analysis." Now the odds are that Charlotte won't see another hurricane like Hugo in the next two hundred years, but the announcement surely gets viewers' attention.

Everybody Has An Axe To Grind
I tell a story about me to suit myself, or I don't tell it at all.
  Kenneth Hoots

I sometimes listen to Rush Limbaugh. Why? Because he says things I want to hear. Does that make him right? No. In fact, the only topic that I am qualified to critique is the stock market. Occasionally he "explains" stock market movements. And those explanations are nearly always wrong. This makes me wonder about other things he says with such conviction. Even Rush admits that he is at least as much entertainer as he is political pundit.

Regarding the news, the three major networks have had their way for many decades. Now they cannot understand why they are losing market share. Maybe all three anchors on the national evening news have been in place too long. When you have as much power and influence as they do, you get used to being catered to, and that certainly leads to being out of touch. The older we get and the more power we accumulate, the less we want to hear anybody else's opinion.

I am wary of all the media information because there are so many opportunities for bias and error. We watch an endless array of "experts" explaining the news to us. They show us a film clip of something that we can readily see for ourselves.

Then they bring on the "expert" who explains to us what we are seeing. Then they ask the expert to tell us what is going to happen as a result of this. But there are so many factors in any forecast - weather, economy, war, whatever - that the outcome more than three days ahead is totally unpredictable. Yet these people speak as though they are telling us something of real value.

In the Iraq war in 2003, every news channel had military experts explaining what was happening and what was going to happen. They were all wrong, at least wrong enough to be useless. Our local channel news had its own military expert, John Falkenbury, a retired army officer and now Vice President of an international communications company. I was very impressed by his analysis. He wisely limited his comments to explaining various weapons in the U.S. arsenal. He talked about a very technical subject so that lay people could understand. He did not try to project the outcome of the war.

Information Overload

Most of us suffer from information overload - we read too many newspapers and watch too much television. And we get worthless information. At any moment, I can lay out a bullish or a bearish forecast. If my forecast was correct, the Dow Jones average could move 2000 points. And no matter whether it goes up or down (probably not that extreme in either case) a year later the move would be forgotten by the people who at this moment deem it the most important factor in their investment life.

Gurus – Market Direction

We can get a sense of the value of brokerage "gurus" by examining their forecasts in two very crucial years when it was important to be right, or at least reasonably close. And since these two years were major market turning points, it would have been helpful to at least get the market direction right. Many of the major brokerage houses have "strategists" who tell their customers what the market is going to do. You need only look back over these last few years to see how little value these forecasts provided. With results like this, you don't want to depend on experts to tell you where the market's headed.

Nine major brokerage firms' gurus forecast the S&P 500 for the calendar year ahead for the years 2001 and 2002. In 2001, the firms' forecasts ranged from +30% to –2% with an average of +15%. The market was down -13%. But not to be discouraged, and only slightly less bullish, in 2002 the brokers' range of forecasts was from +37% to -17% with an average of +12%. The market was down -23%. Over the combined two-year period, not a single firm got the direction right and only two brokers got the direction right for either year, a 2/18 success ratio. The best forecast for any broker for either year missed the market result by 6% and for the two years missed by 13%. The worst forecast missed by 52% for the two years.

Linking the two years, if you had followed the brokers' advice you expected a return of 29% over the two-year period and got an actual return of –32%. In the first year alone, brokers expected a $1.00 investment to grow to $1.15 and the market gave you $.87. If you had decided to follow the brokers' advice again after the first year (although it's hard to understand why you would), you would have taken the $.87 left from your investment dollar at the beginning of the year and expected to grow it to $.97. Instead the $.87 shrank to $.67.

Most of these firms remain largely optimistic year after year. Perhaps because in most years the market does go up, and therefore they will be right more than they are wrong. But it doesn't help much to know that. In fact you can make a forecast yourself just by saying on average the market goes up 5-7% a year (excluding dividends). Your result would be as good as these brokerage firms. But people still heed the advice of these highly paid experts. Why are these people paid millions of dollars each year for advice that is worthless? Because their comments are not worthless to the brokers; they encourage trading, and brokerage firms make money when people trade.[xxx]

Useful Idiots
The insight that I would have and I think for it to be productive, I would hope that this would not be a political commentary on my part but more a human commentary...

Sean Penn to CNN critiquing his trip to Iraq.

Huh? Josef Stalin called the Sean Penns of the world "useful idiots". It is amazing how we hang on every word of celebrities – movie stars, television personalities, talk show hosts, as though they have informed opinions. They know no more than you or I; they simply have a far better forum to advance their views. All we really know about these people is that they are very good at one thing – giving an excellent performance.

Responsibility - Again
As for the mass media, newspapers and television – the recent fiascos at the *New York Times* and CBS Television News should certainly give us pause when we are inclined to take at face value anything we see in print. Most amazing is the reaction of the *New York Times* CEO. He first said the scandal at his newspaper was only about one bad reporter, not the management. Then two top editors were forced to resign because of internal strife, and he said this is still not about "me." As the man in charge who set the policies and picked the people, who does he think it's about, if not about him? And this is the person who is shaping public opinion at the newspaper considered by many to be the best in the world.[7]

---

[7] See Appendix Two.

Movie Rules

When you listen to actors talk about their craft, it is apparent that some of them can't separate reality from the roles they play. I was watching an actor describe the filming "The Perfect Storm." He told how he feared for his life and thought he might drown. He gave the impression that they were really filming on the ocean in a storm. Then they showed how the movie was made. For heaven sake, they were all on a <u>piece</u> of a boat in a big swimming pool with artificial waves. He wasn't any closer to drowning than he would have been in his own bathtub, but apparently he couldn't tell the difference between that and a real storm.

LEGAL ISSUES

Tobacco – The Great Boondoggle

Some see an irony in any federal challenge (to a tobacco company merger): After all, if it is a national goal to discourage smoking by raising cigarette taxes, making the habit more expensive wouldn't seem to be such a bad thing.

Vanessa O'Connell and John R. Wilke, *Wall Street Journal*, May 28, 2004, p. C4

A Strange Industry

I went to work for R. J. Reynolds Tobacco Company in 1965. I soon learned that tobacco was a strange business Each morning I drove by the showcase cigarette factory on my way to the office. I noticed that out front were a number of flags, the American flag, the NC State flag, etc. But there was a flag I didn't recognize, a dark blue pennant with a single white letter "E". I asked what that flag was, and the answer was surprising. It was an award from the Department of Commerce. The "E" was for Excellence in Export. We were good corporate citizens, shipping cigarettes overseas and helping the U.S. international balance of payments. The first smoking and health studies had already been published. Apparently the government thought it was okay to give cancer to people, just so long as they were foreigners. Washington was paying farmers to grow tobacco and praising RJR for exporting its product overseas, and at the same time spending more money to discourage the use of cigarettes in the U.S. This was your tax dollars at work. Is this a great country, or what, where we could afford to throw away billions of dollars on directly opposing programs? And over the next forty years, the government's official position on tobacco hasn't been clarified one bit. Do uncoordinated policies like this make any sense? Being a cynic, I expect government policy will get much worse before it gets better, if indeed it ever gets better.

Big Bucks For Everybody

In 1998, the four biggest American tobacco companies settled lawsuits with forty-six states by pledging to pay the states about $206 billion over twenty-five years. But Wall Street has come up with a way for states to get their hands on the money immediately. The solution is a tobacco settlement bond, a tax-exempt bond backed entirely by revenue from the settlement. The bonds are beginning to catch on with individual investors.

Cigarette Sales - Who Gets The Money		
Distribution of Sale	$/Pack	% Sales
Selling Price	$3.89	100%
Mfg. Cost	$1.47	38%
Federal Income Tax	$0.10	3%
State Income Tax	$0.01	0%
Profit for Shareholders	$0.17	4%
Federal Excise Tax	$0.39	10%
State Excise Tax Avg.	$1.25	32%
MSA Agreement	$0.50	13%
Summary		
Mfg. Cost	$1.47	38%
Profit for Shareholders	$0.17	4%
Federal Taxes	$0.49	13%
State Taxes	$1.76	45%

Because the bondholders receive payments from four tobacco companies, the creditworthiness of the investment depends on the ability of these companies to keep selling cigarettes for another generation. The major companies backing the bonds are Philip Morris; R. J. Reynolds; Brown & Williamson, a division of British American Tobacco; and Lorillard, a division of the Loews Corporation. Revenues from seventeen other companies are also providing part of the settlement payments.

Special-purpose corporations, set up to issue the bonds, take in the payments and pay the bondholders. The bonds are tax-exempt because the proceeds are used for public purposes. More than $4.4 billion in tobacco settlement bonds have been sold by various states. These bonds transfer to bondholders the risk of not being paid.

The $246 billion, 25-year tobacco-settlement deal did not dictate to the states where the money must be spent. But the forty-six states that sued did so on the pretext that the money is to care for sick smokers and fund anti-smoking campaigns. Most states are directing the funds to all manner of spending programs unrelated to tobacco. California, for example, is using some of its windfall to fix sidewalks. Many states are re-directing the money into state budgets to cover deficits. Only sixteen are using substantial shares of their settlement money to fund smoking-prevention programs. Critics say the real surprise is that anyone believed state officials and politicians when they promised they would use the money for smoking-related programs.[xxxi]

And the court system is completely out of control. In a Florida case, the trial and the verdict had a sense of unreality. Jurors are asked to make decisions about billions of dollars. Like most of us, these jurors would have great difficulty in actually conceptualizing what a million dollars represents, let alone a billion dollars. One hundred and forty-five billion dollars! It was the biggest punitive damage award in U.S. history – and it resulted from a "fundamentally unfair" trial in which plaintiffs' lawyers "succeeded in inflaming the jury's passions," most notably through "egregious" appeals to racial sentiment, to the point that its members "ran amuck." That's what a unanimous state appeals court said when it struck down the award against the tobacco industry purportedly on behalf of all sick smokers in the state of Florida.

The appeals court says that virtually every aspect of the verdict flunks on grounds of basic fairness and legality. It found the damage award grossly excessive and that the case should not have gone forward as a class action. Separate trials are needed because of the vast differences among individuals on such issues as why they decided to smoke or quit.

At trial the judge had barred tobacco companies from arguing that their $246 billion settlement with the states had already resolved the punitive damages issue. But the appeals court pointed out that the state of Florida's lawsuit against the tobacco industry asserted claims of fraud, conspiracy, addictiveness and demanded punitive damages. By consenting to a lucrative settlement of those claims, the court said, the attorneys general of Florida foreclosed further claims for punitive damages.[xxxii]

Yet another case shows the conflict of interest woven into all the tobacco legal maneuvering. States attorneys general recently worked to protect Philip Morris from bankruptcy in an Illinois case that would have required Philip Morris to post a $12 billion bond. Yet the Washington state attorney general said in 1996, "The tobacco industry has targeted our kids, withheld safer products, and deliberately misled the public about the safety of smoking."

Now the states have switched sides. The $246 billion fund was to be paid over twenty-five years by cigarette manufacturers. States were to spend the money to educate kids not to smoke and to pay for state citizens suffering from tobacco related illnesses. Less than five percent of the payment money is going into smoking control. It has been spent on other health programs, college scholarships, flood control, and general state budget deficit reduction. Some of the money has gone into state pension funds, which is reinvested into tobacco stocks. [One of CornerCap's clients said when the settlement was reached, "The tobacco companies are still in business, but they now have just fifty significant stockholders, the states' attorneys general." And it looks as though he was right in his assessment.] States have come to rely increasingly on the tobacco money, which they need more than ever since the economy turned down and income tax revenues fell. And a big portion of the settlement went to attorneys. In Texas, the five attorneys who represented the state received $3.3 billion in fees.

Again, we need to take some responsibility for asking ourselves and our leaders – What is important to us as a people? What can we afford to spend our finite resources on?[xxxiii]

For Some Lawyers There's Never Enough

A managing partner of a Wall Street law firm shared with me his experiences with tobacco litigators. He jokingly said, "I don't deal with plaintiff's attorneys and I don't let my kids play with their kids."

He once was a partner with a huge law firm that represented the tobacco industry, so he is well acquainted with the controversy surrounding tobacco. He now does securities law and works with any number of firms and governments who are securitizing their funds from the tobacco Master Settlement Agreement (MSA), so that they don't wait for years to get their billions. They want it now.

A law firm that got a piece of the MSA became his client. This firm, like many others, didn't want to wait twenty-five years for their "lottery" money so they had his law firm put together a security offering. $4 billion over twenty-five equal annual payments, discounted at 8% would be $1.7 billion in "up front" money for the tobacco lawyers. A number of points came from his experience:

The plaintiff law firm's MSA money represented about $60,000 per billable hour, not a bad rate for legal services.

The plaintiff law firm balked at the bill from the securities lawyers. They said it was too much and asked for a courtesy discount as fellow attorneys. [It was a relatively small bill considering the money involved, about .01% of the offering]

Eventually, the plaintiff attorneys grew unhappy with their internal split of the $1.7 billion. The law firm dissolved and the partners are suing each other over how much each should get. Of course, equally divided it would be about $85 million each for twenty attorneys, and if you threw in support staff and gave them an equal cut, then fifty people would get $32 million each. Even at the smaller share, they can live like royalty for the rest of their lives. But apparently, that isn't enough. With any justice, most of their take will be eaten up in legal fees as they sue each other. [There is irony in these convoluted agreements between tobacco growers, cigarette manufacturers, consumers, and governments. For a really humorous take on this, see Appendix Three.]

What Comes After Tobacco – Food, Soft Drinks, Alcohol?

This is a good question, and it looks like the answer is "yes to all of these." There are parallels here to tobacco. Too much fat food is a national health problem. Consider the statistics: (1) Obesity caused 300,000 deaths and $117 billion in healthcare costs in 2000. (2) 14% of all children were overweight in 1999, up from 6% in the late 1970s. (3) Obesity is associated with an average annual increase in medical spending of $395 per obese patient.

Food companies are considering warning labels telling people not to overeat. Where do we stop? Does the waitress in the restaurant cut off the customers when she thinks they have eaten too much, and if not is the restaurant liable? Can the waitress refuse to serve a customer she considers too fat? Does this sound ridiculous? Of course, but no more insane than many of the other rules we have in place.[xxxiv]

As a society, we have no more discipline in this area than we do in our financial lives.

3:   TECHNOLOGY REVISITED

We stressed in our Technology Bubble report four years ago that nothing grows forever and that investors shouldn't count on a single investment sector no matter how attractive - that people were too enthusiastic about "technology" stocks. This is not to say that technology is bad. In fact it is great, but it's the customers who tend to benefit, and not the investors.

FALLEN ANGELS

It's A Long Way Back To The Top

We warned four years ago that, if history was any guide, technology stocks would not lead the next bull market. Fallen angels seldom soar to their former heights. Let's look at some portfolios of technology stocks and how they've done for the last four years.

Name	7/29/00 Price	12/31/00 Price	%Gain	12/31/04 Price	Since 7/29/00 %Gain	Since 12/31/00 %Gain
Accelerated Net	$20.06	$2.78	-86.1%	$.09	-99.6%	-96.8%
Ariba, Inc.	$107.63	$53.63	-50.2%	$16.60	-84.6%	-69.0%
AudioCodes Ltd.	$49.13	$13.56	-72.4%	$16.61	-66.2%	22.5%
Next Level Comm.	$89.88	$11.38	-87.3%	$1.04	-98.8%	-90.9%
Powertel, Inc.	$86.06	$61.94	-28.0%	$0.02	-100.0%	-100.0%
Sonus Networks	$65.00	$25.25	-61.2%	$5.73	-91.2%	-77.3%
Average			-64.2%		-90.1%	-68.6%

Small Tech Favorites

The table above shows six small technology stocks from a news article in mid-2000. The writer warned that they were good candidates to lose 100%. He was wrong, slightly. By the end of that year, they had declined 64%, and four years later they are down -90.1%. So the person who picked this portfolio still has $.10 left for every $1 invested four and a half years ago. And since our last review four years ago, this portfolio would have cost you –68% by trying to buy them for a "comeback."

Analysts' Favorites

These six stocks were picked by noted security analysts in early 2000. All were predicted to rise, an average of 79% over the next year and a half. The highest they reached on average was a gain of 27% (due to Priceline

ANALYSTS' PREDICTIONS MADE IN EARLY 2000				
Company	Predicted Gain	Highest Gain	12/31/2000 Gain/(Loss)	12/31/2004 Gain/(Loss)
Lucent	112%	19%	-76%	-93%
Priceline	168%	86%	-98%	-93%
PSINet	102%	43%	-98%	-100%
Red Hat	29%	6%	-93%	-85%
VA Linux	35%	4%	-96%	-99%
Yahoo!	26%	5%	-87%	-84%
Average	79%	27%	-91%	-92%

which rose 86%). At the end of 2000, the average of this group was then down 91% from the price at the time of the prediction. We cautioned that technology stocks would not likely return to their former glory. Once the bloom is off, an industry group almost never leads the next recovery. There were plenty of investors in these stocks who were still hoping that the market would eventually prove them right. We said that they would be better advised to take their losses and move on. In the following four years, the S&P 500 has given a return of –1.3%. The Russell 2000 has returned a strong 43.8%. And this portfolio of six stocks has declined -12%, but only another -1% from the original price. Investors had already lost 91 cents out of every dollar they invested a year earlier, so a -12% decline from that point only cost them another 1 cent on their original investment, but -12% of what they had left at the end of 2000. Those who disregarded the fundamentals of these stocks and waited for them to "come back" have continued to lose.

Cisco, Everybody's Favorite

Cisco has $21 billion of cash on hand, and the debate is whether it should pay a dividend. Stockholders said "No."

Cisco has remained profitable for most of the downturn, including the last six quarters. Cisco is debt free. It spends heavily on R&D – 17% of revenue in the last quarter. It has trimmed inventories, reduced head count, and pressed suppliers to reduce prices. It outsources 90% of its boxes, up from 60%.

The stock hit $8.12 at its low. It is now about $15. Still it isn't cheap. It is 28 times trailing earnings and 25 times the projected EPS for fiscal 2004. In March 2000, Cisco hit $80 a share, briefly the largest capitalization of any company, $550 billion. Of the $6 trillion in lost market value in this bear market, Cisco stock alone accounts for 7% of that total. New competition may erode the strong profit margins and 70% market share that Cisco enjoys in its product lines.[xxxv]

Major Tech Stocks

We picked thirteen tech stocks at random in 1999. After dropping -46% in

2000, this portfolio recovered, but was still down -37% after another four years,. The decline would have been -65% without the spectacular performance of EBay, which increased 272%. EBay is the only stock in the group that is higher now than at the end of 1999. Of course there are winners in the technology sector, but no one could have predicted which of the thirteen it would be.

Name	12/31/1999 Price	12/31/2000 Price	1 Year % Gain	12/31/2004 Price	5 Year % Gain
Amazon	$76.13	$15.56	-80%	$44.29	-42%
AOL	$75.88	$34.80	-54%	$19.45	-74%
Cisco	$53.56	$38.25	-29%	$19.32	-64%
Dell	$51.00	$17.44	-66%	$42.14	-17%
EBay	$62.59	$33.00	-47%	$232.68	272%
Intel	$41.16	$30.06	-27%	$23.39	-43%
JDSU	$80.66	$41.69	-48%	$3.17	-96%
Microsoft	$116.75	$43.38	-63%	$53.44	-54%
Motorola	$49.08	$20.25	-59%	$17.20	-65%
Oracle	$27.84	$29.06	4%	$13.72	-51%
RF Micro	$34.22	$27.44	-20%	$6.84	-80%
Sun Micro	$38.72	$27.88	-28%	$5.39	-86%
Yahoo!	$216.43	$30.06	-86%	$37.68	-83%
Total			-46%		-37%

Selectron – A Dream Deferred

In 1999, on a flight to Charlotte, I sat next to a young man who worked for Selectron. Being an old economy, value investor, I had never heard of the company. It definitively had not become a buy on our Fundametrics® screen. The company contract manufactures for many technology businesses. At that point, things were going great for Selectron shareholders and employees. This fellow had lots of stock and options. He had a great job, a great house, and two Mercedes. He was thirty-eight years old, and his plan was for Selectron to double one more time and he would retire, presumably before age forty. And the way Selectron stock was rising, maybe before he was thirty-nine.

What was wrong with this picture? He didn't ask and I didn't share my thoughts with him – they probably wouldn't have made much of an impression anyway. His whole plan depended on a single stock. As we say again and again, this is dangerous. And this particular stock, at that moment, was selling at a P/E ratio of 50, $40 per share.

Five years later, we know that a funny thing happened on the way to that lad's retirement. Selectron stock didn't make it to the required $80. It did get to $45 and then started down. It touched $1.50 a share at its low and is now $5.33. I suspect the two Mercedes are now history, perhaps along with the young man's job. He will probably have to put his retirement plans on hold for thirty years.

This story has been repeated millions of times since 1999. This one especially interested me because of the conversation on the plane. I began to follow Selectron stock and the Alice-In-Wonderland nature of the technology industry at that time. Even company management was caught up in the delusion. As demand began to plummet for technology products, the CEO of Selectron issued a press release explaining that this environment was _perfect_ for his company. As demand for their customers' products declined, those customers would be inclined to lay off their own workers and turn to Selectron to manufacture for them because the cost would be lower. In other words, customers would idle their own plants, lay off their own work force, and farm their manufacturing out to a third party. Not a likely scenario, and it didn't happen.

The Living Dead

Stock	Recent Price	Bubble High	Following Low	% Off All-Time High	% Off S. Low	% To Recover To High	Years @ 20% Growth
Akamai	$13.03	$345.50	$0.56	-96%	2227%	2552%	18
Corning	$11.77	$112.63	$1.10	-89%	977%	857%	12
InfoSpace	$47.55	$1,385.00	$3.70	-97%	1185%	2813%	18
Iomega	$5.54	$137.81	$7.70	-96%	37%	1207%	14
Novell	$6.75	$44.56	$1.57	-85%	330%	560%	10
Priceline	$23.59	$990.00	$6.30	-98%	274%	4097%	20
Selectron	$5.33	$48.00	$1.48	-89%	260%	801%	12

Barron's Technology Week, June 23, 2003

Barron's called these seven stocks "the living dead." They are tech stocks that sank when the bubble burst but have since had impressive turn-arounds. All of them dropped more than 85% and then, from those lows, delivered staggering rates of return up to more than 2000%. But those great increases were enjoyed only by those bold enough to buy at the bottom, and we're willing to bet that wasn't many people. For those who think this increase confirms that the techs will "come back", the last column shows the years it will take each stock to attain its former high, assuming an excellent return of 20% each year. For example, Novell will take _only_ about ten years to get even. It would take over twenty years for Priceline. Twenty years is a long time to wait to get your money back.

Henry Blodget Revisited

Even the biggest culprit in the technology boom and bust may have learned a measure of personal responsibility, although it comes too late to save millions of people's money. Henry Blodget has begun writing as a journalist/researcher, not as an analyst. He was barred for life from the securities business and paid a fine of $4 million. In his first report his disclosure section may be the best part. He admits he will mess up from time to time, saying, "Sometimes this fallibility will result from the uncertainty of predicting events and forming conclusions with incomplete information. Sometimes it will result from mistakes, ignorance, and/or idiocy."[xxxvi] If only his research reports on Internet stocks six years ago had carried such a clear warning to his readers!

TECHNOLOGY IS GREAT – TECH STOCKS MAY, OR MAY NOT, BE

I have always wished that my computer would be as easy to use as my telephone. My wish has come true. I no longer know how to use my telephone.
Bjarne Stroustrup, computer science professor, designer for C++ programming language (1950-)

Fears About Technology

Forbidden Fruit
1628 William Harvey publishes description of blood circulation but the theory isn't accepted for years.
1632 Galileo is put under house arrest for arguing that the planets orbit around the sun.
1847 Scottish obstetrician James Simpson is attacked by the British Church for using anesthesia to block pain in childbirth.
1925 John Scopes is convicted and fined $100 for teaching evolution to high school students.
1963 Keith Reemstma, a New Orleans surgeon, is criticized after he transplants chimp kidneys into humans.
1975 Cambridge, MA, and Palo Alto, CA, temporarily block construction of gene- splicing labs.
1978 Louise Brown, first baby born by IVF, triggers world-wide fears.

Technology is scary. Cloning is the most recent of a slew of new biotechnology tools, one that is especially powerful but no more outlandish or immoral than in-vitro fertilization, gene splicing, or organ transplantation. These too were frightening when first introduced but have transformed modern medicine without harming the essential sacredness of being human. Cloning may help treat Alzheimer's disease. It may allow nerves to regenerate.

While many people are upset about scientists who experiment with embryos, the fact is fertility researchers have been fiddling with – and destroying – embryos for years without causing a public stir. We may someday feel as comfortable with cloning as we do with a host of once ghoulish-seeming therapies, such as transplanting a dead person's still-beating heart into a living person's chest.[xxxvii]

Technology may provide more advantages to the old economy companies than to the new economy. Old line companies are using the internet and technologies to serve customers and cut costs in many operating areas.

Efficiencies are being gained across the board by the Dow Jones Thirty companies which just two years ago were being derided by their dot-com competitors for "not getting it." Most of those rivals, which once sported multibillion-dollar market values, have fallen by the wayside. But their arrogance served as a wake-up call for big, established companies.

The emergence of the Internet has prompted far more uses among America's corporate leaders than were originally foreseen. Online purchasing has dramatically streamlined supply chains. But the Web has also brought companies and consumers closer together. As great as the progress on the Web has been, there's far more to go. And greater efficiencies are achieved, the results will be magnified in corporate earnings – and ultimately stock prices....the Internet revolution has only just begun.[xxxviii]

History Of Great Technologies – Lessons For The Internet, Present and Future

In a software design meeting, we were using typical technical jargon to discuss a data exchange interface with a vendor. One co-worker said the programming we had ordered was delayed because the vendor was suffering from a "severe non-linear waterfowl issue." Curious, the team leader raised his eyebrows and asked, "What exactly is that?" The programmer replied, "They don't have all their ducks in a row."

Summarized in the following table are four other great technologies that changed the world of their day. It is interesting to see how they compare with the Internet.[xxxix]

Great Technologies – Lessons for the Internet

	Printing Press	Telegraph	Railroad	Radio
Description	Created 1450s Helped create the modern world Spread through Europe in 15 years Craftsmen found a market for books, circulars, sermons	Created 1830s First telecom network – erased limits of time and distance Transformed the news business making it timely. Helped create the modern stock market and led directly to phone, radio, electric power Initially seen as a novelty	Created 1820s Linked markets and people faster than anything before Huge economic, social, impact – lowered shipping costs, created national economy Concentrated wealth Early frenzy of building – but created lasting industry	Created 1906 Reinvented idea of mass culture, with major audience From first technology it was ten years before first radio station, then quickly grew RCA was darling stock, led market boom of the 1920s
Parallels	Loosened grip of the church on knowledge, created a mass market like media today Cost and convenience won big market Forced legal definition of "copyright" and plagiarism	Inspired enthusiasm and hype Success bred congestion – message delays Users created shorthand to keep messages brief Sub-culture of operators grew, long-distance romances. Predictions that newspapers would become obsolete	Transformed the stock market Stock market bubble First commercial railroad in 1825 in northern England Transformed retailing – made Sears and allowed cheaper goods for consumers nationwide.	First modern mass medium, closely parallels Internet Early users were hobbyists Skeptics recognized it, but doubted is commercial value Early skepticism morphed into irrational exuberance Napster of its day, ripping off Composers and programmers
Differences	No struggle with business model Printing was profitable from beginning Printing was done by skilled artisans (same today), but internet publishing requires no special skills	Very quick commercial adoption only 8 years, vs. 25 for Internet Never a mass market, stayed in hands of professionals Was largely a monopoly Never overcame serious bandwidth shortage	Required huge upfront capital and was not dominated by small individual entrepreneurs Operators could amass great power and wealth	Federal government has mostly left Internet alone, but airwave congestion forced the government to control radio through the FCC. Government got to pick winners and losers by choosing who got stations.
Lessons	Internet not likely to be as revolutionary as printing Speed of information will change access to information and increase understanding	Information wants to be free, unless you must pay someone to deliver it; with the internet, it costs almost nothing to send a book or paper, but it's still expensive to produce them.	Technology survives mania, the best days for the Internet are still ahead The pioneers wont' be the big financial winners – later entrants get the big money, never a mass market	Caution for internet companies and investors –early startups were driven out of business by consolidation Government probably can't control Internet, but look for greater government regulation

4:   INVESTMENT CHOICES

Several types of investments have come under great scrutiny by the SEC, the New York State Attorney General and other regulatory bodies. Much of this is simply the aftermath of the Bubble. Some of the "sins" of the investment business were going on long before there was a bubble, and are only now coming to light. The limited worth of security analysis has long been recognized. But the scandals in mutual funds and other investments have highlighted the many creative ways the investment industry can part unsuspecting customers from their money.

When elephants dance, it is best for the mice to step aside.
   Old African Proverb (Frank Power 1975)

MUTUAL FUNDS

The money taken by late trading and market timing is in many cases criminal. But it is insignificant to the damage that investors do to themselves. The average investor probably lost less than .1% a year from these schemes. The real damage is to investors who constantly move from one fund to another, trying to get better results. This is partly because these people never educate themselves about mutual funds, and partly because they get poor information from industry advertising.

Hopefully investors are coming around to a saner view of the markets and advisors. A survey of those with portfolios of at least $5 million found that 27% fewer were taking advice from a broker, with a commensurate rise in the number seeking out "unbiased" advice from … investment counselors. If it makes sense for someone with $5 million to stop being a stock speculator, it makes even more sense for somebody with $100,000.[xl]

Four years ago, I cited Jack Bogle for his insightful comments on investing. The former head of the Vanguard Funds is back again, pointing out the continuing need for the mutual fund industry to clean up its act. His comments are just as applicable to investment advisors and investors. The statistics on market returns are disappointing, even downright appalling.

The mutual fund industry with over 7,000 funds is unlikely to collectively do better than the market. The S&P 500 returned 12.2% from 1985-2000. That is about what funds did in total, before costs. The average mutual fund had costs – fees and commissions of about 3% and the industry under-performed the index – 2.9%. This is an important shortfall, but criticism about it should be tempered somewhat because there are always costs to investing. Even if you invest only in an index fund, it isn't free – there are some fees and commissions, albeit, much less, at .25% per year.

The really disappointing news is that the average equity fund investor made only 2.7% per year. This is the result of moving in and out of funds at the wrong time. That cost investors twice as much as the 2.9% in operating costs. It cost 6.6% a year in return. This record looks even more dismal when expressed in dollar terms. $1,000 invested at the beginning of 1985 in the market would have earned $7,910. The average stock fund earned $4,420 and the average investor earned $660.

Bogle continues to make the case that low cost market index funds are the way to invest. And I have no doubt that he is right, in theory. The problem is that even with his approach to "cheap" investing, he offers no remedy for the 6.6% a year that investors are going to lose by their own bad, emotional decisions. I suspect that Vanguard shareholders do little better than the average investor in capturing that 6.6% of return. It is easy to say to people, "Now this is all you have to do to be a successful investor - just put your money in the market and forget it."   At CornerCap we know that there is almost nobody with the discipline to do that. We are paid, in large measure, not for beating the market (although we hope that we will) but for trying to capture the 6.6% of annual stock market return that our clients will probably forego if they do their own investing.

The Investment Company Act of 1940 is the foundation of the modern mutual-fund industry. It requires that funds be "organized, operated, and managed" in the interests of fund shareholders, rather than in the interests of their managers and distributors. What is "strange" about the law is that the Act failed to establish a structure that would facilitate the realization of its noble purpose "Put the fund investor first."

In the mutual fund industry, asset-gathering replaced prudent management as the industry's prime focus. Fund expenses rose. Nearly 500 new, largely speculative, "new economy" funds were organized and offered at the recent bubble's peak. The fund failure rate soared, with some 1,900 equity funds disappearing in the last decade alone, lost in the dustbin of history, often merged with other, better performing funds, under the same management.

Stewardship for other people's money is a sacred trust, it is high time for structural reform in the fund industry. For by allowing funds to be organized, operated and managed in the interests of their management companies rather than their owners, the fund industry has defied the principles of the 1940 Act.[xli]

Portfolio Pumping

Just when I thought I'd heard about every lunatic idea that can come out of the mutual fund business, I'm confronted with one more. This time, it's something called "portfolio pumping." This is a scheme that portfolio managers have hit on to give their fund an extra boost in value just at quarter end, when they must publish their portfolio results. As the quarter end approaches, the fund will buy some extra shares of the stocks it already owns in an attempt to manipulate the price just a bit higher for reporting purposes.

Never mind that as soon as their buying stops, in the first few days of the next quarter, the shares will fall right back to their former price. Of course this costs the fund shareholders money because they have bought some stock at prices that are set for reasons that have nothing to do with the value of the company, but everything to do with creating a good marketing brochure for the fund at quarter end. As John Bogle says, mutual funds have ceased to be about taking care of the shareholders; it's all about distribution and getting more money under management for the fees.

CornerCap's CEO, Tom Quinn, addressed this problem in an email to the firm:

Many large fund groups regularly merge or liquidate poor performing mutual funds. This allows the investment firm to "bury" the poor performance and cull the fund offerings down to the most attractive funds (i.e. the ones with the best numbers). From a business perspective, many people in our industry justify the practice. This does not appear consistent with a firm that says it always puts investments and the best interest of clients ahead of the firm's near-term profitability.

A fund company's priority is to sell what is in demand with investors. Inevitably, this means the funds with the hottest numbers. The funds with lower returns are folded into another fund or closed. This business approach says the buyer is always "right." As investment advisors, should our policy be to give our best investment advice or to react to supply/demand defined by the marketing department? Some long-term investors may be in a value fund that has under-performed, but the fund company may merge that fund into one with more growth attributes that has performed better, possibly at the wrong time. In order to make a change, the client is forced to override the actions of the fund company in order to stay with his discipline.

The fund company makes no effort to consider what is best for its clients. The business objective is to consider what is best for the fund company's near term profitability and let the buyer beware.

CornerCap's marketing people feel a strong responsibility to our clients. It is critical that we do a quality job for them. In contrast, we do not know the clients that brokers bring us, and if our quality declined for them, it would be of much less concern. These are natural feelings we all have. If you know someone personally, you will care more about him. However, that is an attitude that we should work to avoid. Should we discriminate about the level of service we give a client because of the way we feel about him personally? We want to deliver the same high quality product to all our clients, regardless of personal feelings.

The danger of not having this goal is that you justify selling inferior products to certain classes of clients. That will have an impact on the reputation of our firm. Why not sell small portfolios? Because we're not set up to handle them, and we don't believe it would be good for the client. Why not set up a Market Neutral hedge fund if that is what the market demands? Because our research indicates that it would be a high cost, low return product for the clients. Would we recommend such products to our close personal relationships? No. Then we shouldn't deliver them to people we don't know.

It's difficult, and maybe impossible, to care about and deliver the same service to clients we don't know. Still, this is an attitude I would like for the firm to have. It is the ultimate in "doing the right thing when nobody's looking."

If we want to build a firm with the best reputation in the industry, then we must always start our thought process with what is the right investment decision and what is the right client service for every client. This can only be done if we decide to treat every client the same way we would treat a close friend. We examine our actions as fiduciaries, using as a yardstick the "prudent man rule" that states that whatever we do must meet the test of an action that a prudent man would take.[xlii]

We have relationships in the Channel Islands where our client is a trust company. Their administrative officer explains that Guernsey is bound by Norman law, going back to an age before Anglo-Saxon law. Attorneys must take a six-month course in the ancient Norman language. In this body of law, there is a phrase that I like much better than our "prudent man." It is "a bon père" – as a good father. This strikes me as a much better standard to measure behavior.

Survivorship Bias

"Survivorship bias" sounds like the name of a new television show. But it actually tells a great deal about how the investment industry misleads investors. It is a technique that allows mutual funds and investment management companies to enhance reported performance. It is perfectly correct, mathematically; it is factual. It is also grossly misleading.

This term refers to the practice of showing the returns of all the existing portfolios or funds that a company has. The catch is that it uses the survivors, live funds, and doesn't show the results of the dead ones. And those dead ones are dead because their results were poor. A Standard & Poor's study shows that this bias adds more than 1.5% a year to the reported historical returns of stock mutual funds. And the problem may be getting worse, with all the new specialized funds that have sprung up and then been "killed" in the last few years. The 1.5% calculation was based on forty years of data. In the last five years the spread has been 3.1% a year for specialized, sector funds. So when you buy mutual funds and your actual return over the years falls short of the published results for all mutual funds, the reason may be this method of reporting results. The average investor knows nothing about survivorship bias. It's just one more thing to be aware of in the investment process.[xliii]

The best thinking in financial economics should have taught us long ago that we can't outguess markets on a regular basis. We blame the SEC. Its whole philosophy of enforcement and rules suggest to the small investor that he should be picking winners and losers in competition with the most cold-blooded speculators in the world.

The fund industry paints itself as the salvation of Mom and Pop, then drowns them in brochures for specialty funds. These are nothing more than an invitation to commit the same mistakes that small investors have always made. The SEC should inform the public that it's wasting its money. But the agency considers itself the protector of the "active" small investor so it can't very well tell him his "activity" is the single biggest menace to his investment returns. Don't get us wrong, active fund managers are highly useful people. They do their research to make sure prices reflect the latest wisdom about what companies are worth. They make the world safe for "indexers": smart investors who stick their money in cheap funds.[xliv]

ANNUITIES AND LIFE INSURANCE

Annuities

The annuity is another investment that has been widely abused. Like any other investment product, annuities have a place in specific, special circumstances. They can protect a person who fears that he may "outlive his money." A true annuity provides an income stream each month for life, just the reverse of an insurance policy. Insurance protects your heirs if you die too soon. An annuity protects you if you live too long.

In the last few years, annuities have been oversold – often where they are not a good fit. Today, variable annuities work very much like an IRA. If a person has money to invest that would otherwise generate taxable income, he definitely should consider an annuity. The money placed in an annuity can grow tax-deferred until it is removed, like an IRA. Unfortunately, annuities are complex and difficult to understand.

When money is withdrawn from an annuity, like an IRA, the money is taxed at ordinary income tax rates. There is also a life insurance feature added so that if the investor should die and the investment has lost money, the annuity would pay back the original investment and there would be no loss.

These features come with a price tag however. The commissions can be quite high, typically around 8%, and this is a great incentive for salesmen to sell annuities even when they are not totally appropriate. For example, there is virtually no reason for an IRA to buy an annuity since the investments are already sheltered from income tax inside the IRA. The only value in this case comes from the life insurance feature, and if the investment is even modestly successful and the value of the account rises above the initial investment, the insurance feature is worthless.

Annuities are usually sold as having a great benefit by deferring income tax. There is a catch here. At the end of the line, when the money is withdrawn, all the increase is taxed at ordinary income tax rates. But if the investor chose instead to invest in a portfolio of stocks, then the profits from those stocks would not be taxed each year at ordinary income tax rates. Capital gains would be deferred for some portion of the portfolio and capital gains and dividends may have favorable tax rates that are much less than half the ordinary tax rate. So the sales pitch for the annuity doesn't always compare apples to apples.

Industry regulators are becoming increasingly concerned about advisers who sell variable annuities and also get fees for the investment management. The total of all these annual fees can run as high as 4% to 5% on the assets, and at this level, it is nearly impossible for the investor to net a decent return on his money.

Life Insurance

A whole life insurance policy is not easy to analyze. The typical whole life policy gives cash surrender values, guaranteed values and insurance values each year. All these values are projected to grow steadily. However, an analysis of the rates of return shows a very interesting result. Recently, looking at a life insurance policy, I concluded:

In the first few years, the return is negative due to the commission that is paid. Also, the earning assumptions on the portfolio are suspect. This insurance portfolio is about 85% in fixed income. Therefore, whether the insurance company says so or not, the entire projection is based on about 4% inflation, a very high assumed rate. If the insurance company earns less with poor investments, then the payouts will be smaller. Any investor with this kind of cash for a capital outlay for insurance premiums could build his own portfolio with a higher expected return over this multi-year period.

One of the few ways such a policy makes economic sense is if the insured dies very soon after taking out the policy, and the sooner the better. The same financial result can be achieved with a much cheaper term insurance policy.

The one advantage of this whole life insurance program is that the money can be compounded tax free in an insurance policy and can be left to heirs outside of the estate, if the insured lives many years. For estate planning, life insurance can be useful and profitable. But to build a nest egg, whole life insurance has limited value. If the assets are withdrawn, income tax must be paid on the increase.

Under most circumstances, if you need cash at death, use term insurance.

PENSION FUNDS

Consultants (Style Police) have led many pension funds astray over the last five years. They have committed too much effort to style type and not enough to common sense. In addition, funds have used far too high actuarial earnings assumptions, some up to 13%. This is likely to lead to big adjustments to profit & loss statements and probably some executives being fired for the huge losses. Consultants may become less powerful than in the past.
Rodney Mitchell

I managed a corporate pension fund for ten years. In the nineteen years since I left that side of the industry, much of it has changed. How corporations account for their pension funds is very different now. Until 1986, pension funds could only be cost centers – the most favorable impact that a pension fund could have on the income statement was to not create a loss. In 1987 a new rule allowed pensions to be profit centers. This has created many changes in the way pension funds are managed and accounted for.

With his usual clarity, Warren Buffett explains the problems that even pension funds have with long-term investing.[8]

HEDGE FUNDS

Thirty years ago hedge funds were private partnerships that invested money for a limited number of wealthy clients. They could buy or sell short (bet against stocks) and they were generally unregulated. In my first investment incarnation, I envisioned the forerunner of CEF to be a hedge fund, and did indeed sell a few stocks short in the 1969-74 bear markets, with limited success.

Today hedge funds are very different animals. They do not necessarily "hedge", meaning they do not reduce risk and volatility by being both long and short at the same time. Some hedge funds today do employ such "market neutral" strategies, but many others simply make enormously risky investments and also borrow money, or "leverage" to increase the returns. This also increases the risk.

Dullsville
Hedge funds have become popular as the markets have dropped over the last several years. We are in a great lull. Most people are reflecting on the last few years and saying, "Okay, I bought into technology and lost a bundle, now the market has been seesawing down and back up and back down, going nowhere. What I really need is a steady performance of 8-10% a year with no volatility, so that I can sleep at night. I don't care if I never see another 20% up year (That attitude will last only until they miss another 20% up year) just so long as I don't see a 20% down year. I want to be in Dullsville."

This is ideal for the promoters of hot new products. As we have noted in the past, there is an army on Wall Street whose job is to keep you out of Dullsville. You know these people. They are paid to peddle financial products and so they must create an atmosphere of excitement. They must convince you that they know where the market is headed next. They know that, in times of greed, they can make lots of money, and, in times of fear, they can make lots of money. Dullsville is not where they want you to be.

Ben Graham said in his book, *The Intelligent Investor,* first published in 1949, "Nearly everyone interested in common stocks wants to be told by someone else

---

[8] For his detailed history of pension funds and their accounting, see Appendix Four.

what he thinks the market is going to do. The demand being there, it must be supplied." This was true then, is true now, and will be true forever.[xlv]

The hedge funds promote an absolute return that is stable and well above money market. While the funds employ widely different investment strategies, they all have one thing in common – extraordinarily high fees to their investors. It is not uncommon for a hedge fund's fees to be 1-2% on the asset base and an additional 20% of each year's profits.

Hedge funds are not regulated and their reported performance can be suspect. As the number of hedge funds grows, many more of them will be managed by inexperienced people, and some by less than ethical people. Many tend to focus on the fee income for themselves more than on the return that the clients will get.

Since the bear market of 2000, hedge funds have been a hot property. As people lost money in conventional stocks, they wanted to get in on the game that they think is the domain of the very wealthy. But the investor's problem is always the same – identifying in advance the fund that can give a good return. The entire hedge fund category might under-perform because it is flooded with too much money to invest. One of the most successful hedge funds managers of all time, Julian Robertson, reached a peak of $22 billion under management. He suffered major losses in 1999 and early 2000, and he returned his clients' money and closed his funds.

No doubt hedge funds have been a good investment over the last decade. Since the market started declining in early 2000, hedge funds have looked far better in comparison to stock indices, which have declined markedly. And it is the concept of absolute return that is so seductive. People always look for a way to prevent their last mistake from happening again. And investors' last big mistake was the stock market. People lost so much money. And the hedge funds promise that it will not happen again– that they are careful and you can be sure that they will never lose money. Well, we have news for them and for all their investors. Nobody can make that promise with any assurance. And the fact that there are investors who believe that, is a scary sign in itself.

There is no guarantee that a hedge fund will be successful. Today there are over 7,000 hedge funds. In 1998 there were only about half that number. Assets managed have grown to approximately $1,000 billion, and money continues to pour in. In 2003, new money is estimated at $75 billion, more than twice the previous record year. And with this growth come changes in the funds' structure. Fees are moving up from 1% annually and 20% incentive fee to 2% annually and 25% incentive in some cases. Also, funds are demanding that new investors lock up the money with them, sometimes several years. This means that if you become dissatisfied, you can't get out.

As more money searches for opportunities, the returns must necessarily shrink for everybody, from sheer competition. The easy way to increase returns is for the hedge fund to borrow money to add to the investors' money. This gives great rewards to investors if all goes well, but if it doesn't go well, borrowed money, or leverage, is disastrous. If you have $1 of your money invested and $5 of borrowed money, then if you go down 16% (which isn't unheard of in this business) you are broke. It's happened before and will certainly happen again.

In an interview with *Forbes*, John Bogle (whom we have cited before) said: All investors over time get the market's return, before fees. After costs though, the market is a loser's game. The croupier rakes too much out. It is inconceivable that you could take 6,000 different hedge funds and expect them to be smarter than the rest of the world. If they are, say, 20% smarter, you're even. Or maybe you're losing a little bit, because they're taking an average annual fee of 2% in addition to the 20% carry. To equal a 10% market return, a hedge fund must make 17% before fees, assuming a 20% carry on gross return, a 2% annual fee and half the gain being long term, half short term. I don't think that 6,000 funds have any remote possibility of making 17%.

Why So Many New Funds?

One reason hedge funds are so popular is their use of leverage, or borrowed money. We examined our Small Cap Value Equity Fund, using historical results compared to an illustrative example if we had turned our mutual fund into a leveraged hedge fund. Using $2 of borrowed money for every $1 of investors' equity magnifies the returns – up and down. Given that assumption, over a seven-year period, one bad year can wipe out the advantage of the hedge fund. Over the same seven years, the operating costs and management fees of the hedge fund would be five times what they are with the mutual fund. In our example, the investor makes the same money, but the advisor makes five times as much. That's a good deal for me, but not a good deal for you.

What Can Happen To Hedge Funds Now?

Sometime (as usual, the date can be five months to five years) hedge funds will have a major decline. All the signs are there. Investors lost a great deal of money in the bear market of 2000-2002 and they want to find something that will prevent that unpleasant experience again. Enter the hedge fund as a solution.

The hedge funds are for investors who now say, "I don't' want to be greedy anymore. I am not shooting for 15-25% a year returns. I just want to make a 'modest' 1% a month, 12% a year, with little risk.[9] I don't want to lose more than 5% in any one year." Of course this expectation flies in the face of all past experience about markets. In order to make even 10% a year in a 3% inflation environment, an investor should expect to have years when his portfolio loses 30%.

But money is flooding into hedge funds. And they are no longer the domain of the very rich, very savvy investor. Hedge funds are being offered world-wide, and are packaged so that people can own them with as little as $20,000. And a huge

---

[9] This is almost exactly what Bernie Madoff offered and billions of dollars rushed to him about this time, though the world did not yet know who he was.

number of new funds are opening, looking for some small niche or inefficiency that they can exploit to make money.

Unfortunately, most of these funds base their investment strategies on models that are backward looking. They are set up to succeed in a period that has just passed. This is true of nearly all investment strategies. But financial markets are dynamic, the future is always very much like the past, but just different enough that what worked last time won't work again. And this always leaves investors shaking their heads at the disaster they have gotten into, and asking, "Who would have ever believed that this could go wrong." The answer is, "Almost nobody. That's why we're all in this mess."

And the more funds there are and the more money they manage, the more they will begin to look and act alike. In addition, as competition increases the funds will be pressured to deliver the promised returns. If the investment opportunities narrow, then the only way to make more money is to use leverage, borrowed money. This is what brought down Long Term Capital Management. As any market becomes popular, people figure they can make even more by borrowing money to invest. Why not? If you think you're going to make 12%, or perhaps 50% a year, then what's the harm in borrowing money at 4% and putting that to work too?

At the moment, investors are focusing on the promised returns, and are ignoring the risks – the funds are unregulated and need not meet any reporting standards. Liquidity is limited, and in some cases there is <u>no</u> liquidity. All this should raise caution flags, but it doesn't seem to.

At some point, there will be a publicized malfunction at a hedge fund. This is likely to cause the same people who have rushed into hedge funds to want to rush out. And as always in panics, prices will suffer, the weaker hedge funds will go out of business, and people will again ask, "How could this have happened to me?"

There will be sound hedge funds that have a good, solid record, but in a panic that won't matter. It never does. People just want out and will carry down the good with the bad.

One investment advisor warns that a wave of cash withdrawals by guaranteeing banks could lead to a "house of cards effect." Hedge funds of funds would be forced to pull their money from individual funds. Those funds could then be forced to dump stocks and other holdings in the market. Banks providing the guarantees say such scenarios, while theoretically possible, are unlikely.

People have a hard time learning from the past, even the not so distant past. A similar technique was offered by various consultants in the mid-1980s and it was applied to traditional portfolios of stocks. The academics dreamed up the idea; they called it "portfolio insurance." They said the same thing – while it was theoretically possible for the house of cards to fall, the market was efficient and it wouldn't happen. Many institutions bought into the portfolio insurance idea. Then on October 19, 1987 all of them tried to sell. And – surprise! The market wasn't efficient, there were no buyers, and the Dow set an all-time record, a - 23% decline in one day.

Hedge Fund Mania?

Yet here are investors who naively believe they can get high returns without taking any downside risk. It is a recipe for another disaster if enough people decide they want to play this game. There is a big rush into hedge funds by colleges endowments. For example, University of North Carolina- Chapel Hill's investment officer has been in the media spotlight for his innovative restructuring of the school's endowment assets from a traditional stock/bond mix to a very high 84% in hedge funds. "There's also a trend toward hedge investments by smaller schools, especially with the downdraft in the market. It's troublesome…Hedge funds can look like they make steady, low-volatility profits and then there is a catastrophe and hedge funds go out of business."[xlvi]

Always Give The Suckers What They Want

Once again the industry is gearing up to give the public what it wants, at probably what will turn out to be the very worst time. New funds will start and begin to boast about their ability to protect in down markets, money will flood in and rise to astronomical levels as people see this as the next sure thing. At about the same time, the bear market will end, leaving investors once again in the wrong place at the wrong time. They will not participate in the first leg of the next bull market when profits usually are big and quick.

Beacon Hill

This hedge fund ran into real trouble, seemingly overnight. In late 2002, Beacon Hill management announced that their losses were over 50% in a few months, although they had been reporting profits until shortly before. One month the firm reported client net assets of $756 million and a total of $1.3 billion in investments when assets bought with borrowed funds were added. At month's end, an outside prime broker reported that net assets had fallen to $257 million, a decline of almost 2/3 in a matter of a few weeks. Hedge fund investing is not for the fainthearted. Such sudden loses serve as a reminder that investing in hedge funds still carries risk, and that there is volatility even in the bond market. For example, hedging mortgages with Treasuries is inherently risky, especially when you use a substantial amount of leverage. The danger is that the treasuries rise more than the mortgages or decline less. If you have leveraged your bet 5 to 1, and the Treasury rises 5% and the mortgages only rise 1%, you lose (5%-1%) X 6 = 24% in very short order.[xlvii]

Beacon Hill now is closing down its biggest hedge funds and liquidating its remaining positions, even as the firm sells other bond investments in hopes of averting further losses that could threatened the entire firm. And in an unusual move, Beacon Hill has told its investors they can't pull their money out of the foundering hedge funds, or even receive updates about how the hedge funds are doing for the next six months…

The firm also disclosed that some of its losses occurred before September, even though investors had been told that the funds were up 10% through the end of August. The losses, as of September 30, were 54%, not the 25% as initially reported, according to the letter.

This points up a danger in hedge funds. You can't tell what they are doing. And they have ample opportunity to lie to you. Most investment advisors know at the end of every day what their portfolio is worth and how much they have made or lost in any given period up to and including that day. For the advisor to say that they didn't know about losses year-to-date through August in a letter written in October acknowledges that the manager has either incompetent record keeping or very dangerous investments if they can't tell what they're worth two months after the fact.[xlviii]

Long Term Capital Management

And there are spectacular blowups – most notable was Long Term Capital Management, which almost toppled the worldwide banking system. Its near collapse in 1998 pulled open the curtain on hedge funds. A handful of Wall Street insiders launched Long-Term Capital in 1993, with some of the best minds in the business. After a few good years, the fund was ravaged by miscalculations and unforeseen circumstances, touching off a global financial crisis. A meltdown was averted only after the Federal Reserve Bank of New York organized a consortium of banks and Wall Street firms to engineer a $3.5 billion bailout.[xlix]

What went wrong at LTCM, run by some of the most brilliant mathematicians and traders in the investment world? Peter Bernstein explains in his book, "Against the Gods" what happened to the Nobel laureates in economics, Myron Scholes and Robert Merton of LTCM. Merton was prey to a trap with his mathematical models. For stocks, there are many more days of extreme price movements than would occur in a normal distribution. Stocks are like a world in which most people are average height but every twentieth person is either a giant or a dwarf. There are too many extreme readings, or "outliers", that random distribution cannot explain. An extreme price movement that should happen once every seven thousand years in fact occurs about once every three or four years.[1] This quote may be the most important statement about investing that you ever read.

> Merton's theories were seductive not because they were mostly wrong but because they were so nearly, or so nearly often, right. As the English essayist G. K. Chesterton wrote, life is "a trap for logicians" because it is almost reasonable but not quite; it is usually sensible but occasionally otherwise". It looks just a little more mathematical and regular than it is; its exactitude is obvious, but its inexactitude is hidden; its wildness lies in wait.

If you heed this truth about the market, you will avoid a great deal of misery. The market is like Chesterton's description of life because the market is life. The market reflects the rational thought and the emotions of millions of people. The market is not going to change until human nature changes, and that hasn't happened in a million years. The market looks very sensible and mathematical, so people think that it will accommodate them by following their "rules." Then the market delivers a big surprise – a crisis erupts, not once every 7,000 years as the math would suggest, but every three or four years. So, beware! Investing is not the simple business that most people imagine. Only those who haven't tried think it is easy.

Still the money continues to flow into the hedge fund sector. A lot has changed about hedge funds, but the risk hasn't. Nor has the potential for fraud. Managers have incredible pressure to satisfy investors' appetite for double-digit returns. And they operate in virtual secrecy, with no federal oversight. In short, all of the ingredients are in place for an explosion, but it may be years in coming or just around the corner, nobody can foresee exactly.

A Successful Strategy

Certainly, successful strategies can be used with hedge funds. One well-designed strategy involves using a group of specialized hedge funds as a substitute for the fixed income portion of a portfolio. A group of funds is selected that do in fact hedge and attempt to capture small market inefficiencies. Clients expect to get an annual premium over the bond market of perhaps 1 or 2%. This offers a better-than-bond return with what should be little more risk, well worth the effort if the hedge funds perform as expected. There still can be significant risk of a "systemic" meltdown of the hedge fund industry in which all investors want out at the same time regardless of performance. Even then, properly chosen hedge funds can weather such a downturn without long-term ill consequences. This is a conservative approach, and far more reasonable that strategies that are really high leverage, high volatility.

Regulation

As a final word, you still may find that a well-chosen fund or fund of funds provides balance to your over-all asset mix. But in this field, the watchword is responsibility. Do your own investigation; get to know the people you are investing with. There is no substitute for this – certainly not the SEC. In fact the latest efforts of the SEC to "help you" may be counter to your interests. Hedge funds serve a great purpose in the market in that they are often contrarian in nature. They provide liquidity for the market by offering up buyers when there aren't any others. The SEC recently required that hedge funds of a certain size must register. 40% of them, mostly the giant ones already were registered. Requiring the other 60% to register may give them so much red tape and paperwork that they are driven out of business. The SEC maintains that its efforts may prevent a melt-down in the industry. This is doubtful. If the SEC couldn't figure out the scandal that was going on in the already highly regulated mutual fund industry, it's not likely that they will be more skilled in finding wrong-doers in the complex world of hedge funds.

REAL ESTATE

A Third Investment Leg

Real estate falls between a stock and a bond on the risk spectrum. It is tangible and does best in inflationary times since the supply of buildings and land cannot easily be increased the way financial assets can. People sometimes talk about a "shortage of stocks", a ridiculous idea. The shortfall in supply can be remedied by any company with access to a printing press. Not so with real estate.

Real estate is an excellent third leg to the investing stool, along with stocks and bonds. And a home represents that leg well because there are tax advantages in buying it with debt. Real estate does have several characteristics that are markedly different from stocks and bonds:

Real estate is likely to be a more "inefficient" market, another way of saying that real estate is more likely to be mispriced than stocks and bonds are, meaning that you may be able to find a real bargain if you are an astute buyer or seller. I have known individuals who have this knack. But real estate successes tend to be much like all investment successes – people brag about the great deals they have made and keep very quiet about the deals that haven't worked out well.

Real estate is not readily valued every day. You can't open the newspaper and see what your property is worth. This can lead to a false sense that it isn't fluctuating in value, when it really is. The returns can look huge when comparing the selling price to the purchase price. But real estate is often held for long periods and this can make the returns look exaggerated. In addition, with non-income producing real estate, such as raw land, there are carrying costs associated with the property. These costs give you a small negative return each year. As a result, the true rate of return is often smaller than it appears when comparing only the selling price to the purchase price.

Real estate is illiquid and cannot readily be converted into cash. Often there are large commissions on real estate transactions.

So while real estate has a proper place in a portfolio, it is important to understand its true return when comparing it to other investments. Historically the return on real estate falls between the returns on stocks and bonds, as it should. Its risk level is somewhere between stocks and bonds, and in a reasonably efficient market, returns should reflect that risk level.

Another Bubble?

In the recent stock market downtown, the economy has arguably been fueled by cash that came from people refinancing their homes with new low rate mortgages. Even as stocks fell, the net worth of most U.S. households held fairly stable or increased because of the increase in their home values. Could this lead to a housing bubble similar to the stock market, with rapidly and steeply falling home prices? Of course, anything is possible, but it is less likely for a number of reasons.

Unlike stocks, there is an industry that reliably produces new houses. There is no industry that reliably produces new profit-making firms. Home construction costs are very predictable and very much in line with inflation. But home prices move around with more volatility than this steady construction cost would suggest because home prices are the price of the house <u>and</u> the land. And while the house can be reproduced, the land is unique.

So housing bubbles tend to be limited to areas where the land is high-priced. In places like Boston, New York, and San Jose, a change in outlook for business prospects in the area can lead to price declines of 10%. But it is unlikely that home prices would drop nationwide. In the last few decades there has never been a nationwide price drop. There are too many places with a history of home prices tracking construction costs, and of real estate markets that are dull and consistent. Only the high-flying cities need worry about a real estate bubble.[li]

5:   LESSONS LEARNED

Honest criticism is hard to take, particularly from a relative, a friend, an acquaintance, or a stranger.
   Franklin P. Jones, businessman (1887-1929)

We should learn from our mistakes. We need to survey the last five years as not just a bear market, but also as a learning experience. There may have been a hefty tuition in the college of hard knocks, but if we learned a lesson it was worth the price to now know something valuable that we can use in the future.

THE CLIMATE AT THE PEAK

What Investors Thought Five Years Ago
   Five years ago, investors were optimistic. In early 2000, they were euphoric. They were certain that stocks in general, and technology/growth specifically, would go to the moon. They dismissed any dissenter as an "out-of-touch has-been who just didn't understand the new economy." Investors told me:
   "I'm not afraid of stocks." My unspoken thought, "Well, you should be. The stock market is a very dangerous place. It has not seemed so for the last few years, but it always has been, and now it's more dangerous than ever, because people believe it is benign."
   "Technology is still the way to go. It beats everything else over any ten-year period." My response to this one actually was spoken, "No, technology has beaten everything else over the last ten years. In other ten-year periods other stock sectors led the way. Each of those leaders fell by the wayside. They were replaced by the next 'new' thing. So be careful thinking that these great leaders will save your portfolio. If they do, it will be the first time."
   The 75% decline in the NASDAQ from its peak is one of the great collapses in market history. Some of the speculative technology stocks declined virtually 100% from prices that were in triple digits to pennies per share. After nearly five years, the NASDAQ was still 57% below its peak of 5,048, as of December 21, 2004.
   The broader market also caused investors much pain and fear. The decline was near panic. But the market was in a normal cyclical pattern wringing out the excesses created in 1998 - early 2000. Market psychology shifted from euphoria to despondency. People now have a great distrust of the market, corporations, business leaders, and accounting firms. Indeed, a small percentage of these institutions and leaders have betrayed investors. But, it was always thus. There

have been scandals throughout the history of organized markets, and this time is no different. There were scandals during the late 1990s. But the market was going up then, so nobody cared. Now investors say, "I have lost money. But it couldn't possibly have been my fault, and someone is going to pay."

We got a few requests from clients to sell everything. In the bull market, clients asked why we would not buy the great technology stocks. Now they ask why we would not go to cash and get completely out of the market.

What CornerCap Thought Five Years Ago

Our CEO, Tom Quinn's comments in July 1999 express how we felt. 'The Gold Rush - 1999 Version: We told the kids to study hard, work hard. We didn't know that so many twenty-five year old day traders could create multi-million dollar wealth. Expectations are so high for a quick-and-easy American Dream. More than half of upper class college students believe that they will retire between ages forty and fifty. We have never seen such expectations for significant wealth from little effort. Hard working people show their disappointment and envy, and many are determined to rapidly grow their investments to make up for opportunities lost.[10] The end of this gold rush will have many similarities to the one in 1849.'

After Tom's comments, the market went straight up for another eight months, a long eight months for Tom and me. In our business, <u>early</u> looks just like <u>wrong</u>.[11] Investors were rapidly losing patience with people like us. But this is nothing new. It's all happened many times before. Over three thousand years ago, a very wise young man named Joseph told his boss that seven fat years should be used to prepare for seven lean years - that the good times wouldn't last forever. But according to the story, most people didn't believe his warning then any more than they did ours in early 2000.

Holiday From History

This great bull market and speculation was partly fueled by unwarranted optimism. The world was enjoying a holiday from history. We should have known that economies don't grow at 3-4% a year forever; companies don't compound growth at 30% a year for very long either; wars and war-like people are a danger in this world – peace is a sometimes dividend at best; and <u>all</u> those young technology companies could not possibly be successful.

In the years between the end of the Cold War and the terrorist attacks, we let ourselves be lulled into believing that risk was a thing of the past. Defeating the Evil Empire had been unthinkable ten years earlier, yet America had done it. The Gulf War was almost a surreal combination of the Baja 1000 auto race and a video game. Almost nobody on our side died. All that American ingenuity and energy

---

[10] This is called greed.

[11] I was asked if I ever doubted my convictions about the market? No. What I doubted was whether the Bubble would burst in time to keep CornerCap from being destroyed.

that won us the title of sole superpower needed an outlet, and there seemed to be nothing serious to address, so we played. We played with the health care system in 1993, we played "Government Shutdown Chicken" in 1995, we played with interns in 1996, and we played with the stock market – with IPOs of zero-earnings, zero-revenues companies like Netscape and with day trading. We were invincible and infallible. The terrorist attacks reminded us that the world is not a safe place and that nothing is certain.[lii]

WHO'S TO BLAME FOR THE BUBBLE?

Responsibility belongs to individual investors. We are responsible for our own money and our own life. Lawsuits and threats will not solve the problem.

Embarrassing Wall Street into changing its business model is a good idea, but Eliot Spitzer, New York's attorney general offers fixes that would do little more than add a layer of rouge to the Street's flawed approach to the small investor. He wants to make an honest woman out of Wall Street's research departments, but he's only kidding himself and the investing public. He ought to be reminding investors of this rather than flattering investors that their own bad financial decisions were really somebody else's fault.[liii]

THE "EFFICIENT MARKET" – IT WASN'T EFFICIENT

Burton Malkiel's "A Random Walk Down Wall Street," has been a popular book for decades. It strongly implies, even in its title that the market is efficient, that all price movements are random, and that you cannot outguess the market. He seems to see no contradiction between his earlier book and what he writes here - in short that there was a Bubble:

I have long believed that our securities markets are extraordinarily efficient. Stock prices generally reflect all relevant information about the economy. But I also recognize that sometimes markets go haywire. This was certainly the case in Japan during the late 1980s. It was also the case in the US in the late 1990s during the internet-telecom bubble, when much unproductive investment was directed to nutty "New Economy" companies and to building telecom overcapacity.[liv]

Every market crisis produced laws to stop abuses. Some of the laws were clearly beneficial. But there is also a danger that legislators can overreact. After the South Sea collapse, the British Parliament passed the Bubble Act, which prohibited new issues of stock certificates for more than a century, until 1825. Certainly, the proper solution for abuses then was not the prohibition of new issues. Laws will not fix some of the current abuses. The securities industry itself must provide a solution.[lv]

This reaffirms the need to look at stocks with the same skepticism that you would look at any purchase. I believe that Malkiel has it right this time when he says that new laws won't protect investors or solve their problems for them. The only thing that will help investors is common sense and the discipline to avoid foolish investments. Does this mean that you won't sometimes be wrong as an investor? Of course not – anyone can be wrong. That is why we diversify.

BROKER RANKINGS

We have known for years that brokerage rating systems do not predict what stocks will do. As long ago as the 1970s, one major brokerage house touted its stock rating system. But when asked to show the results, they said that the numbers were confidential. Could you doubt for a moment that if the system worked the broker would be taking out full-page ads in the *Wall Street Journal* telling how good their ranking system was? They were confidential because the highest rated stocks performed worst and the poorest rated stocks performed best. Of course they measured their results! They just didn't want you to see them.

Our Fundametrics® research has been carefully measured for over twenty years. We know what worked and what didn't. Ironically, the SEC will not let us publish the results because of some technical rules on the records we kept. Yet it is perfectly okay for brokerage houses to make claims about the value of their analysis, just so long as they don't get specific.

NEEDED – LOWER PRICES (AND EXPECTATIONS)

During the long boom, in certain cases, executives were overpaid, analysts were faithless and financial statements were fraudulent. Wall Street was selling very expensive stock certificates. We may think of them as $100 hamburgers. Many will argue that stocks are now cheap. But at 40 times trailing earnings and 19 times estimated earnings, the best that can be said for the S&P 500 is that it is cheaper. It is a $20 hamburger, a bargain only in comparison with the $100 sandwich.

Now comes the call for more federal intervention – more laws, more regulations, and more stimulus from Alan Greenspan. Notice, however, what the extensive existing body of federal securities law did not forestall. It did not forestall what we have today. The government can no more restore confidence than it can impose virtue. Most people are irrational and will never learn how to invest "correctly." To have any hope of beating the market, you must be a contrarian and do the opposite of what others are doing.[lvi]

IT'S HARD TO SAVE TOO MUCH

In a consumer society there are two kinds of slaves: the prisoners of addiction and the prisoners of envy.
Ivan Illich, priest (1926-2002)

Personal bankruptcies are rising fast among the "older, more responsible, mature crowd." For years, people have asked, "How do so many people seem to live so much better than I do? I think we make about the same income and yet they have more 'things' - cars, homes, vacations, whatever." And my answer has always been - a few have more income than you think (in some cases really big income), a few have an inheritance that you don't know about, but most of them are borrowing – either from the bank, credit cards, or their future retirement. Recent data bear this out. From 1991 to 2001 the number of bankruptcies increased 69%. But the number of people under thirty-five years old declaring bankruptcy increased 16% while those over thirty-five increased 113%, with by far the biggest increase among those over sixty-five. Some of these are due to uncontrollable circumstances – unexpected and severe illness, loss of a breadwinner, aging parents. But many bankruptcies have come from poor planning. It is a fact of life - if we are lucky, we will live long enough to send children to college, to retire, to get old and sick. Don't be surprised when these things happen. Plan for them.

RISK

At last, people understand risk. In 1999, people weren't afraid of the market. Most successful investors have a healthy respect for its dangers. Warren Buffett says if you can't stand a 50% decline, you shouldn't be in the market. Most people in 1999 could not imagine a 50% drop. Now they not only believe it can happen; for many, it has happened.

Defining Risk
We have always told our clients that the object of investing is not just making money. The object is to build assets to support your lifestyle. And you should never adopt an investment approach that could jeopardize your lifestyle. Yet many people, some old enough to know better, did so in the late 1990s. There is anecdotal evidence that the market drop caused the average person to postpone retirement by four or more years. We know people who must dramatically reduce their living standard. They believed that making 15%+ each year in the market was their god-given right, and that they could count on that to support them.

"Dow 36,000"
I was critical of the book "Dow 36,000", but a review has made me rethink my opinion. The authors explain that they chose a flamboyant title to sell books. When it was published in September 1999 this title caught the eye of eager investors. However, the authors go on to say the book was a "sober explanation, not a wild prognostication."

Their main points in the book are: (1) Long-term investors, more than five years, should be in stocks not bonds. (2) Stocks are risky in the short term, but not the long term; investors should buy and hold. (3) Stocks are undervalued relative to their long-run trend.

They argue that in the long-term, stocks do much better than bonds because of a "risk premium". This means that investors consistently price stocks lower than they should because they fear short-term losses in stocks that they do not expect in bonds. If investors understood that stocks aren't risky and that there should be no risk premium, then the Dow should immediately go to 36,000. They insist that they never said the Dow would go to 36,000 <u>immediately</u>; they only said it would get there <u>someday</u>. To quote my granddaughter, "Duh! Tell me something I don't already know."

They say that stocks do continue to sell at P/E ratios far above where they have been in the past. In my mind it is not yet proved (1) whether these high P/Es will continue and (2) even if they do, whether these valuations are the result of more knowledgeable investors who have shrunk the risk premium or the result of lower interest rates and lower inflation that make stocks more valuable than when interest rates are high.

The authors do make a point with their skepticism of market timing. They take to task Robert Shiller whose book, "Irrational Exuberance", was published in 2000, an opportune time for him. Shiller claims to have been a good market timer with his call that the market was going to decline significantly. However, the authors of "Dow 36,000" point out that Shiller laid out his bearish theory in 1996 when the Dow was 5,400. He said his data implied that the S&P 500 would decline 38% over the next ten years. Yet nine years later the S&P is up 90%. For Shiller to be right on his original timing call, the S&P must decline to 394 in the next year, a drop of 67% from the current level. It may happen, but it is doubtful.

Both authors seem to ignore the element of human emotion. At CornerCap, we know that people have a great deal less patience than they admit. Our major task is <u>not</u> picking stocks; it is managing the expectations of the clients and helping them control their emotions.

As the market moved up after 1996 when Robert Shiller had already declared that it was rising on irrational exuberance, it took a person of very strong will to not be excited by the fantastic gains the market was producing. Now just the opposite is true - while the market is being carried lower, it is equally difficult to take the long view. People just <u>don't</u> focus on the last ten years or the next ten years. What most people see is that they have lost 15-90% of their portfolio value in the last few years. That goes down hard. So they tend to focus on the last sixty days.[lvii]

One of my favorite stories illustrates the contrast between the investment manager who deals with clients and the academics. It is about Robert Kirby, Chairman of Capital Guardian Trust. Bob had taken a sabbatical to teach investment management at Stanford. One day some of his students asked if he could get them a Capital Guardian research report on a popular stock at that time, Itel. The company was based in San Francisco. Its stock had plummeted recently. The students were concerned about an investment they had made in it, having lost

80% of their money. Kirby, with his understated humor that always made a practical investment point, told them, "Don't worry. Just go next door and talk to Bill Sharpe (Stanford faculty member, later the winner of the Nobel prize in economics for his work on modern portfolio theory) and I'm sure that he'll explain to you that 'risk-adjusted' you've made a profit."

People may become better educated about market risk and reward, but we doubt that enough of them will overcome their greed and fear to shrug off 50-75% swings in the market, up or down. That means opportunity for those few who do.

CONFIDENCE IN MANAGEMENT AND MARKETS

We ask why major companies fed us bad numbers. The answer comes from that well-know philosopher, Pogo Possum who said, "We have met the enemy and he is us." But how can we be responsible for what happened? By our demands that company managements deliver steadily rising earnings quarter after quarter. Management got stock options so that they would benefit as their stock (and our stock) rose. We had faith in these quarterly numbers. If a management failed to deliver those numbers for ninety days, the stock and their personal wealth got severely punished. So managements got the message – deliver the quarterly numbers or else.

Anyone who has worked at a huge company can tell you that it is impossible to produce operating results that rise steadily without some quarterly dips. The world just doesn't work that way. Yet investors demanded steadily growing earnings, and corporate managements delivered them – by fair means or foul. Those companies that didn't play the game suffered the consequences; their stock was ignored during the great rush to growth investing.

DON'T PAY FOR PERCEIVED GROWTH

There is benefit in buying low P/E stocks. High and low P/E stocks in the NASDAQ behaved very differently during the rising market and the falling market. In the two years ending March 2000, the lowest P/E stocks went down while the highest P/E stocks rose more than 80 percent. In the following two years this trend reversed and the low P/E stocks did well. For the entire four years the group made only a 3.4% gain, but the low P/E stocks rose 21% and the highest P/E stocks fell 12%.

MARKET HISTORY

Over the last century extreme market irrationality periodically erupted - and investors who want to do well had better learn how to deal with the next outbreak. What's needed is an antidote, and in my opinion that's quantification. If you quantify, you won't necessarily rise to brilliance, but neither will you sink into craziness. When I was talking about the market in 1999, I ventured then that the American public should expect equity returns over the next decade or two (with dividends included and 2% inflation assumed) of perhaps 7%. That was a gross figure, not counting frictional costs, such as commissions and fees. Net, I thought returns might be 6%.

Today the stock market is cheaper. The country's economy has grown and stocks are lower, which means that investors are getting more for their money. I would expect now to see long-term returns run somewhat higher, in the neighborhood of 7% after costs. Not bad at all - unless you're still deriving your expectations from the 1990s.[lviii]

The above is from Warren Buffett. He gives a long-term history of the market in far clearer terms than I ever could. Buffett always amazes me at how simply he can explain a very complex subject.[12]

---

[12] See Appendix Five for his great review of the stock market in the 20th century.

6:   KEY ISSUES IN THE FUTURE

Troubling issues are lurking on the horizon. You should be aware of them and how they may affect your investment life. We will discuss several that are likely to be important, not necessarily over the next year or two, but over the next several decades.

SOCIAL SECURITY

Our society must make it right and possible for old people not to fear the young or be deserted by them, for the test of a civilization is the way that it cares for its helpless members.
  Pearl S. Buck, Nobelist, novelist (1892-1973)

Social Security is debated emotionally, with very little understanding of how the system works. My information is gathered mostly from anecdotal evidence and is not necessarily the complete story. Mine is not a government, academic, or political viewpoint. This is an effort to help you understand what the social security system is likely to do for you, or to you, for the remainder of your life.

The Need For A Safety Net
Social Security was born during the Great Depression when 25% of the workforce (mostly men) was unemployed. Many thought the capitalist system had failed. The answer in such desperate times was government programs. Social Security was introduced by the Roosevelt administration in 1934 as a fund of last resort to help those in great need. Even in a time when most people were suffering economically, the System reflected the basic generosity of Americans toward their needy fellow citizens.
Such a "safety net" undoubtedly had been needed for a long time. A distant relative of mine in Yadkin County in the early 1900s was a widow with two small children and no means of support. The story goes that she hired out by the day to hoe crops. She would take the children with her and place one at each end of the field to play alone. As she worked, she could check on one child at the end of each row. She worked for money, food, or anything else to keep her family alive. Her son grew up to become one of the most successful and respected businessmen in the county, but no one would deny that such people needed a safety net.
Like so many grand plans, Social Security suffered from the law of unintended consequences. But a few economists envisioned the worst problems early. In one

economics class a student asked, "But who will pay for this program." The teacher answered, "You and your children, and grandchildren." My generation is the children, and those under forty are the grandchildren, and it is on these grandchildren that the real burden will fall.

Current Status

20% of Americans who are over sixty-five rely on Social Security as their only income. The money for current benefits comes from the people who are now paying into the System. Your payments are not being set aside for you. They are being paid out to people who are already retired. The government spends any excess on other things in the federal budget. Contrast this to the private pension system. In 1974, Congress passed the Employee Retirement Income Security Act (ERISA). That law forced companies with a pension plan to fund that plan with a trust containing real assets – stocks, bonds, cash, real estate. This fund is managed separately from the company's operations and investments. Government guidelines dictate how much money must be in the fund to keep it fully funded, and if the company goes broke the pensioners will still get what they are promised. Funds must have enough assets to cover those pensions. And if they don't, they must contribute new cash on a timely basis to meet the future obligation.

If companies reported the status of their pension funds the way the government reports on Social Security, then the pension officers and financial executives of those companies would surely be in prison. The people in Washington do not intend to discuss the pension system in any way approaching a fair representation. They talk about a "trust fund" and a "lock box" as though these terms mean something. There is no trust fund and if the lockbox is opened all you will find in it is an IOU from the government. The fund is on a pay-as-you-go basis. Money that comes in goes out immediately. For decades most of the pension funds in the U.S. operated the same way. Then a number of companies went broke and the retirees found themselves to be nothing more than general creditors of their company, and their pensions disappeared. Of course, the government has the power to raise taxes to pay the benefits, and that is what must happen if the Social Security promises are to be met.

Social Security started as a low cost supplementary pension system for the truly needy. It is now a Ponzi scheme. As cited before, such investment schemes take their name from Charles Ponzi. In Boston in 1920, he used money contributed by new investors to pay enormous returns to early investors. Such a Ponzi scheme can continue so long as the number of new investors increases fast enough to pay off old investors. Eventually it must fall from its own weight; there is never an unlimited supply of new investors.

When Social Security began, twenty workers contributed for every person who was retired. Now because of the increasing coverage of various groups and because people are living longer, there will soon be only two workers for every retiree. That ratio is going to slowly get worse. There are now 47 million people getting Social security checks. In thirty years, that number will grow to 77 million. The system is outdated. For example, a retirement age of sixty-five was set because in 1874 a railroad company set up the first private pension plan, and sixty-five was believed to be the oldest age one could safely operate a train.

One Family's Experience

Over the years, more people wanted to get in on this "good deal." In the 1950s, Congress recognized that farmers had been an excluded class. Farmers had usually not earned W-2 wages and had not contributed. But they were allowed into the system. If a farmer was over sixty-five, he only had to contribute for five quarters and then he could begin to collect benefits. What could be fairer? Fair! Unbelievably generous would be more like it! My grandparents paid in about $25 for five quarters and then began to collect. My grandmother lived to be 97 and got $2,000 a year for over 30 years - a $60,000 return on a $125 investment. The compounded annual return was 1,600%. That's a "good deal" by anybody's measure!

When my children started to work as teenagers, they asked , "What is FICA?" I didn't want to burden them with the truth at their tender ages. I knew that they would likely contribute huge amounts each year for decades and then get little or nothing in return in their old age under the current system. So I answered, "If I really told you, you would probably protest and might go to prison. So you should simply think of FICA as a gift to your great-grandmother through a middleman, the federal government."

Social Security has been on my mind this year because I reached the magic age, and I now draw benefits. (I think of myself as another pig at the public trough.) I started paying into the system in 1957, $19 that year. My earnings have been typical of most middle class professional people. Over my lifetime, if I had been allowed to deposit my contributions in a 401k account, earning just 5% a year, it would now be worth $400,000. Instead all I have is a government promise to pay me a monthly check for my lifetime. My wife and I must live to age eighty-five in order to draw out enough money to make a 5% return on my "investment" in Social Security.

The system has created real inequities among age groups. Most people who now draw benefits never think of themselves as being on welfare. The average retiree will tell you, "Look, I paid in for years, and I'm entitled to collect. I earned it!" In fact, this is not true. Many older retirees today have gotten back all their contributions and a decent return on the money in as little as nine years. After that time, they have been on "welfare" – meaning that the government is supplying them funds that they did not really "earn."

But for younger people, the outlook is grim. For every person who made a greater than market return on Social Security, like my Grandmother Maude, there must be a young person who is going to make a below market return. There is no free lunch. In the end somebody is going to pay the bill. In Maude's case it hasn't been her son or her grandson, but it is going to be her great-grandchildren and great-great-grandchildren.

Trouble Ahead

The debate about what to do is emotional rather than rational. For example, a lady who heads the National Committee to Preserve Social Security and Medicare says, "There's no crisis. There's a 'shortfall' of 30% of the benefits starting in 2042 when the trust fund gives out. The system could be shored up with changes similar to those undertaken by Congress in 1983, such as increasing the payroll tax." So it's all a matter of how you look at it. To her, there is no 'crisis', there's only a 'shortfall'. It's only a crisis if you have to come up with 43% more money to pay for this. Since it isn't going to be this lady, then for her there is no "crisis."[lix]

Options to cure the problem are few, and none of them are palatable to politicians who must tell voters the bad news. We always come back to the premise that eventually somebody has to pay. The solutions really boil down to some combination of only two actions: reduce benefits or increase withholding taxes:

Cut the payments or increase the age at which people become eligible for benefits. This is very hard on people who are retired. They planned for decades to have this money and it would be disruptive, in some cases disastrous, to deny them at this late date. But people are going to realize that they can't afford to retire so soon, that they must work an extra few years.

Increase withholding taxes. The amount has risen from its initial level of 2% of the first $3,000 earned to the current level of 15.3% on the first $87,900. (The tax is greater if you earn more. There is no cap on the Medicare tax.) At some level the taxes become counterproductive and people will refuse to work.

The only politically acceptable solution is to pay current retirees and near retirees, but begin phasing out the system for younger people. Much is made of the fact that if individuals are allowed to keep this money they may lose it in the stock market. However, a system can be set up for a portion of their funds that would work like an IRA does today. It isn't feasible to allow young people to keep all their money because some of it must be paid in to support current retirees whose money has already been spent to support those who participated in Social Security before them (the Ponzi concept.)

One thing is clear - young participants today should expect to get nothing from the system. Social Security is becoming a wealth transfer system from the "successful" to the "have-nots." It is likely that when today's young contributors retire, a "means" test will be imposed, and those who have contributed most will be deemed to have the "means" to do without the benefits.

Social Security is described as the "Third Rail" for politicians - the electrified rail that will kill you politically if you touch it. Just because politicians don't discuss the problem doesn't mean it isn't there. If you are unacquainted with the details of how this system is going to work, you owe it to your children and their children to become better informed. They will pay the price if an older voting populace selfishly mortgages the future of the young so that the older generation can have something now that they did not earn.

We can never insure one hundred percent of the population against one hundred percent of the hazards and vicissitudes of life, but we have tried to frame a law which will give some measure of protection to the average citizen and to his family against the loss of a job and against poverty-ridden old age.
> President Franklin Delano Roosevelt, August 14, 1935, Signing the Social Security Act.

My advice to young people – do everything in your power to abolish Social Security. It will be a burden to you and to your children, and it's current structure will mean that you eventually could pay as much as 25% of everything you earn to keep up an older generation that did not earn what they are asking you to provide for them. (None of this discussion considers Medicare and Medicaid – with far greater potential costs than Social Security since there is no limit on how much money we might spend on health.) Outright abolition may be politically impossible. Short of that you should fight to have benefits reduced, taxes lowered, or individual accounts set up for yourselves. As a concerned grandparent, I will gladly make a bargain with the government – I will give up all the benefits that I will ever receive from Social Security if my granddaughters are freed from having to pay. Of course, that isn't a deal that the government can afford to make.

The Social Security numbers are so astronomical that they are almost impossible to appreciate. A study done in the last few months shows that this year, Social Security and Medicare combined will spend, over and above what they take in, 3.6% of all federal taxes raised. Now that doesn't sound so bad, but if the system is left the way it is, in another sixty-five years Social Security and Medicare will require just over 100% of all taxes raised (based on the assumption that taxes will be 10.9% of GDP, the last fifty-year average). This means that we must either cut benefits or levy a tax burden on our grandchildren that will be beyond any reasonable ability to pay.[lx] Do we really want to demand an entitlement in our old age that is going to leave our grandchildren bankrupt? It should concern us all. There is a moral issue here in taking something we have definitely not earned and leaving the bill for someone else to pay, someone who has had absolutely no voice in the decision.[13]

A Proposed Solution

It will be difficult for any politician to meet the challenge of changing the Social Security system head-on. But we have people in Congress willing to try. One is Paul Ryan. Following are comments he wrote about a bill he was

---

[13] See Appendix Six for an excellent description of the system written by a former Director of the Government Budget Office.

introducing in mid-2004:

Without improvements to Social Security, our government will be left to choose between several painful options: endlessly borrowing more money, cutting benefits, raising taxes or a combination of these. Fortunately, there is an alternative – empowering workers with the freedom to choose a large personal account option for Social Security, with no benefit cuts or tax increases of any sort, now or in the future. These personal accounts will increase future retirement benefits and cut future taxes for all workers.

Other Key Points:

The short-term Social Security surpluses projected until 2018 would be devoted to financing the transition – instead of being used for other government spending. This will stop Washington from raiding the Social Security trust fund.

A national spending limitation measure would control the growth rate of federal spending to an average of 3.6% for eight years, rather than the current 4.6% projection. Those savings would be devoted to the transition. In comparison, spending grew at an average of 2.6% during the Clinton years. This is an effort to get federal spending under control.[lxi]

Many in government will vigorously oppose such a proposal. It will remove their power over enormous pools of money. The Social Security debate reflects just what kind of country we want to be and what kind of government we want. Do we want independent choices where we are responsible for our own future and well-being? Or, do we want a system where we depend on someone else to see that our needs are met?

CRISIS IN HEALTHCARE

The Bell Tolls

. . . never send to know for whom the bell tolls, it tolls for thee.
Devotions upon Emergent Occasions (1623), John Donne, Poet (1573 – 1631).

Many people in their forties and fifties will dismiss these comments on health care as irrelevant. They will be making a big mistake. The years have a way of passing quickly, and one day we suddenly find that we have turned into our parents and grandparents. Yes, it will happen even to the forever-young baby boomers. We can't predict much with accuracy in economics, but as consultant John Rutledge said, "One thing I can predict absolutely – Everyone who is fifty-five years old today, will be fifty-six years old a year from now."

My wife Judy and I had enjoyed good health. We had little experience with medicine or doctors. We paid our insurance premiums, got our annual physicals, and forgot about the doctor for another year. All that changed in August, 2000. Judy was diagnosed with breast cancer. For over four years, she has been battling this terrible disease with courage and dignity. She has impressed everyone who knows her, and has amazed many – including her doctors. The struggle is time consuming and frustrating. Dealing with the health care industry up close and personal has made me aware of the broader issues of health care.

Anxiety

As we enter the world of hospitals and doctors, at first everything is alien – the surroundings, the people, and most of all the terminology. It is difficult for the average person to comprehend what is happening. You're initially in shock just having to confront cancer, and are certainly not in a receptive frame of mind. Mostly we are scared. The medical community, like other professions, has developed a shorthand vocabulary to make their work easier. With the job pressure and time constraints, they tend to speak to patients in this shorthand. We often have absolutely <u>no</u> idea what they are talking about.

Judy and I are grateful for the technology that has brought her this far. Our criticisms are not based on some unreasonable bitterness. They are, hopefully, a realistic example of what can happen in our circumstances. I admit that, early on, I was sometimes frustrated and angry. My behavior wasn't always gentlemanly. But it was necessary to be sure that Judy was getting the treatment she deserved. As months and years passed, I learned that there was a better way, and that people in the system are not our enemy. But we had a few confrontations at first.

A Flawed System

Health care in the U.S. is badly flawed. And it is well on its way to completely broken. Without major reforms, it will become a disaster. I am not given to rash statements or dramatic hyperbole. But when millions of aging baby boomers confront the problems that Judy and I face now, the system will break down and become unworkable without major changes. That time is only ten or so years away. I certainly can't offer major solutions. But there are some pretty definite conclusions from our experience. This critique of health care fairly belongs in a financial report because much of the problem centers on money. Providers want to bill more, and patients want to pay less. And something has to give.

The entire structure to deliver and pay for health care - that's doctors' offices, hospitals, and insurance - is broken. My comments are not meant to be critical of the people who operate within that system. On the contrary, nearly all the doctors, nurses, and administrators that Judy and I have met are caring, concerned people. They have been much nicer to Judy than I had expected. They are professionals who genuinely want to help her.

Just as there are bad investment advisors, there are incompetent or unethical doctors and nurses, but I'm sure that they are a very small minority. Early on, I had one memorable example of professional dedication. Judy's surgeon called me at home at ten o'clock one evening to give me the results of a test he had run on her. I expressed surprise that he was still at work. He said that he customarily performed surgery or saw patients during the day, and evening was the time he cleaned up his administrative work. That is <u>real</u> dedication to the patient/client, no matter what the profession. I would certainly have understood had he delayed his call to me until the next day, although we <u>really</u> were anxious to know the result.

In the next few decades, almost everyone will either have a severe illness himself or be a caregiver to someone who does. The coming crisis is partly because people are living much longer. In my hometown, Winston-Salem, there is a Moravian cemetery. The tombstones are laid out in rows and the burials generally take place chronologically. A walk through that cemetery and a quick look at the tombstones reveals much about medical progress. Forty years ago, many people died in their fifties and sixties. It is easy to see that the life expectancy has increased markedly. We are living longer and will require much more health care.

Doctors have talked with me about Judy's case and their own views of the health care industry. They are as frustrated as their patients by the bureaucracy that makes it nearly impossible for them to deliver the service they were trained to provide. The problem is not the people working in health care. The real problem lies, as it so often does, with ourselves. The industry is suffering from much of what is wrong with the rest of the U.S. - we expect too much and are unwilling to pay for what we want. I am not smart enough to know everything that needs to be done, but I can offer a partial solution. And that solution goes back to the theme of this commentary - personal responsibility. We will address that in some depth later on.

Some people just won't accept that modern medicine cannot cure them. This has its roots in the "me" generation who believe that whatever they want, they deserve and can have. I talked to one young professional who was amazed that there is not some cure for Judy. I found his attitude naive. Yet doctors have told me that people demand, "Fix me, and fix me now!" Do they think life is television and every problem can be solved in an hour? Their attitude toward medicine is not unlike our client who saw his portfolio decline in one of the drops that hit stocks periodically. He called and <u>demanded</u> that I give him my plan for recovering his money in the next ninety days. He viewed the investment process as though it was a manufacturing plant and we could simply speed up the machines. Of course, we can't. It isn't much of a stretch to think he will make the same ridiculous demands of his doctors.

The medical problems in America are going to lead to knotty issues that we must eventually address. We may face having to put a price on people's lives. Consider Judy's case. She has lived with cancer for more than four years, and the cost has run into the hundreds of thousands of dollars. Much of the time she gets chemotherapy every week and radiation five times a week. Just the small bag of medicine she receives intravenously costs $1,300. Now, I thank God that I do not have to put a price on her life. We have insurance. But the truth is that others, in this case <u>many</u> people through insurance premiums, are paying for her treatment. So far society has not forced me to ask, "How much can I afford?" And even worse, what if I had to pay and it took more than I have or could get? Outliving your money is very possible for almost anyone with a serious, lingering illness.

The cost of medical services will rise dramatically as new treatments are added to keep us alive longer. THEN society may not be able to afford to give everyone all the health care they want – and there will be rationing. But which of us is to decide who gets to live and who does not?

We also must consider that some people will not be capable of deciding life and death issues for themselves? Medical technology is outstripping our ethics in these matters. When does a loved one say, "This person is no longer 'alive,' and we must cut the life support systems that stave off death, but don't really give any quality life?"

Rather than face these long-term issues that are critical to our society, our country prefers to go along with short term, expedient fixes. That is the way a democracy works. A new Medicare entitlement is a transfer of $400 billion over the next ten years from young people to old people. And this cost is probably greatly understated. When the baby boomers age and demand "free doctors and medicine," such programs are going to cause resentment when young people discover they are going to have to pay for it. And again, so long as it is "free" to the user, there is no incentive to cut back.[lxii]

Costs

It is difficult to determine who is responsible for higher costs. Is it the drug manufacturers? Or is it the pharmacies? Or is it perhaps the doctors who prescribe way too much and way too expensive drugs? But how do we get the consumer involved so that people know what health care costs? Not by going the way we are headed - more government control over the health industry. We need a consumer-driven system.

The politicians and health policy "experts" who have unprecedented power over our system don't like consumer-driven health care. They question our ability to purchase health care and doctors' and hospitals' ethics and competence. We would be lost without them, they say. But somehow, consumers and providers of other complex items – cars, computers – succeed without their help. Their costs plummeted while quality shot up. (Anyway, if these guys are such geniuses, how did they get us into this mess?)[lxiii]

Now, all this sounds simplistic. But the open market will provide better answers than all the bureaucracies, planners, and politicians that this country can muster. Because as long as they are involved, they will continue to construct a system that pretends to provide something for nothing to those who demand it in exchange for their votes.

We are debating such things as soft drinks or "sports" drinks for kids at school. There is no common sense applied in these situations. Both drinks are loaded with sugar. A letter from a sports drink company executive explains that such drinks are important to keep kids hydrated. Active kids are prone to dehydration and heat illness and research shows they only replace about half of what they lose in activity when drinking water. Whose research, for heaven sakes? I did my own research fifty years ago – we only drank water – no sugar added. If this drink company's research was accurate, every time my generation played a ball game, we would have lost half our hydration, whatever that means. We would have been dead after a few practices. Of course their research is going to support more of the sports drinks, when any idiot would see that water is better for you than drinks with sugar. But the sports drink executive explains that all their marketing is focused on sports – implying that they encourage sports and this justifies their product.

Obesity and disability are increasing in younger adults. One in six children is overweight.   They will likely grow to be ailing adults. Children, and adults, apparently need to be taught about what and how much is healthy to eat. This epidemic can be prevented. But the ignorance is amazing. I had no idea how many calories I consumed each day, or how many I needed, until 2002. I was sixty-three years old and still totally ignorant about nutrition and exercise and how much they affect long-term health. I had been consuming 30% more calories daily than I needed.

Our health care system is burdened with costs from cases that are preventable:

A man has $900 of medicine each month for diabetes. He is thirty years old and weighs four hundred pounds. He has borne no responsibility for his poor health himself and can't understand why society can't pay to keep him alive.

One U.S. adult male in fifty is 100 pounds overweight. One in two hundred is 200 pounds overweight. This is two million men and their average health care costs are $2,000 a year more than those who are less than 100 pounds overweight. If you add in adult women, the cost is running $8 billion dollars a year. And it is only getting worse as costs escalate.

Annual medical costs in the U.S. are over $5,000 per person. One roadblock to better cost containment is a system in which we don't pay for health care from our own pocket. We pay through private insurance, Medicaid, Medicare, etc. As a result, most people think the Tooth Fairy brings them health care. We think differently about health now than we did fifty years ago. Back then, you got old and sat home for twenty years complaining about sore joints. Now you've got to stay better than well to cycle, jog, and hike. This is all great, but it's ridiculous to think that it is free.

Lawsuits
Sure you have rights, but you don't have to insist on using every one of them every day.

Kenneth Hoots

Of course patients have rights, and people deserve good treatment by doctors and hospitals. But the ability to sue has its price - a reduced level of health care services.   Doctors and hospital services are disappearing because malpractice insurance is too expensive for them to stay in business. In some states the annual insurance for delivering babies is $200,000 a year.

To the doctor, every patient is a potential plaintiff in a suit against him. Whenever a sick person gets sicker, a lawyer can come up with something different that might have been done. The possibility of a claim from virtually anyone – with years of litigation – would drive most normal people into defensive cocoons. It's driving many doctors out of the business. Letting anybody sue for anything is not law, it is anarchy. The rule of law is supposed to set boundaries on what suits can be about and for how much.[lxiv]

One surgeon said, "Despite the fact that I have practiced for twenty years without incident, it would take only one slip to wipe out my net worth and my professional reputation." There is no doubt that frivolous lawsuits have added greatly to medical costs. In many courts, medical malpractice attorneys have found a wonderful lottery. They can spend lots of time and get nothing. Or they may hit the jackpot for a multi-million dollar payoff if they can find a sympathetic jury and a doctor with plenty of malpractice insurance.

Some doctors now find malpractice insurance so high that they decide to go "naked" – they choose not to have insurance at all. This is not necessarily a bad approach for the doctor. The theory is that plaintiffs will only go after cases where there are "deep pockets" – there must be somebody to sue who has lots of money or the suit isn't worth the effort. If the doctor has relatively little to take, why bother to sue him. If this approach works, it will fairly well make a lie of the argument, "It's not about money, it's the principle of the thing." When you hear this, you can be pretty sure it's really about the money.

Nearly all Judy's doctors seem reticent to discuss her outlook. They tend to say very little about her case, even though we are hungry for information, for reassurance. Why would they say so little? Again, probably fear of being sued. Of course any reasonable person knows that they can't predict the future course that a patient's disease will take, any more than I can predict the course of the stock market. The difference is that if I speculate on market direction, no one is likely to sue me. But in the doctors' world, any comment no matter how well meaning or innocent can be the basis for a major suit. Suppose the doctor tells a sick patient that he is probably going to live five or ten years. And then the patient dies in six months. The family of the deceased can then argue that they had made specific plans based on the "promise" that the patient would live several years and they are entitled to monetary rewards for the disappointment. In contrast, suppose the doctor tells the patient that he will probably live only a few months, and the patient recovers and lives several years. Then the patient can sue for the pain and suffering of expecting to die when he really is healthy. So even the most innocent comment can be turned against the doctor in a lawsuit. Is it any wonder that doctors are cautious about saying only what they absolutely must? If investment professionals were sued for every wrong forecast, then the world would have almost no money managers and economists.

Judy's surgeon gave me an example of how better technology, along with concern over suits, has driven up the cost of a simple appendectomy. Twenty years ago he diagnosed by physical examination. Nine times out of ten he would correctly diagnose appendicitis. Each time he would operate, and in the worst case, he would remove the healthy appendix and that one patient in ten might suffer a bit from a "needless" operation. The operation cost about $1,000 total. Therefore the total cost of removing nine bad appendixes was $10,000 – ten operations. But now all sorts of tests are available, MRIs - Pet Scans, Ultrasounds - to be sure that the one healthy appendix is left alone. And if he operated on a healthy appendix without performing this battery of expensive tests, then it is likely that he would find himself in a malpractice suit. The tests cost about $2,000. So now the cost of taking out nine bad appendixes is $29,000, $20,000 for the tests and $9,000 for the operations. The unnecessary operation is avoided, but the cost of each successful operation has increased 190%. This is how technology and potential litigation drive up costs for everyone.

Cheap, Fast And Good

One doctor put in a nutshell what is wrong with the healthcare system. It's simple. I was surprised that I had not heard his explanation before, and also surprised that it came from a medical professional instead of an economist. "There are three things people want from healthcare – cheap, good, and fast. You can have any two, but you can't have all three." In the U.S. we have good and fast, but it isn't cheap. In Canada they have good and cheap, but it isn't fast – it might take months to get a routine surgical procedure. In the U.S., we have not yet decided which two we want. We are like spoiled children, demanding that we have all three.

Baby boomers are moving into the years where they will need/demand health care. Costs per capita for the thirty to sixty-four year olds have risen much faster than any age group over the last thirteen years. This group has grown accustomed to living well. They buy whatever they want – cars, vacations, clothes. They spend on discretionary, luxury goods that were unknown to their parents. Now health care has become a luxury good, and the boomers don't mind spending on that either. In a few years, the system will be dealing with the demands of these people who are sick and want to be cured and also with the "worried well" who will pay for the reassurance that they are okay.

All The Care Other People's Money Will Buy

People behave differently when it isn't their money they're spending. A company set up its own in-house health care and gave all employees and their families ready access to a doctor. A visit to the doctor was virtually free. After many years the company changed the practice, and began to charge $10 per visit. The number of visits dropped by a third. Apparently the members' believed that a visit to the doctor was worth the price so long as the price was nothing, but at the nominal price of $10, one third of all visits were deemed unnecessary. We must learn – this stuff isn't free, even if we aren't writing a check.

Several years ago a heart surgeon at Duke University wrote an Op-Ed piece in the *Wall Street Journal*. He said that he had operated on an elderly man, and as the patient's recovery progressed, he noticed that the man was not regaining weight as he should. On examination, the surgeon discovered that the patient's false teeth didn't fit properly and he was not eating enough because of the discomfort of chewing. The doctor told the patient that he would send a dentist by later to see him. On his next visit, the surgeon asked if the dentist had come by. "Yes," the man said, "But I'm not going to buy those teeth, they cost $300!" The patient wasn't willing to spend that much money to help speed his recovery. The doctor checked the patient's file later and discovered that the heart surgery had cost $500,000, paid by insurance. So the patient was perfectly willing to spend a half million dollars of somebody else's money on his health care, but he wasn't willing to spend $300 himself. Hence, all the health care that other people's money will buy.

So we point a finger at doctors and accuse them of greed, incompetence, and outright fraud as they treat our illnesses and complaints. And undoubtedly, some are greedy and dishonest. But the bad ones are no greater percentage of their population than in any other profession, and maybe far fewer than in my own.

In many ways doctors are victims of our system. We overburden them with our healthcare demands. While it is important that doctors become better business people, for their own well being, this is a sad departure from what their role ought to be. They are highly trained to care for the sick.

When I choose a doctor, I am not looking for a well-rounded person who understands economics, billing procedures, and the stock market. That's probably true when a doctor seeks out an investment advisor. The doctor isn't overly concerned that the investment manager understands and speaks fluent "medicine".

No. If Judy must go under the surgeon's knife or get chemotherapy – I'm looking for a doctor who spends one hundred percent of his or her time devoted to medicine. I'm not looking for someone who has lots of time for side interests and hobbies. This is very serious to us, literally <u>deadly</u> serious, and I want a doctor who takes it just as seriously. I have met very few investment managers who spend time in the operating room or examining patients. And when I'm sick, I want to see doctors who don't spend a great deal of time picking stocks or running investment funds. I've not met many people in this world who do even <u>one</u> thing really well, and it stretches my faith in human ability to believe there are people who are <u>really</u> good at <u>two</u> or more professions.

Who Is To "Blame"

We refuse to educate a workforce and then expect good treatment anyway. We demand that they fix us <u>now</u>; they can't – they are highly trained technicians – but they are not miracle workers. We demand that they be held accountable for errors.

The costs go up to cover those errors.

In a case of medical malpractice at New York's Mt. Sinai Hospital:

A healthy fifty-seven year old man dies. What happened?

A medical resident, a medical school graduate, fails to recognize that a patient who is vomiting blood after a surgical procedure needs the care of a more experienced member of the surgical team. She doesn't inform the surgeon. Blame her!

The surgeon doesn't appear for three days. Blame him!

The family brings in a lobster dinner one day after surgery and doesn't ask the nurse if this is acceptable. Blame them!

The nurse fails to observe the written order for clear liquids. Blame her!

The hospital has the temerity to staff this area with one inexperienced resident for 33 patients. How many nurses were on duty? Blame the hospital![lxv]

Many people played a part in this tragedy. It is impossible to really know who is to blame. But one thing is certain. The man's family played some role in not following the diet rules; he might still be alive if they had played a very different role. They could have decided that they would be responsible for being with him and challenging the decisions of the hospital staff all along the way. They wouldn't be popular, but the patient would still be alive, and nobody would be placing blame for the death that didn't happen.

It's All About Money

Yes, it's about money. Is that a surprise? What business isn't about money? The health care givers want to continue to make a good return. The health care payers want to squeeze them. When a doctor does a procedure in order to get paid he must fill in one of 7,000 five-digit code numbers for that procedure and submit it to the insurance company. If the code is wrong the insurance company just says it is miscoded and the doctor's office frequently just bills the patient, with no communication with the insurance company.

Cost efficiency goes out the window. Hospitals will spend hundreds of dollars repeatedly sending you a bill for $15 they say you owe when you sent them the check two years ago and followed it with a copy of the cancelled check and an explanation that you already paid. This actually has happened to Judy and me.[14]

The oncology group that treats Judy is not adding new doctors. The business manager at the group says that with the burden of all the new rules, she cannot see

---

[14] This happened in 2003. After a year, the monthly bill stopped. In 2007, I got a call from the hospital billing office. They were searching for Judy. I explained that she died two years ago. The billing clerk had gone to great length to locate me in another city on the chance that I might be related to Judy. The clerk explained that Judy was due a $265 refund from the hospital. She was very sympathetic when she learned of Judy's death. I never understood how there could have been a refund when I had only paid $15 which was a legitimate bill. Is there any wonder that hospitals say they can't make money?

why anyone would enter the practice of medicine. New patient privacy rules are an example. As if we didn't have enough to read and sign on every visit to a doctor or hospital, now we have to sign forms concerning the privacy of our information. The rules appear ridiculous. I suppose they are intended to protect those who, for any number of reasons, want their medical records to remain private. But there is an unintended consequence – a mountain of new paperwork. Before this law, when I went to the oncologist with Judy I could walk down the hall and say hello to the doctors, nurses, and staff – (we are pretty well acquainted after four years.) A nurse stopped me and explained that I was passing by examining rooms with patients in them (behind closed doors) and that as a non-employee non-patient, I was forbidden to get within x feet of these people, so I couldn't come into the area any more.

Each time you enter the hospital for a test or whatever, a receptionist will dutifully ask you to complete a set of forms that has the same questions you answered the last time you were there. This procedure is repeated no matter how many times you go to the doctor. The hospital should have a computer system that contains all the historical patient data; when you arrive; you should get a printout with your data and you should be asked to mark only changes, rather than start from scratch each time.

The insurance companies say they would pay if the doctor would only code correctly. But these medical people shouldn't use their time doing billing work and interpreting insurance codes. All this adds up to extra costs that you and I must pay. But so long as it doesn't come <u>directly</u> from our pocket, most of us aren't overly concerned.

The Nightmare

Health care costs are rising rapidly, and, sad to say, the deck is really stacked against those least able to pay – people without insurance. There are catchy phrases for the rules that cause this, but it seems to boil down to the concept that those who are covered by insurance have rates that the insurance company negotiates at "wholesale" prices with the health care providers. Those who have no insurance are often charged "retail" prices that are much higher.

If you read your policy carefully, you discover that even when the insurance pays for a procedure, it will pay only what is "usual, customary, and reasonable." The patient must pay the difference, and this can sometimes run as much as 25-30% of the total bill. You will find that there is no way you can know what is usual, customary, or reasonable. So there is no way to challenge the insurers on this. (In our case, this is especially true because Judy is often forced to go out of network. This means that the insurance company and the health care provider have not reached a working contract with each other.)[lxvi]

In one instance, we are fairly sure we got caught in a negotiation between a hospital and an insurance company. In the fall of 2001, Judy desperately needed to have the extreme stem-cell replacement treatment. This is a radical and very expensive procedure, but a "last resort" that has saved lives in recent years. She showed enough progress to qualify and her oncologist recommended a facility to her. Being still new at this business and desperate to get the medical treatment she needed, I ignored the warning sign that this facility was not "in network."

We had an initial interview with the doctors at the stem cell center and they agreed to take her as a patient. Her doctor, who was very capable and probably prolonged Judy's life, assured us not to worry about the money, "Something could be worked out." He very much believed this to be the case, but financial arrangements were not within his authority as things developed.

Judy was admitted to the program. She began the first task, harvesting her stem cells to prepare for her coming chemotherapy treatments. And then the business office told me that they could not reach an agreement with our insurance company. Insurance would pay only a prescribed "reasonable and customary" amount. [It is likely that the insurance company and the hospital were in negotiations to bring this hospital in network, and neither one wanted to give very much on the pricing. The dollar implications for both of them would be enormous going forward, and Judy was a test case, so both sides were pushing very hard with us caught in the middle.] I asked what this would mean in potential cost to me personally without insurance, and the hospital's finance people said they couldn't tell me. It would be open ended. It might be $50,000 and it might be $500,000 or much more. So here we were, putting a price on Judy's life, asking what we could possibly do, and feeling totally helpless. And then matters got worse.

We decided to look for another hospital that was in our network. Judy's attending doctor was very helpful and suggested two good hospitals where he knew the doctors. But when we contacted them, they refused to take Judy as a patient saying that she had already begun her treatment at the first hospital (the harvest of her stem cells) and they couldn't be responsible for her now. In effect, they viewed her as "tainted goods." I have never felt so helpless in my life. Here was my wife's life at stake and we were being told that we might have to put our entire life savings on the line before the original hospital would go forward with her treatment. This is a decision you don't want to face!

The discussions with the hospital went on for weeks, and we were negotiating with absolutely no leverage. The hospital held all the cards. I am not sure where the pressure came from to resolve the situation, but finally the hospital and the insurance company reached a special agreement that quoted me an out-of-pocket cost of a set dollar amount that we could live with, actually a very small number compared to what it might have been. This insurance agreement was good for one year. Fortunately within that year, Judy's treatment was a success and insurance paid for the majority of the treatment, but getting to that point was more frustrating and frightening than you can imagine.

Personal Finances

When you enter the world of medical economics, forget everything you ever learned about finance. I've worked over forty years as a number cruncher, a person who deals with P&L statements, balance sheets, and budgets every day. But keeping track of the medical bills is by far the most challenging analytical assignment I have ever had. Bills come from sixteen health providers plus statements from the insurance company. (Judy has used an additional five doctors, but they were only for immediate problems that were non-recurring such as a gastroenterologist for digestive problems brought on by repeated chemotherapy and radiation.)

Bills

I keep the account of each doctor or hospital on a computer spreadsheet and attempt to reconcile the statements. These bills generally conform to the dates and procedures of Judy's treatment. They are always difficult to understand, but not impossible. There is the occasional "mystery" bill that arrives – for example, one from a billing agency in California for $275. It doesn't have the name of a doctor, or a date of service, or a medical procedure described. It just states that I should pay them. I ignore it, and I don't hear from them again, at least to this point, three years later. Hopefully they simply went away. But a follow up bill may come any day bearing no more explanation than the first bill.

The insurance company sends statements called Explanation of Benefits or "EOBs". I receive, on average, one of these daily. I have a file nine inches thick. It is impossible to match the EOBs with the bills that come from the various doctors and hospitals. Sometimes insurance pays the bills without explanation. Other times the insurance company will refuse to pay part of the bill for various reasons that are usually not clear. The reason can be as straightforward as an annual deductible on the insurance. It can also be related to the notorious "usual and customary" charges.

Networks

Use health care providers that are in network. If you have a major insurance company, your insurer has negotiated favorable rates with a group of hospitals and doctors and has placed them "in network." You will not be charged for using these services, except for standard deductible amounts, which you must pay for each visit to a doctor or hospital.

However, anyone who uses a doctor or hospital that is not in network will probably be charged a much greater price. They have to make money somewhere, and unfortunately it is often from those who can least afford it – those without insurance. There are documented cases where these poor souls have been hounded into bankruptcy because they could not pay these bills.

Even if you have excellent insurance, you will still face a challenge from out of network providers. Sometimes your doctor will refer you to an out-of-network doctor or hospital for a test or procedure. You may receive a surprise, huge bill. It represents the difference between what you have been charged and the amount that the insurance company will pay. That amount is what the insurers call "reasonable and customary." This is a convenient way for insurance companies to reduce their costs. And there is no way for you to get a list of what is considered "reasonable and customary." If possible, you need to be sure that you are sent to in-network providers.

In the event that you face such huge bills, my advice is: do not pay immediately. Document what was done and what the cost has been. Send letters to that provider explaining that you are out of network and suggesting that they negotiate with your insurance company to agree on a price the insurance company will pay. Occasionally the provider will write off the difference.

Rule For Paying Bills

In medical economics, the time value of money is not even a consideration. It takes months for bills to arrive and for doctors to receive payment from insurance companies. And any thought you have about paying your bills on a timely basis should be tossed in your mental trashcan. Your new rule of medical economics – never pay any bill until you absolutely must under duress such as threat of lawsuit or court action, and perhaps not even then.

Why? This is so alien to most of us who have always paid every bill when due. But you are now dealing with a system that is complex, slow, and inaccurate. In many cases you may pay bills that you do not owe. Thankfully, early on I was instructed by the office manager at one of Judy's doctors. She was straightforward and helpful. She called me after I had paid a $1,500 bill that had later been paid by the insurance company. She cautioned me about responding too early to bills sent to me. If she had not refunded the money, I would never have known that she had been paid twice, once by me and later by the insurance company. And not all medical practices are so honest with their patients.

So after gaining some experience, we never pay a bill without being sure it is correct. In one case, we received a bill, which I was about to question with a letter, but before writing, I decided to call the business office of the medical practice once more. And the person in charge of billing reviewed the account and said, "Wait, this has been paid by the insurance company, and in fact has been paid twice. I need to check on that." I told her that I had a bill in hand that said I also owed them money, and while my bill was quite old (due to my 'no pay' policy) shouldn't I have gotten a new statement showing that the bill had been paid. She explained, "You would not receive such a statement. It is our policy that once a patient account reaches a zero balance (or in this case a credit balance), then we stop sending out statements." In other words she is saying, "So long as we get paid, we don't care who it is from, and we wipe the slate clean. If you decide to pay us based on old information, then we'll take your money too, along with the insurance money". I'm not sure that is really the policy of this medical practice, because such a policy is clearly unethical, but that's the way she explained it to me. I don't think she understood what she was saying.

How Do We Save The System?

Unfortunately I have no answer. But I can tell you what <u>won't</u> work – continuing to allow the level of services to grow and grow and let people continue to pretend that it is free. I do believe the answer lies in a market driven system - where people are aware of the costs. If individuals bear at least a portion of the cost they will begin to demand competitive services. When large numbers of people get involved in a debate and the outcome affects their pocketbook directly, things tend to change. This will lead to a more rational system.

Certainly the government proposed Health Savings Accounts (HSA) is a step in the right direction. With whatever form such an account would take, at least the individual will decide how that money is spent. The government will not decide for him. HMOs will not decide for him. Once this shift takes place, people will begin to demand value for their money. Health care can work in a system where people compare prices and quality. It wouldn't be perfect, but it would be much better than a system set up with a bureaucracy to decide everything. We already have that with Social Security – a system that is itself clearly broken and in bad need of overhaul and privatization. The only reason it isn't fixed is that elected politicians don't dare admit to their voters what a mess it really is and how much it is going to cost the next generation to keep it going.

It will also help if medical facilities become more high-tech. This is already under way. There is no reason that the medical industry cannot benefit from the efficiencies and productivity that many other industries have enjoyed. Many areas have been identified where new computer technology can cut costs dramatically. These include:

Prevent overdosing with medicine

Prevent unnecessary surgery and serious medical errors

Promote preventive medicine – there are no rewards in the system for doctors who prevent disease, they are only paid for treating sick people, not for keeping people well.

Manage diseases – helping people help themselves

Reduce Intensive Care Unit costs with technology that allows more patients per worker through better monitoring.

Get patients involved.[lxvii]

Value Of A Positive Attitude

Being an analytical person, I admit that I had put little faith in a positive attitude at first. Yet most of the medical people I talked with stressed the importance of maintaining a positive outlook. Initially I believed that the doctors had misinterpreted a positive attitude. I thought that it was primarily the doctors who benefited from the patient's positive attitude, that the doctors simply had less trouble dealing with a patient who didn't complain. However, given Judy's results, I have come to agree more with the doctors about attitude/outlook. I still am not convinced that a positive attitude does much to cure cancer. It seems to me that the cancer sits inside a person and does what it is going to do, regardless of whether the person thinks positive or negative thoughts. I don't think the cancer cares whether your attitude is good. But the positive attitude, the mental toughness to address the issue, does give the patient strength to fight the disease in much more aggressive ways. I think it has been this positive attitude and willingness to continue a fight against long odds that has allowed Judy to go through the rigors of daily or weekly chemotherapy and radiation. At times, these have produced severe side effects and discomfort for her, yet she continues. The overall result has been quite positive. Even with the difficulties, she has had four years of life that on balance she would say has been much more positive than negative.

What have those extra years been worth? To me, they have meant the companionship of someone who had supported me in every aspect of my life for thirty-eight years before her problems began. I don't want that love and support taken away. And to her granddaughters, it meant the opportunity for their Nana, who loves them so much, to be with them in their most formative years. It has meant that Nana could be there for their soccer games, their school plays, movies, and overnight visits. It has meant that they could take trips with Grandmother – to New York at Christmas, to Disney World, and even to France to visit their uncle. These are memories that will last them a lifetime. They would have been denied these memories without Judy's fight to stay alive.

So, yes! There are many benefits to a positive attitude.

Personal Behavior

Everyone had heard horror stories about hospitals – the wrong medicine administered, the wrong kidney removed. We don't want to dramatize this. When Judy was admitted for her mastectomy, I was prepared for the worst - uncaring staffs and the big errors that they made. But nothing happened much out of the ordinary, to the great credit of the doctors and nurses.

Take Charge

But it could have. Easily. Hospitals are confusing, complicated places. Occasionally there are big mistakes, like giving a child the wrong heart. You can't do much about that if you are a caregiver and aide to a patient. But there are small things, like giving the right medicine, in the right amount, at the right time. These can mean life or death too. A patient should have someone with him almost constantly to monitor what is being done.

Demand (and Earn) Respect – Thankfully we have dealt almost exclusively with good people. We have had little contact with the stereotype of the "arrogant, aloof" doctor. In contrast, nearly all the health care providers we meet are caring and kind. Still, it is easy for them to dismiss you and your concerns, just because they are extremely busy. You earn their respect by being informed about your own treatment and illness and asking intelligent questions so that they don't feel you are wasting their time. Also, be nice to the staff. They are like sergeants in the army – they make everything work. Do not take them for granted or abuse them, even when they frustrate you.

Ask questions. Learn about your medicines and treatments. Doctors say that patients are much better informed now with the advent of the Internet. Much information is available via computer today, probably too much. You can be overburdened with all sorts of things from websites, much of which may be useless in a specific case, or worse, just plain wrong. Good physicians welcome this increased information available to the patients. Unfortunately, a few see it as a challenge to their authority; they do not want patients who question them. My advice to them is "Get used to it. It's here to stay."

The letter below was addressed to Judy's hospital and oncologist. It was written when I was frustrated and angry. It could have been written with much more diplomacy. But when the stakes are life and death, it isn't easy to be diplomatic. The letter did bring positive results and the hospital staff and the oncologists became our allies and, in some cases, our friends over the next few years. But nowhere is our recurring theme of personal responsibility more important than where major health issues are concerned. At the risk of repetition – Do not trust anyone else to do what has to be done. It may or may not be important to the person who is expected to do the work, but to you it is critical. And if someone else makes a mistake because they don't care or are incompetent, it will not be that person who bears the consequences. It will be your loved one or you, and all the lawsuits in the world after the fact won't compensate for the suffering and loss.

January 21, 2002
Mr. James Smith
President and CEO of National Healthcare

Dear Mr. Smith:

Attached is a completed Outpatient Services Survey that you sent me. My generally negative evaluation has prompted me to write you this letter of explanation about my wife's specific case.

My wife, Judith, has had a lengthy bout with breast cancer, beginning with surgery at National in the fall of 2000 – followed by radiation and a variety of tests in your nuclear medicine area. During surgery and recuperation, her treatment was excellent. We had heard many stories of patients who received less than satisfactory care in hospitals. We were both very pleased at the caring attention she received from doctors, nurses, and the entire hospital staff during her initial hospital stay.

However, in subsequent visits, when she had tests such as CT scans, MUGA scans, and X-rays, we have been far from happy with the way she has been managed. Her oncologist describes Judith as "stoic". She is disinclined to complain about anything, ever. Seeing such a genuinely agreeable person subjected to poor treatment is especially bothersome to me.

It is apparent that in many areas of the hospital, staff members are overworked, are not properly trained for their job, or both. Whatever the reason, far too many errors occur in both the administration and the testing. Any layperson, dealing with a life threatening illness, is extremely concerned about what is happening to him any time he is in the hospital. Naturally, he or she will see small incidents as larger than normal. One incident can be overlooked. But we have experienced an ongoing pattern.

When checking in, there is usually confusion at the desk about what we are here for. In taking the tests, there is usually great delay in getting the task completed. And finally, there is no understandable pattern to the billing procedures.

Judith is a candidate for the stem cell transplant program at American Stem Cell Clinic. Her survival may literally depend on getting into that program. In order to admit Judith, American requires a number of tests, which her oncologist in Charlotte scheduled at your hospital. If this weren't such serious business, her experience would be comical. The last several days illustrate the problem very well:

We receive a call three days before Judith's first visit for tests explaining that we need to "pre-register". I call and leave a voice mail three or four times each day for the next three days, requesting that someone call again about pre-registration. No one ever returns those calls.

We arrive first on Thursday afternoon, January 10, for a MUGA scan and a CT scan - My wife begins the MUGA scan. After 15-20 minutes or so, she is told that they forgot to hook up the machine properly and it didn't record her data. The reason is, "We are short of staff today." The process is repeated. My wife moves on to get her CT scan. While she is drinking fluid and preparing for the CT, a person comes from the MUGA scan area and says that during the second MUGA test, there was a power failure and the process must be done a third time. Apparently this third effort is a success.

She returns to the CT area, and has the CT scans (we think). So after about five hours, we are finished with what easily should have been a two-hour procedure at most.

We await the results. We are apprehensive. Will they show more cancer? American stem cell staff is insistent that they need the results immediately before they can move forward with the approval for Judith. We are assured that the results of all these tests will be available the next day. Days pass, and no results arrive for the oncologist to pass along to American. We can never determine whether the problem is with the oncologist or with your staff. No one seems to know – everybody says it's someone else's job. There is absolutely no consideration that these results can spell life or death for patients. The people involved appear to treat this information with no more seriousness than if it were, say, a driver's license score. Some of the test results finally get relayed to American via our oncologist on Wednesday, January 16.

Based on those results, the oncologist decides that Judith needs an exercise MUGA scan. This is scheduled for Thursday, January 17 at 8:00am. Again, I get a call about "pre-registering". This time a real person tells me that Judith IS pre-registered, whatever that means. When we arrive, we can see no difference between showing up pre-registered and not being pre-registered. We get asked all the same repetitious questions either way. But they forgot to mention in this pre-registration phone call that Judith should not eat before the test. They postpone the test until Friday morning and send her home.

Please remember, again, you are dealing with laypeople who know nothing about medical procedures. Hospital staff cannot simply assume that the patients know when, and when not, to eat.

On Friday morning, January 18 at 7:30am, we show up again for the exercise MUGA. Judith is sent to a room and placed in position for the test. It is an uncomfortable position to hold for long. Nothing happens for a half hour. Regarding your question about privacy, no one makes an attempt to draw a curtain across the open door while Judith is lying there. Then the technician returns to tell her that the machine can't be operated because someone has removed one of the cables that connect the machine to the recording device. The technician calls a young man to help. It takes him another half hour to find a cable and figure out how to connect it properly.

Once again, a one-hour procedure takes over two hours. As a courtesy, the technician apologizes for the delay and gives us each a ticket for a complimentary meal. We stop by the dining area for a delayed breakfast. When I present the tickets, the clerk says she cannot accept them. They haven't been properly filled out. This is our final indignity for the morning at the hands of hospital staff, but unfortunately not our last for the day.

On Friday afternoon, my wife must go back to the oncologist. She is experiencing severe chest pain, probably unrelated to her cancer. But the oncologist orders a chest X-Ray. We return to National Hospital on Friday afternoon. The lady at the front desk checks us in, and we give her the note from the oncologist who referred us. She sends us back to nuclear medicine. At that desk, the check-in lady there wants to know if we have any instructions?

What instructions? The note from the oncologist that the lady at the front desk kept, of course.

So I must go back to the front desk and retrieve it. The lady in nuclear medicine, Susan James, tells me that the front desk person failed to code my insurance information properly and Ms. James must correct it. I ask her how long she is going to do someone else's job for them? Why doesn't she just insist that the people up front learn to do it correctly before sending it to her? Because I'm obviously angry, she diplomatically ignores these questions.

At this point, my wife has her chest X-Ray. A doctor reads it immediately and explains the results. This quick service is much appreciated.

In the meantime, Ms. James is very helpful in answering my questions about what is happening with Judith's test results. She determines, to my distress, that Judith did NOT receive her bone scan during the visit on January 10. Rather than completing the entire CT scans at one visit as we were led to believe, she was scheduled to have the bone scan done the next day, January 11, at "Randolph Road". I learn later there is NO Randolph Road facility. No one ever told us that the scan was not done or that she should have met an appointment the next day. I cannot determine whether the scheduling fault lay with the oncologist or the hospital. Of course, everyone always assures me that whatever the problem, they certainly didn't cause it. Their condescending look and tone always imply that it must actually be Judith and I who are messing everything up because unfortunately, we're just not smart enough to be "medical" people.

A moment's thought would show that someone, ANYONE, at the hospital or at the oncologist who followed what was happening could see on the schedule that Judith needed to be somewhere on Friday, January 11. They could have told us so. Or when she didn't show up, a simple phone call could have alerted us that the test hadn't been done. Such action requires a sense of urgency about your patient's well being. Obviously nobody involved cared enough to make the effort until Ms. James investigated. Now we are several days behind the schedule that American has laid out.

Above, I mentioned billing procedures. This is a totally separate area from Judith's treatment as a patient. I can read a bill with at least as much understanding as the average person, but your billing procedure is totally beyond comprehension. My medical insurance provides for a deductible and a co-pay up to a fixed amount annually. We have a right to assume that our insurance will pay what it is expected to pay. Yet shortly after any visit to the hospital, I begin to receive bills showing amounts that are due, obviously well above what I should be expected to pay out of pocket. Most annoying, the bills keep coming, each with an increasingly threatening tone regarding my delinquency.

When I search for an explanation, National says the insurance company will not pay the bill – no reason why. When I call my insurance company, they tell me that National will not code the bills properly and the insurance company will not pay until the bills are submitted with proper codes. Who am I to believe?

After eighteen months of being subjected to this bureaucratic finger pointing, and paying bills that I later learn were NOT my responsibility, I have developed my own plan. I simply file the bills and wait. I expect that sooner or later, regardless of threats to me, the two parties who should be solving this problem, the insurance company and you, will finally get it right. It is not my place as a customer of both institutions to do your job for you.

I have concluded that the health care system is, indeed, badly broken. I suspect that the dedicated line people bear the brunt of this disrepair. It is unfortunate that we, and countless others, develop such a negative impression of a system when many fine and dedicated professionals do care about treating sick people. As individuals we feel almost helpless to defend ourselves against this system, at a time when we already feel extremely vulnerable.

You must know, unfortunately, the average person subjected to this kind of care will believe that the solution is more government control over the healthcare system - a solution that I am certain will not work.

But as customers of the system, we simply can't excuse or overlook its faults. It is our lives that are at stake. It is unfortunate that we should have to take on so much responsibility just to protect ourselves from an incompetent system we are forced to use. Even sadder, we see many people in the hospital who have absolutely no means to call attention to the shoddy treatment they are receiving. They just have to take it. I would pose to you this question – Would you, or any of your staff, be pleased to be clients/patients in your own facility if you were treated the way your patients are treated? I suspect that you would not.

Your letter described me as one of a "limited number of patients who receive this survey." I have taken you at your word that you really want feedback, and have probably given you more feedback than you have time to digest. As you suggest, I have expressed my opinions frankly. It does not matter to me that my comments be kept confidential. In fact the broader you distribute them, the better, if they might result in positive change.

I look forward to your response.

Sincerely,
Gene Hoots

Addendum to Letter, January 30, 2002

As if the previous difficulties in getting Judith's tests completed weren't enough, this afternoon, American staff called to tell me that there is still a pulmonary function test that has not been run on Judith.

The administrative staff at Oncology Specialists has been at least partially responsible for this chain of events. At my request, American just faxed me a copy of a fax that they sent Tammy on January 22 requesting the results of the pulmonary test. I had already talked days before with Anne and Tammy about the difficulty in getting all Judith's tests scheduled, run, and results sent back.

Much of this delay could have been avoided if someone in Oncology Specialists had simply done a small amount of follow-up. A phone call to National Hospital requesting the results (supposedly on a test done on January 10 and already 12 days late) should, and probably would, have revealed that the test was never run.

I called this afternoon, and Anne tells me it is the Hospital's fault for not running the test. She is trying to get it scheduled now. Trying is just not good enough under the circumstances. Judith must have these tests, and we are now twenty days behind schedule. It may be the fault of the hospital, but certainly, it is apparent that no one at Oncology Specialists is following up to get an explanation for these delays.

Between Oncology Specialists and National Hospital, I always get the story that it is someone else's responsibility to follow up. Nobody wants to accept the initiative to recognize that work isn't being done and ask why. Nobody but me. I do not consider it my job to monitor the lists of tests sent by American and assure that they are being done. I'm not the medical authority here.

It breaks my heart to see this gracious lady treated this way. It is an extremely difficult time in her life, and she is dealing with it with more patience and understanding than the medical community deserves, given the lack of service you have provided.

I find this last delay and miscommunication absolutely indefensible in light of all my calls and requests to be sure that everything is on track. We can draw no conclusion except that nobody dealing with this problem at either the oncologist or the hospital really cares enough to solve it.

I don't know what our options are in dealing with this. I do know that if it were the business I am in, my clients would fire me in a second and go to a competitor. In this case of course, we are essentially held captive by the system. Patients have little option but to simply bear the abuses and excuses. Despite that, be assured that I will not tolerate Judith receiving any more of this shoddy service.

Strange Vocabulary

Do not allow medical people to intimidate you with their vocabulary. There will be many unfamiliar terms and procedures Do not be afraid to say that you don't understand. Request a simple explanation in plain terms. Usually the doctor or nurse will be happy to go over things so that you are comfortable, but they forget that you are not one of them. We had an instance where I asked a doctor a question, and the response was, "We already talked about that." Now, that conversation had been two weeks earlier when we were anxious, even upset. I politely reminded the doctor that we are laypeople who are not familiar with all the terms. We need to be told more than once. The doctor was happy to oblige.

Medical people are not the only ones with their own shorthand language. They do seem to use this shorthand in an effort to speed up the process rather than to impress people with their skills that others do not possess. I can't say this is always true in my own industry. For example, in 1979 I listened to a very bright group of investment research people talk at a major bank conference. I was very new to the business and like most novices, I was awed by their vocabulary. I listened for two days to them use the phrases, "Ex ante", and "ex post ante." I finally figured out that the terms actually meant "before" and "after." Why didn't they simply say "before" and "after" if that's what they meant? Apparently because it was more impressive to speak Latin even if ordinary people in the audience didn't know what they meant. In fact, it was probably because most people didn't know what they meant. Many people believe it is more important to impress than to communicate.

The Occasional Jerk

I have mentioned the caring attitude of doctors and nurses. We did have one experience that is so negative it is worth mentioning. If you find yourself in a situation with someone who is not respectful of you, don't be intimidated. Let them know how you feel in no uncertain terms. We met with a radiologist, a department head in a major hospital. He was the stereotype of the insensitive, cold professional with no bedside manner whatsoever. He actually went beyond that – he was rudely insensitive. A junior doctor had examined Judy and had explained to her what her treatment options would be at this point. But he said, this was a serious case and he wanted to have his superior, the department head, review the situation. So the boss showed up, and listened briefly to an explanation from his subordinate. And then in my and Judy's presence, he said to the junior doctor (as though we weren't in the room), "Okay, but you know what's going to happen." His manner and words conveyed clearly that he meant that Judy would die shortly, regardless of their treatment. The comment was crass and grossly inconsiderate. I'm sure it was his best medical judgment and he was certainly entitled to it, but he wasn't entitled to say so in front of a very sick, disturbed patient and her family. I was so taken aback that I did nothing. A comment like that shouldn't pass without some reaction from the patient's caregiver. Now, more experienced, I would not tolerate it. In fact Judy's oncologist, whom I have come to respect enormously, told me I should have told the radiologist to "Go to hell." Today, I would invite him out of Judy's presence and he'd get a lecture on insensitivity that he would remember. This type incident is very rare, hopefully. But remember, you as a patient/customer, don't have to tolerate such rudeness.

Take Charge - It's your life at stake.

Being Sick Takes A Lot of Time

A serious medical problem can take all your time. There is no quick fix, and often no really dramatic positive outcome can be expected, short of a miracle. Your life will be absorbed by the events related to the disease. Much of your thinking and energy will be diverted from routine things – job, family, recreation, and other usual activities. You ride an emotional roller coaster, moving from the shock of bad news to hope from the latest treatment to the next round of the fight.

A disease like this provides a never-ending challenge for the victim, the caregivers, family, and friends. There are pressures involved in dealing with life and death issues daily, on a long-term basis. While dealing with the medical side, you must also deal with the day-to-day details of bills (they are in the mailbox every day) and wondering whether this will destroy you economically.

Often a new symptom arises. Each ache or pain, or lump, or skin color change brings a flood of thoughts that this is yet another cancer attack. Of course, it usually isn't, but it is still very disturbing. Radiation and chemotherapy become weekly routines. But these "little" routines take precious time out of your life. On every visit to the doctor, the wait can be anywhere from a few minutes to an hour. Coupled with the travel time, any medical treatment can easily consume a half day. You find yourself planning most of your life around the medical schedule. With cancer, I draw an analogy to war, "Long periods of boredom, punctuated by moments of pure terror." Each negative reading is one of those terror moments. And all the times in between, you try to live a normal life, but in the back of your mind, you know somewhere down the road, another serious battle is coming, and you're never sure you're going to make it through alive.

Our case is <u>not</u> atypical. Remember for whom the bell tolls. It tolls for thee.

NATIONAL SECURITY

Just What We Need - A New Bureaucracy

Does anyone who has traveled through an airport believe what is going on there will really deter terrorists? What we have from all this homeland security is a <u>new</u> federal bureaucracy that is entrenched and that we will be paying for forever.

There is a parallel here from a former national "crisis." – the energy crisis in the 1970s. This crisis began with inflation largely caused by government policies in the late 1960s. Nixon created an energy crisis by imposing price controls in 1971, a government response to the inflation it had already made. This led to OPEC raising the price of oil in late 1973. To "solve" this problem, Nixon then appointed William Simon as the Energy Czar. The oil problem didn't go away, so in the late 1970s, Carter created the Department of Energy. The energy crisis was finally solved by the market when supply and demand were allowed to come into balance by natural economic forces. But did the Department of Energy go away? No! Today it still exists with a budget of $20 billion a year, and thousands of employees making and enforcing new rules. To what purpose? The Department of Energy never produced one drop of oil or did much to make our supplies more secure. But inside the beltway in Washington, all this is seen as a great leap forward because it creates jobs and power there.[lxviii]

It is always amazing how it takes very little decrease in demand for a commodity at the margin to cause a precipitous drop in prices. As one of my friends said, "We were worried about energy policy and consumption, and all we had to do was learn to cut off the lights when we left a room."

But back to the Transportation Safety Administration. As described earlier, on a trip last summer, Judy and I were held up for three hours because we missed a connecting flight out of Newark. Our bags didn't miss the connecting flight but the airline assured us that they were still somewhere in Newark airport with us. I could understand that happening – they only held the flight for us about fifteen minutes and then it left without us. (The bags were carried over by truck, but we had to run through the terminal, and we weren't fast enough.) But the next night we took the flight after waiting twenty-four hours, and the plane was delayed over an hour because two people who had checked bags at Newark didn't get on the plane. Yes, the circumstances are somewhat different – but not that different. I thought the airline was certainly applying policy very inconsistently. (I had some justification because in that twenty-four hours they certainly did a great number of things that were wrong.) As it turned out, on this point the airline was right. I checked with the TSA office, and was told that if a bag is checked through from another airport it <u>can</u> go on a flight without its owner, but if a passenger is not on the flight at his point of origin, the bag <u>cannot</u> go on the flight without its owner. The TSA representative assured me that while this policy may be inconsistent, it <u>is</u> the policy. With policies like this, how much luck do you think we are going to have preventing terrorists on airplanes?[15]

Intelligence Agencies

The CIA and FBI are taking heat from people who are disappointed in their ability to identify and stop terrorists. Anyone who ever worked in a large organization can appreciate the problem. An article in *Forbes* described the state of our national security agencies - no surprise, they suffer from the bureaucracy you would expect. Several years ago I talked with a man in England who headed his own small private investigative agency. He took great pride that his company could investigate quickly and with limited manpower. He had little use for government investigative organizations. In fact he said that he would not hire people who had worked for them because they had already developed a bureaucratic mindset – they thought that any problem always needed more people and more money for a solution – an approach that would assure no profits.

No matter how well intentioned at its beginning, if <u>any</u> organization grows large enough it finally reaches the bureaucratic state. The *Wall Street Journal* reported in July, 2002 that the FBI's files and computer systems are so outdated that they cannot function on a timely basis. Agents are not made aware of each other's work even though shared information might lead to a more complete picture.

Many case files are stored in hard copy folders. Unbelievably the bureau's case-numbering system dates back to the days of J. Edgar Hoover, who worked at the Library of Congress before joining the FBI in 1921 and imposed a kind of Dewey Decimal System on the bureau for classifying criminal acts. The system, which is issued to each FBI agent in a little blue or yellow booklet, still includes offenses related to Prohibition, white slavery and sedition.[lxix]

The latest idea is to create a cabinet level post, National Intelligence Director. This person will head the CIA, the NSA, part of the FBI, the Defense Intelligence Agency, and other units. He is to bring all these forces under one roof and force them to cooperate with each other. For reasons we've already addressed, this is likely to be a fruitless exercise. While people are already working hard, and at great expense to protect us, this new post will not add much to the project if past

---

[15] See Appendix Seven for a Review of Our Security Procedures.

experience in bureaucracy is any indication of future results. Already Homeland Security has spent $70 billion and wants $40 billion for fiscal year 2005. And the bureaucrats grind on. Tom Ridge, Secretary of Homeland Security, had to testify to eighty congressional committees and subcommittees in his short time in office.

RETIREMENT PLANNING

A Case History

An example of one family's experience will illustrate today's retirement planning problems. The challenge they face is not at all unusual in today's affluent society. The family is spending about $700,000 a year after taxes and is living "the good life." The breadwinner is nearing retirement age, and they have a nest egg of $7 million, a sum that seems enormous to most of us. But the numbers don't work for retirement here. Part of this nest egg has not been taxed, and there is perhaps a $1 million unrealized tax liability that will have to be paid at some point. But more important, the $7 million portfolio must generate a return of about 13% annually to provide enough money to support this lifestyle and keep up with inflation. That high 13% return is not realistic. Their financial advisor has run the numbers and is going to deliver some bad news to this family.

Even when their portfolio was a bit larger, before the Bubble burst, it could not have realistically thrown off enough cash for the spending the client wanted to do. This investor probably: (a) didn't think at all about a long range plan, or (b) expected the funds to continue to compound at the 15% rate they had during the 80's and 90's, or hopefully (c) looked at the $700,000 spending level as temporary for a couple years while the family caught up on all the good things they had been postponing.

Such news is usually not well received. The client may look for an advisor who will deliver them "good" news that they can indeed earn 13% or more - not good results, but good news.

Retirement Deferred

Millions of people's lifestyle has been dramatically impacted by the bear market. I continue to tell people that my major concern as an advisor is to be certain that their lifestyle continues in the way they want. If expectations don't meet reality, there are two ways to remedy the problem. One is to make more money for them and the other is for them to control their spending and work longer. And speaking of working longer, here's a sobering thought. Over the next three decades, the proportion of the U.S. population age sixty-five and older will jump to 20% from 12%. There will be just 2.7 working age people for every person age sixty-five or older, compared with the current ratio of 4.7 to 1. Even if every baby boomer has saved for retirement and even if the government cuts them all generous Social Security checks, we still have a huge problem. If all these folks retire at sixty-five, there won't be enough workers. The elderly retired are going to be bidding against a lot of other retirees for services. To fill the gap so that there are enough workers to produce what we need as a society, the average retirement age will rise from sixty-five to seventy-two.

Even if they want to retire, their demands coupled with fewer goods and services produced will create inflation and will force the retirees to sell off their investments and trade down to smaller homes. The only way to beat the game is to save more than other people so you can outbid them for what you need.

EDUCATION

We can put television in its proper light by supposing that Gutenberg's great invention had been directed at printing only comic books.
Robert M. Hutchins, educator (1899-1977)

They have an amazing proliferation of TV channels now: The all-cartoon channel, the 24-hour-science fiction channel. Of course, to make room for these they got rid of the Literacy Channel and the What's Left of Civilization Channel.
Dennis Miller

A Failed System

A nation is as strong, as productive, and as smart as the collection of its citizens. To build a strong economy, education standards must rise. We are "dumbing down" America. And the poor education system impacts us all. If a country's citizenry can't read, write, and count, then that nation is in trouble. Now, I'm old enough that it would be easy for me to say that the education of our youth doesn't concern me. But it concerns all of us. Everyone has a stake in this crisis. And as usual in a democracy, we are trusting the solution to politicians who look only as far ahead as the next election.

Young people who aren't getting a proper education are the ones who will be running the country in a few years. Many young people don't know how to make change or how to talk with enough clarity that you can converse with them. They are going to be waiting on you at the fast food counter and filling your drug prescription or giving you food and medicine at the nursing home. They probably can't read a thermometer, and they won't know how to measure doses of medicine or read the instructions on your chart at the foot of your bed. They also are going to be your banker, your doctor, your lawyer, your car repairman and a thousand other things.

One certainty - the schools are caught in a bureaucracy that exists to protect itself – its jobs, its work rules, It does not care very much about the quality of education. And as usual, the politicians throw more money at the problem, even though we know that it doesn't work. The answer is, again, responsibility. Parents need to be responsible for their children's education, and also make the children responsible.

College Loyalty

As one of those people just old enough to communicate with Paul Tibbets, I have always been put off by trivial conversation. I am appalled at the number of people whose only interest in their college is the quality of their sports teams. Many players on those teams are an educational and moral embarrassment. In no way do they represent their school's primary mission to produce people to be leaders and/or useful citizens.

When I was a child, I spake as a child, I understood as a child, I thought as a child: but when I became a man, I put away childish things.
First Letter from Paul of Tarsus to the School at Corinth, Chapter 13, Verse 11.

News magazines, books, and television talk shows discuss the problem that parents have saying "no" to their children. They don't know how to be adult, mature parents. They want to be their child's best friend and see that their child gets all the things they wish they could have gotten when they were children. And they seem to have absolutely no sense of the damage they are doing to their children. All they know is that the kids are out of control, and their parenting approach isn't working. Sadly, we have a generation of parents who are themselves children. They have not been made to grow up. They are like so many Peter Pans and Wendy's, and their children are the Lost Boys (and Girls). Unfortunately, that may be what the children become – lost boys and girls.

What is important seems to have changed. I suspect that in the years ahead, America will be forced to put away childish things if it is going to survive. Instead of studying the sports and entertainment pages of the daily paper, we may need to focus on the International section. It may be more important to learn the mindset of those who are determined to kill you than it is to know who hit a home run or scored a touchdown or what Paris wore last night, or what she was arrested for.

The literary award is the "Pullet Surprise"
Student at Penn State University

America's long-term problem isn't too few jobs, it is education for the jobs that are available. The solution is to help spur upward mobility by getting more Americans a good education, including access to college. Unfortunately, just the opposite is occurring. There will be plenty of good jobs to go around. But too few of our citizens are being prepared for them. Rather than fret about "losing jobs" to others, we ought to be fretting about the growing number of our young people who are losing their footing in the emerging economy.[lxx]

WEALTH, CHARITY, AND ESTATES

Lottery Winners usually believe that when they hit the jackpot all their troubles are over; actually their troubles have just begun. Wealth brings an unimaginable set of problems. It is not surprising that many lottery winners later file bankruptcy. Managing wealth requires special skills and very hard work – something that the lottery winners are not prepared for. Money definitely changes the relationship between rich people and everyone around them.

How Much Wealth Should You Give Your Heirs?
Your children need your presence more than your presents.
    Jesse Jackson, clergyman and civil rights leader (1941-)

Warren Buffett, one of the world's richest men, said in *Fortune* in 1986 that he was leaving the bulk of his fortune to charity because you should leave "enough money to your kids so they can do anything, but not so much that they can do nothing." While few have fortunes approaching Buffett's, there are many families who wonder how much they should leave their children, and in what form. Many of these families are young – forty-five percent of today's millionaires are younger than fifty-five. They worry about whether giving their kids a large amount of wealth will undermine their work ethic. More and more wealthy people are following Buffett's advice: they're giving more to charity and less to their heirs.

I regret that my multimillion dollar worth will not buy my children the thing they need most to succeed in this world - a childhood of abject poverty.
    Jim Walter (Mobile Home Manufacturer)

While Jim Walter's words might be a little strong, the idea certainly seems on the right track. Giving children too much is not love. It deprives them of one of life's greatest pleasures, pride that comes from having built a life that includes earning one's own way with worthwhile work. When we see people who have been denied this opportunity, they always strike me as drifting aimlessly and somewhat to be pitied, no matter how big their trust fund might be. How difficult life is for them. They lack a sense of purpose. They have often been sheltered from the real world by their wealth, and they have great difficulty in dealing with the normal challenges that most people face every day. I remember a young man, barely out of his teens, who was the scion of a wealthy family. He commented to a friend, "I can't imagine wanting something that costs as little as $50,000 and not buying it."
    One wealthy person described his life – "When most people want water, they just go to a faucet and turn it on. They take it for granted. With my family, money is like water; if we want some, we just turn a handle and out comes as much as we

want." If anything in life comes that easily, it soon has no value at all.

Some people think they are worth a lot of money just because they have it.
     Fannie Hurst, writer (1889-1968)

     When I was quite young I lived on a farm with my grandparents and uncle. This was the early 1940s and even then the rural South wasn't that far removed from Reconstruction. A farmer's life was hard. Decades later, I mentioned to my Uncle Kenneth how I remembered my grandfather and him plowing corn in the Yadkin River bottom land with horses. They would be so hot that their blue shirts would sometimes get a white layer of salt from the evaporated sweat. Like most farmers, they worked harder than people can imagine today - sun up until dark, bone-wearying labor. And I commented to my Uncle how hard that must have been. And then Kenneth said, "You should <u>never</u> feel sorry for your grandfather and me. Both of us were doing <u>exactly</u> what we wanted to do <u>every</u> day." That is a wonderful thing to be able to say about a lifetime of work. Everyone should be so lucky.

There's no sauce in the world like hunger.
     Miguel de Cervantes, novelist (1547-1616)

Charity
You make a living by what you get; you build a life by what you give.

     We all know, at least intuitively, that it is blessed to give. But only recently have I come to see the real benefits of charity – and more for the giver than for the recipient. One of our friends, Pauline Carter, at her death left funds in a charitable foundation. Her niece and nephew are the trustees who determine each year which charities receive its gifts. When they talk about their giving, it is impossible for them to contain their enthusiasm. It has become a labor of love, and they describe the joy they get from their work – the satisfaction in seeing their gifts helping those in need in many ways – food for the hungry, care for battered women, support for a children's hospital and education for those who could not otherwise afford it.

A true measure of your worth includes all the benefits others have gained from your successes.
     Cullen Hightower, salesman and writer (1923-)

     When you hear the Carter Trustees describe their experiences, you see that they have learned a great deal from meeting with the beneficiaries of their generosity. And that they have been blessed at least as much as those to whom they have given. True generosity is important, giving - and giving with the right spirit. Taking satisfaction in seeing something accomplished that enriches the lives of others in a meaningful way. Everyone doesn't understand this.

A wealthy miser died and found himself at Heaven's Pearly Gates.
St. Peter said, "Can you tell me any generous act you did on earth that would allow you to enter here?"
The man thought and said, "Once I saw a beggar standing on the street, ragged, hot and thirsty, and I gave him a nickel."
St. Peter said, "Can you think of anything else?"
The miser replied, "Yes, Once I was in a fine restaurant and outside in the snow I saw a little girl, cold and hungry looking in at me as I ate my dinner. I was so moved, I went outside and gave her a dime."
The archangel Gabriel was standing by listening to the conversation. St. Peter turned to him, "Well Gabe, what do you think we ought to do with this man?"
And the angel Gabriel said, "Pete, I think we ought to give him his fifteen cents back and tell him to go to hell."

Estate Planning

Preparing for one's estate is not a pleasant job; sadly many people neglect it. The rules governing estates are complicated and the financial penalties for doing it wrong are severe. Yet the typical person knows as much about nuclear physics as he knows about estate taxes.

The Death Tax Is Probably Here To Stay

The so-called "death tax" is likely to be with us for a long time. In spite of efforts to abolish this tax, it is an emotion charged issue. And surprisingly, many very wealthy people, among them the world's richest person Bill Gates, believe the tax should be kept. As a conservative who never met a tax I liked, I'm still of two minds on this one.

On the one hand it seems unfair for people who have worked hard to accumulate a nest egg or build a small business to have a lifetime's efforts diminished by about half. They were already taxed when the money was earned. On the other hand, the tax proponents make the valid point that I have made above – that it is no favor to leave enormous wealth to people who have done nothing to earn it, and it will probably do them more harm than good. I can't quite sign on to this argument, because I still believe that the wealth people earn should be theirs, and that taxes should only be used by the government to provide for the common good; taxes should not be used to redistribute the nation's wealth or conduct social engineering.

But I concede that the supporters of this tax have a point. For one thing, it is not certain how much charitable giving would be curtailed if such gifts didn't get tax breaks.

You Better Know the Rules

So long as the tax exists people who have worked hard to accumulate wealth and who do not want to see it reduced by half at their death had better beware of this tax. With proper planning, over a normal lifetime this tax should touch only the very wealthiest. The tax laws have generous allowances for gifting to family members and charities, and for establishing trusts at death. These can reduce or avoid the tax altogether.

But problems arise because: (1) the tax rules and techniques to avoid the estate taxes are complicated and it takes great effort to understand them and act on them. And (2) it is an unfortunate quirk of human nature that most people won't confront their own mortality and so refuse to even think about estate planning. Many people don't have a will. This, despite the legal entanglements that are caused when someone dies without a valid will. Refusing to prepare a will is a very selfish act. It leaves a great burden on loved ones at exactly the time when they are emotionally least able to deal with legal and financial problems. If you don't have a will, get one, no matter how young you are and how little you have.

Planning

Here's some rules to help decide who, how and when to give away your estate.

Start your children young. Whether you already have a fortune or hope to have a fortune, or just want to help your kids, start teaching them about the value of money and how to manage it. The best way you can teach them about money is to set a good example in the way you manage money, give to charity, avoid excessive spending and so on. Teaching your children how to manage their money well may be the best gift you can give.

Give during your lifetime. Passing money on to your children when they are young and middle-age adults offers several benefits. As long as estate taxes continue, there are tax benefits to lifetime gifting. With more and more people living well into their 80s and even 90s, waiting until death to pass on your wealth probably means your children are themselves retired or nearly retired, and the need for the gift may be greatly diminished. But more important, lifetime gifting is an opportunity to see how your children handle wealth. If they handle it well, you may feel more comfortable in passing on more.

Let your children know your plans while you are alive. This is particularly important if you plan to give much of your wealth to charity or you want to give more to one child than another. Perhaps one child has lifetime medical needs while the other is already well-off financially, or you want to pass the family business on to a particular child. By explaining your intentions and reasoning, you can eliminate misunderstandings that may cause squabbles among your heirs or angry memories about you.

When you communicate with your family, you may want your financial advisors to help explain the money issues or have the family work with a therapist to air out the emotions that so often cloud estate planning. The wealthy sometimes delay taking important planning because they fear dredging up these issues. And look at matters from the viewpoint of your children, as well. Some young adults are uncomfortable inheriting wealth they themselves haven't earned.

Use estate planning tools. Consider using trusts to help manage your wealth for the benefit of your heirs. There are many kinds, including incentive trusts that require an heir to accomplish specific tasks on their own (say earn a certain amount of money, complete college or even pass drug tests) before receiving assets from the trusts. Do not try to over-control the child by using trusts. It's one thing to use a trust to help a young adult who's not ready to manage money, and another to control the money until the child is in his sixties.

Above all, create an estate plan and a will. Otherwise, your estate will be distributed according to state law after your death, and it may not go where you want it to.

Savings, Investment, and Tax Philosophy

How does one get to be "wealthy?" By saving a little bit every day and living a long time. That applies to families as well as individuals. Here is one family's philosophy. It is worth noting:

Our philosophy for work and investing can be summed up in two ideas: 1. Without active, productive work a person has no sense of self worth. 2. The *Bible* is right – "To him to whom much is given, much is expected."

Our family has always been workers and savers. Our goal is to carry on that tradition - not because that is the way we've always done it, but because it is the right thing to do. The happiest people are gainfully employed at something, anything! Every family member should be productive at a job, raising a family, or whatever. Life is only a collection of memories, and we would like for our family to have good memories of our lives and of each other.

We continue to work and save because it makes sense on several levels. The greatest danger with thrift is that it will be bad for children. It is not easy for wealthy people to raise productive children. The best reason for continuing our family program of savings can be illustrated by past events. Each generation worked and saved for future generations. A strong financial base is the best way you can generate continued success. We want to leave that opportunity to our grandchildren, but we want them to know that their financial good fortune didn't happen by accident. Our prior generations could have elected to spend everything, and we would have been much the poorer for it. We have been given much, and much is expected of us in return – we ought to do the same for our future generations.

It is important to build substantial savings today, because nobody knows how long he will live and how much he may need to support himself in his lifetime. People are living much longer, and no one wants to be a financial burden to the next generation. As a result, no one knows how much is enough, and it is better to err on the side of having saved too much.

We also feel strongly about the need to plan carefully. The deck is clearly stacked against any family trying to save today. With current tax laws, in three generations the government will take 92% of nearly everything a wealthy family earns in either income tax or estate tax. This means that under normal circumstances, it is impossible to pass along money to future generations. We must plan to protect assets from taxes. We don't want to work most of our time for the government. We don't want to be victims of a tax system that destroys people's desire to work and save.

It is important to never depend on the accumulated nest egg for a living. It is far better to supplement wealth with productive jobs and earning power. Many wealthy families start with enormous fortunes, and when a work ethic is not fostered, the wealth disappears in a surprisingly short time. We will do our best to see that this does not happen.

INFLATION

A report on financial management must have some discussion of inflation. Inflation can be defined as "too much money chasing too few goods." But a simple definition is not enough to deal with this complex subject. The general price level has risen rather steadily, sometimes dramatically, for most of our lifetimes. Economists debate the nature of inflation, what really causes it, whether it is good in small doses, can it really be controlled?

I believe that inflation is caused primarily by the way governments manipulate the money supply, coupled with their borrowings. However, this is still a very simplistic explanation that will get lots of argument, deservedly. If we look just at government borrowing, the U.S. ran huge deficits during the Reagan years and yet inflation was low. Then the Republican Party essentially switched its stance in the last few years; they used to say a balanced budget was critical, but now they say deficits don't matter.

I won't attempt to explain inflation, because I can't. Nor am I going to defend any political position, because no political party maintains a strong stance on it for long. What we can provide is a little history of inflation that may surprise many, as it did me. And we can discuss the implications on our investment policy going forward, which is what really matters anyway.

History

Let's put the last 404 years of inflation in a long-term perspective. For well over three hundred years (1600-2004) there was very little inflation. Major inflation is a relatively recent event, beginning just after World War II. Prior to that time, inflation had usually been associated with financing war, but after each war prices dropped back to their base level. After 1945, this did not happen. There was no economic contraction after that war and prices have risen steadily for decades.

In the three hundred years (1600 – 1900), there was almost <u>no</u> inflation. Prices rose 27%, that's about .08% a year. There were periods when prices rose dramatically, usually during major wars, probably resulting from war financing and a shortage of goods. But notably, after each such event there was a long period when prices settled back to their previous level, frequently with an economic contraction.

Inflation accelerated during World War I. Then the depression of the 1930s carried prices back toward their earlier levels, but not in the way that had happened in the previous three hundred years. Prices did not return to their 1900-1915 levels

From the end of World War II until now, inflation has continued more or less unchecked. It rose above 13% in 1980, and then settled back to a 1-4% range for the rest of the twentieth century. But even the inflation at the end of the century that seemed so benign would have been thought astronomical a century earlier. The sixty-four year period 1940-2004) averaged 4.15% a year. Inflation was relatively low for the first thirty years and then accelerated in the 1970s during the energy crisis. Economists are still debating whether oil prices really caused that inflation.

A Deflation Mindset

It took decades for those who lived through the Great Depression to shed the deflation mindset. Even into the 1960s, I remember men who had been alive in the 1930s who said that their investment strategy was to wait for the economic collapse and then buy everything for "ten cents on the dollar." It was years until they realized that their big investment menace wasn't deflation, rather it was inflation eating away at the purchasing power of their bonds year after year – they didn't own any stocks. In their investment world, only an idiot would gamble on the stock market.

In 1971, I worked on a project and dealt with the patriarch of the family that virtually owned Myrtle Beach at one time, and still owns much of it. I asked him about the story that he had been a member of a small group that owned Pine Lakes Country Club and Golf Course and had sold it for $50,000 in 1941. He said the story was true. His group had bought the club for $50,000 and week after week it showed a loss - $5 one week, $10 one week, and so on. He said, "Son you have to remember that in 1941 a man who paid $50,000 for <u>anything</u> was a fool. From the interest on a $50,000 savings account, you could live forever. By 1971, the clubhouse alone had been appraised at $500,000, and the buyer got a twenty-seven hole golf course to boot. I can only imagine the value of that club today in the middle of the Grand Strand.

The Inflation Mystery

Inflation is a bit of a mystery to me. At the same time that we have experienced great inflation, the world has enjoyed a standard of living that has risen dramatically. Is inflation the price we must pay for such affluent lives? Or could we have been even more affluent, if we had inflation under control? These are tough questions to answer.

Has there been a real fundamental shift since about 1940? In past times, every war brought inflation and every peace brought deflation, and prices didn't change much. Are we really in a new world, or could we again experience deflation? Note that there were four periods on these charts when prices dropped about 40% over a period of many years. It's hard to believe, but a 40% decline in prices would take us only back to about 1986 prices. That's what <u>only</u> 2.9% inflation does in eighteen years. It cuts your purchasing power of $1.00 to $.60.

Recent Inflation Trends

In the last few years, the inflation trends have been very different from the last great inflation surge. Understanding the past is important, but it is critical to recognize the differences as well as the similarities in events. It is never safe to assume that this time will be just like last time. It is those small differences that can play havoc with investment plans.

In the late 1970s, as raw material prices – steel, oil, metals, foodstuffs – rose, manufacturers passed those increases along in the prices of producer finished goods and then retailers passed them along to the end consumer. But in this decade it's been a different story. As raw material prices have jumped sharply in the last five years, producer prices have risen only 2.2% a year. Several reasons are offered for this – raw materials are not such a large component of producer prices anymore, producers have realized labor productivity, and foreign competition has made it more difficult for U.S. producers to raise prices.[lxxi]

Forecast?

In Jan 1980, a price of regular gasoline was $1.13/gallon and today it is around $2.04/gallon. Using the CPI to inflate the $1.13 from 1980, it would be $2.77/gallon. So, twenty-four years later we are obviously getting a heck of a deal, especially when you consider that the expectation in 1980 was that prices would hit $2/gallon in 24 months rather than 24 years. We must continually remind ourselves how wrong most current expectations will be. (e.g., interest rates are REALLY headed higher -- like gas in 1980, is it so obvious to everyone that it can almost be guaranteed? I wonder about anything that is so irrefutable.)

Thomas E. Quinn, July 25, 2004

Tom's comment reflects our contrarian nature. We are wary of forecasts. But since we can't forecast inflation, we need to learn something from the past and apply it to the future as best we can. If inflation remains benign as it was in the 1990s, or better yet declines as it did in the late 1980s, then stocks are a good thing to own. Companies can make money in a stable, predictable (that's a relative term - since very little is really predictable) environment. Companies, and stocks, do well in an inflationary environment in the long term because they have the ability to raise prices, but that doesn't always work well in the shorter term. In the 1970s, it took several years for companies to adjust their prices and operating policies to inflationary times.

If inflation is high, then hard assets tend to be the best investments – this includes anything tangible. Tangibles, such as commodities (especially metals and oil) and real property, cannot easily be reproduced to increase supply,. In the last inflationary cycles, real estate did quite well – not only because it was an asset with limited supply but also because investors/borrowers figured out quicker than lenders that they could borrow money at a fixed rate below inflation. They could use this money to buy real estate and get a "double-whammy' return – an asset that was increasing in price, purchased with little money down and lots of cheap debt. This financing probably won't work so well the next time around, because lenders are smarter now that they have been burned once. As inflation rises, interest rates seem to adjust upward much more quickly than they did in the 1960s and 70s.

But what about deflation – falling general prices? This is something that only people over eighty years old can remember. Does this mean it can't happen again? Of course not! We all agree that it's not likely, given the tendency of governments to opt for more inflation at any cost rather than deflation – it's easier to get elected with inflation. A "little" inflation seems to give everyone a psychological lift – a sense of well-being, no matter how false it is. You just feel better if you get a raise, if your house is worth a bit more than you paid for it, if your stocks are going up a bit. But underneath, inflation is quietly chipping away at your purchasing power year after year.

Deflation could happen. Economic cycles can be very long, and we would be foolish not to consider the possibility of deflation. In a deflationary environment, cash and government debt have been the best investments. It's hard to imagine cash being a great investment, but just imagine having cash in hand from 1929-33. By doing nothing you would have received a real return of nearly 66% in just four years. The cash didn't increase but prices dropped so that the same dollar would buy 166% of what it would buy four years earlier. In deflation, government bonds would do even better. They can't be called (repaid early by the government). So a bond that offered an interest rate of, say, 4%, for the next thirty years at a time when prices were falling –12% a year, would give you a real return of 16% a year. (The math is not quite that simple, but 16% isn't far off the mark.) And this return would be tax advantaged as well. If inflation is 10% and you have bonds that pay you the exorbitant rate of 26%, you probably get interest of 16% after income tax and after subtracting inflation, a real return of 6%. But with deflation, in our example above you get 4% before tax, maybe 2.5% after tax, and adjusted for deflation, a real return of 14.5%. You can see that deflation requires a new way of thinking about investing.

So, you ask –What's it going to be, stable prices, inflation, deflation? The answer is: We don't know, so we better prepare for all three. That is why any portfolio should diversify – and the percentages of each asset class will depend on the individual's age, total wealth, and risk tolerance. It would be nice to give you a magic formula to solve this most important investment question, but no one can. You need to be aware that just because something has happened for nearly a hundred years, doesn't mean it's going to keep on happening in the same way.

TAXES

History

Income Tax History				
Year	Cost of House	Cost of Loaf of Bread	Value of $1	Fed. & State Income Tax Rate %	Time Span
1776	$1,000	$0.01	1.00	ZERO	-
1913	$1,000	$0.01	1.00	ZERO	137 years
1923	$1,900	$0.02	0.70	0.5%	10 years
1933	$3,610	$0.04	0.49	0.9%	10 years
1943	$6,859	$0.07	0.34	1.6%	10 years
1953	$13,032	$0.13	0.24	2.9%	10 years
1963	$24,761	$0.25	0.17	5.2%	10 years
1973	$47,046	$0.47	12¢	9.4%	10 years
1983	$89,387	$0.89	8¢	17.0%	10 years
1993	$169,836	$1.70	6¢	30.6%	10 years
2003	$322,688	$3.23	4¢	55.1%*	10 years
2004	$400,000	$3.50	4¢	58.0%	1 year
2013	$613,107	$6.13	3¢	100 % ?	10 years

This table shows the history of the U.S. income tax from its beginning in 1913. Tax increases along with inflation have eaten away at the savings of every American. The author of this table has tried to make the case that income tax increases <u>cause</u> inflation. I'm not a good enough economist to follow that argument, but it's no secret that taxes and inflation have done a great deal of damage to everyone's pocketbook.

After two years in Washington, I often long for the realism and sincerity of Hollywood.
     Fred Thompson, U.S. senator, lawyer, writer, and actor

The only sure bulwark of continuing liberty is a government strong enough to protect the interests of the people, and a people strong enough and well enough informed to maintain its sovereign control over its government.
     Franklin D. Roosevelt, 32nd U.S. President (1882-1945)

Who Pays Income Taxes?

October 14, 2002: Congress is considering a bill to raise to $8,250 the amount of capital losses that are tax deductible each year. The current $3,000 amount has not been changed since 1978.

A second bill would help seniors better protect their retirement savings. It would raise to seventy-five the age when people must make withdrawals from their tax deferred accounts such as IRAs and 401(k)s, now age 70½. In a down market that means the government forces some seniors to sell assets at a loss, and pay taxes on that loss to boot.

Politicians of both parties have spent the past year moaning about the plight of investors. Such a law would help investors more than putting all the guilty CEOs in America in jail. But such laws don't make great headlines like fighting crime by handcuffing CEOs.

Nothing has been done to enact any of these proposals into law, as the tax burden continues to rise. Sure the wealthy are getting bigger tax cuts under the recent law. The bottom 50% of wage earners make 13% of the income yet pays 4% of the income tax. And most of them pay nothing at all. You can't give a cost reduction to somebody who isn't paying anything in the first place.[16]

Our Tax System Is A Mess
Most Americans accept the moral premise that the needs of some are a moral claim on the lives and property of others. Taxes will be slashed only when Americans openly reject this premise and stand for the opposite proposition: that an individual's income is 100% his private property, not to be taxed and distributed to other people.

David Holcberg, Ayn Rand Institute August 12, 2004

Each year, the number of tax forms and the time to complete them grow and grow. There are so many sub-forms and calculations that it is almost impossible to do your tax without a CPA. And each year the politicians talk about "simplification" and each year they make it more complex. Any law that reduces taxes also limits the amount of money flowing to Washington, so you won't get much enthusiasm for tax cuts from the people who are going to get the money to spend. And make no mistake, it's all about the power that comes by controlling that money.

I learned firsthand a little about the power that these politicians experience. In my former life I managed pension funds of $4 billion. The fees that could be earned on that pool of money by various investment firms and consultants could conservatively run to $20 million a year. I had no authority to decide who got that money, but I did have <u>some</u> input into the decision and I was the most visible person associated with the fund. My peer at the much larger AT&T fund in those days was a country music fan. He said that Hank Williams wrote the definitive song that described our job, "If You Got the Money Honey, I've Got the Time." And that was a fairly accurate description of our function. Many, many people wanted to be my friend, and indeed, the friend of everyone in my pension department. In fact, I had to caution my staff that before I entered this work, nobody ever found me particularly witty, or charming, or interesting. But it is surprising how popular $4 billion can make a person.

---

[16] See Appendix Eight for a very good explanation of how tax cuts work.

Also, sadly when the control of the money went away, so did all my popularity. Hank Williams' song has a lyric about that too, "When you got no more money honey, I got no more time." But it's fun while it lasts. You almost feel like a celebrity. Once, my picture appeared in a trade journal, *Institutional Investor*. A few weeks later I was standing in a hotel lobby in New York when a young man I'd never seen before walked up and said, "You're Gene Hoots, aren't you?" He was a marketing person from an investment company on the west coast who recognized me from my picture. That sort of thing gets to be heady stuff; you quickly begin to think you're really important. Of course as ole' Hank said, when the money goes the fun stops. When I left that job, not only were many of the people who contacted me not calling any more, now they wouldn't take <u>my</u> phone calls. But that's only natural, I never took offense, and indeed some were justified in reminding me that I hadn't returned their calls either.

But if ego and self-importance can develop in a minor pension officer, imagine what happens to a congressperson or senator who is constantly in the public spotlight and forever being asked for some favor due to his or her exalted position. It's easy to believe all the flattery. And it is devastating when it stops. Power is addictive.

But as election time rolls around, mostly what you hear from politicians is lip service to tax cutting, and promises of more of this or that for whoever wants money. Of necessity, politicians must − Promise everything to everyone and get through one more election.

Much of our tax policy stems from the economic theories of John Maynard Keynes in the mid-1930s. Keynes was instantly popular with all politicians because he told them that the antidote for recession (in this case the Great Depression) was expanded government spending. The antidote achieved little in America in the 1930s, but that didn't make it less popular with politicians.

Government at every level - federal, state and local - wastes money shamelessly. They waste it on ridiculous projects in unbelievable amounts. As we've already said, much of this has to do with the desire of politicians for power and control. That is why, for the politician in power, there is never enough money. The worst political ideology is that everything belongs to the government, and whatever they allow you to keep at tax time, you should be grateful for. We see this expressed in the terminology that comes out of our tax system. Congressmen speak of "Revenue loss". This is money that you didn't send to them in taxes. It isn't a "loss" to you, it's a gain.

Why am I so certain that our money is wasted? The adage, "Easy come, easy go" applies. I worked for a great company, but it had one major problem, an embarrassment of riches. The business was extremely profitable by any financial measure. And how did the management and employees treat the money they got? We all tried to convince ourselves that we were frugal with company funds. But the truth was that we didn't have to monitor our budgets and count our pennies the way people did in the average competitive, low margin business. We had more jet planes than we needed, and more first class travel than was necessary. People took limos when a taxi would have been just as useful, and probably more so. Once I remember traveling with some company people and we had a number of calls to make in New York City. Having spent a good deal of time there, I was accustomed to walking. It's the preferred mode of transportation for most Manhattanites. But walking was out of the question for this group. We had a limo to chauffer us about town that day. Moving between two meetings on Park Avenue, I pointed out that our next call was just across the street. We could have walked over to the building in forty-five seconds. But instead, we got into the limo, drove down two blocks, made a U-turn and came back. Total lapsed time, ten minutes in New York traffic. Now this was a very small incident but little things get multiplied many thousand times in a giant organization, and before you know it everyone is behaving this way to one degree or another.

This was an enterprise that was supposedly accountable to its stockholders and its purpose was to make profits. Yet we still wasted time and money. Can you imagine the waste in government where there is <u>no</u> effort to make a profit and <u>no</u> accountability by your elected officials?

What we need, and probably won't get, is a completely new tax system that is simplified, fair, and pro-growth, encouraging business to take more risk and invest more. But so far we have seen little from either party in Washington that addresses the tax issue. And a real tip-off is the amount of time all the candidates spent discussing it in the recent presidential campaign. There was a great deal of time spent on who did what thirty-five years ago in and about Vietnam, but very little on what our tax policy might be for the next thirty-five years, or thirty-five months for that matter.

This is our money. We should know what is happening to it, and make those in authority accountable, or things won't get any better.

Capital now moves around the globe literally at the speed of light. It will move to where it's treated the best - the highest return after tax. Politicians will have a great deal of trouble confining capital within political boundaries. We are moving toward a world economy and that is probably all for the better. No longer can a country set up roadblocks to capital coming in and going out. With the flow of money today, if one political or economic climate isn't a suitable home, then capital will move when it finds a place it is treated well. Governments have never liked this, but there is less and less that they can do to control it.

7: OUTLOOK

Now we come to the hardest part of a commentary on investing – addressing what lies ahead. Anyone can pull together data that tell you what has happened. We are not forecasters, but we want to address the future in broad generalities. But remember, "The future isn't what it used to be, and it never was."

HISTORICAL PERSPECTIVE – COMPARISON

This bear market began March 13, 2000.

It is the eleventh bear market in sixty years. It has been the most severe in percent decline, slightly worse than the 1973-74 bear market.

When the NASDAQ index is taken into account, this becomes the worst bear market of the eleven. The NASDAQ declined 75 percent from its peak, rivaling even the 1929 crash. This bear market has had the second longest recovery period so far.

We don't know when the S&P 500 will recover to its previous high. In fact, we don't even know whether the bear market is over. Thirty-one months might not have been the end of it. If the market continues on to new lows from here, then the bear market might easily be tagged with a decline that lasted fifty-eight months or more. (One thing is fairly certain, it will be a very long time before the NASDAQ recovers to its high above 5,000. It could take another fifteen years or more to set new highs).

But the greatest of all bear markets in 1929 ushered in the Great Depression. This wasn't your garden variety bear market. The decline was –85% over thirty-four months, and the recovery took more than twenty-three years.

Bear Markets - Post World War II			
	DECLINE	S&P 500	RECOVERY
Years	Mos.	Percent Lost	Mos.
1946-49	37	-30%	16
1956-57	15	-22%	11
1961-62	7	-28%	16
1966	8	-22%	10
1968-70	18	-36%	23
1973-74	21	-48%	70
1976-78	18	-20%	18
1980-82	20	-27%	5
1987	4	-34%	19
1990	3	-20%	6
Average	15	-29%	19
2000-02	31	-49%	27+?
1929-32	34	-85%	276

INFORMED OPINIONS

The whole problem with the world is that fools and fanatics are always so certain of themselves, and wiser people so full of doubts.
     Bertrand Russell, philosopher, mathematician and writer

We've rehashed the last five years and the lessons they taught us. But looking at the past is of limited value at best. What really matters is where we go from here. We need to ask, "What will be profitable in the future?"

So, what is an investor to do? Most people get their investment information from CNBC or market newsletters. These are the same sources that led us into the market debacle, so why should they be any better now? I am always skeptical of experts, but there are a few people whose investment opinion I value. Two of them are Warren Buffett and Bill Gross. Buffett is famous. Bill Gross is less known outside financial circles. He manages over $400 billion (yes, billion) in bonds at Pimco. For some rational guidance, we have examined their methods of valuing the market. It pays to listen to people with real experience.

It is a wonder that nearly everyone chooses to ignore the advice of these successful investors. Warren Buffett has become the second richest man in the world through stock investing, and he is perfectly willing to share his approach with anyone. He describes how he invests as "simple, but not easy." Bill Gross has compiled a record in bond investing that is unsurpassed in over twenty years at PIMCO. He shares his insights in a monthly commentary. Yet, most people think that they have a better way to invest than these men have. While the Buffetts and Grosses of the world are not infallible, they certainly deserve attention because they have been so right, so consistently. They cautioned us for nearly three years about the stock market before it disintegrated. Theirs is not some "after-the-fact, Monday morning quarterback" analysis. They differ a bit in their approach to valuing the market, but they tell the same story:

Warren Buffett's Approach
Rule 1. If you consider the United States as a business, the stock market can't grow faster than the Gross National Product (GNP) in the long run. Over many decades, the economy has grown with surprising consistency at a rate of about 2.8% over inflation. The total U.S. stock market usually sells at a ratio of about .45 - .85 of Gross Domestic Product (GDP).

Rule 2. For extended periods the value of stocks can grow slower or faster than the economy. In the intermediate run, it can grow faster if (a) profits take a greater piece of GNP (not sustainable for long) or (b) inflation declines, giving a P/E increase. (Inflation is about as low as it can get now; if it were to go below zero, it would cause a whole new set of problems for stocks.)

Starting about 1998, stocks got way out of line by Rule 1. the ratio of stock prices to GNP peaked at more than <u>twice</u> its normal acceptable range in 2000. Stocks and the economy will probably return to a normal balance by some combination of economic growth and/or declining stock prices.

If you buy stocks when this ratio is at .85 or below, you have a pretty good chance of making a decent return on your money, not necessarily next week or next year, but over several years. If you want great returns every quarter or even every year, you are going to be disappointed.

Lots of people simply had to get in on those great returns that the market was giving in late 1999. They got one quarter of good results, but they bought at very high valuations, and now they may have to wait years to get a decent return on that money. Conversely, money invested as this market continues to decline may not earn a good return next quarter or next year, but it should give a good return over the next decade or so.

Bill Gross' Approach

Bill Gross looks at the historical relationship between S&P prices and earnings over a 130-year period that included six other technology driven eras of market "exuberance." In 1999, the market moved to a price that valued a dollar of earnings by over 50% more than the normal valuation. This was a strong indication that people were carried away by their expectations for future market growth.

Dividend Discount Approach

Many models claim to place a "fair" value on the market. One of the most widely used is the dividend discount model: a stock is worth the future stream of all dividends that will be paid to the stockholder - These dividends will be received over many years - You only have to discount these dividends back to a present value, and you will have the "true" value of the stock.

The mathematics are simple, but the models never work very well, because too many things are unknown. Just how much profit can the company make, how fast will the profits grow and for how long, and how much of the profit will the company distribute in dividends to the shareholders? Most important of all is the discount rate for the dividends to assure a satisfactory return. If you change any of these numbers, the "fair" value changes, sometimes by 20-30% with just a small change in input. You cannot put much faith in this kind of forecast.

So why bother with such a model? Because it can give some broad idea about market value. For example, if you examined the outlook for the companies in the S&P 500 near the end of 1999 when the index was at 1450, you just couldn't make the fair value come anywhere near that number, no matter what reasonable assumptions you used. The best that you could expect to earn over the next ten years on an investment made at that time in the S&P would have been in the +3% to –3% range. But, investors believed that they would get 15% to 25% a year, only because they <u>had</u> <u>been</u> <u>getting</u> that return. This was the rear-view-mirror approach to investing, - look in the rear view mirror; what you see there is what you can expect to see up ahead. That doesn't make much sense, does it?

Results Of The Three Methods Of Valuation

The conclusions from these three approaches to market valuation are about the same. They indicate that the market is about 30% overvalued. However, these are only broad indicators of valuation, not exact numbers. In a world with 2% inflation and an economy that is slowly improving and has never really been that bad overall, despite the technology wreck, the conclusions are:

Warren Buffett Approach (Market as % of GNP) – The market is moving toward a reasonable valuation. It is still too high, and a 30% decline is needed to put it in a range that should provide a reasonable return to investors over the next several years. The market could fall another 65% and reach the bottom of the range, but that would be very unlikely.

Bill Gross Approach (Market as a Historic Multiple of Earnings) – The market is still about 32% above its normal range. It would be a reasonable buy if it were to fall by that much.

Dividend Discount Approach – At the current level, the S&P is priced to give an expected return of 3.4% over the next ten years. This is below an historical return of 6% over inflation. With a 33% decline in the market from its current level, the expected return would rise to 8%, very much in line with history. If the market were to continue to fall, it would probably move into territory that could provide a good return, though probably not above 10% a year. There are no reasonable assumptions that could make a case for 15% to 20% a year returns, nor could such a case have been made in 1999 or 2000.

However, the market may be well above its historic norms because of the extremely low interest rates that still prevail. It is not a given that the market must fall dramatically just because these models say it should. However, at best the models suggest that we should expect several years of sub-historical returns for stocks.

RETURN ON EQUITY – HISTORICAL AND FUTURE

One of the most important measures of a company's value is return on book equity. Return on Equity (ROE) is a key financial measure of a business. A good business will earn about 13% after tax on capital employed; a mediocre business will earn 7%. An extremely good business will earn 25-35%.

Over the last fifteen years, the return on book equity for the S&P 500 increased from 15% to 25%, a remarkable increase in return on the business investment in plant, equipment, inventories, etc. It has been so remarkable that it puzzled me for several years. Again thanks to an explanation by Warren Buffett, we have at least a partial explanation for this increased profitability. A small part of these gains is real, and a larger part is probably accounting fiction. The following table explains:

Return on Equity Components	Percent Return on Equity		
	1986	1999	2006 E
Operating Results After Tax	17.5	17.5	17.5
Pension Fund (Cost)/Profit	-2.5	3.0	-3.0
Financial Leverage/Lower Interest Exp.	-	1.0	0.0
Productivity Gains/Technology	-	1.0	1.0
Shift to Intangible Assets/Service Industry/Options	-	1.0	1.0
Accounting Changes	-	1.5	-
Total	15.0%	25.0%	16.5%

The major shift in profitability may have resulted from changes in pension fund accounting. This is a subject that Warren Buffet has recently addressed with his usual clarity, considering that pension accounting is even more complex and difficult to follow than is regular accounting. In 1987, the accounting rules changed and corporate pension funds were allowed to show a "profit". Companies were reporting on average an expense on their book equity of about – 2.5% in 1986. This has now changed to a profit of +3% on book equity, even with the stock market going down. In other words, if you invest in a company that you think is making a profit on widgets, or oil, or cars, you may really be getting a significant part of your reported "earnings" from pension fund gains. Pension funds invest in stocks, and these profits are far less predictable than operating profits – just as you now realize from your own stock portfolio. This accounting change may have added over 5% to the return on equity, about half of the increase.

It is likely that there is a further +1.5% from additional accounting changes that contribute nothing to real earnings. There may be as much as 1% added from increased debt and lower interest costs – both are real, but more debt adds risk for investors. And finally, about 1% is added by real gains in worker productivity and technology that lower costs.

Over the next decade, it is possible that only the 1% from productivity and technology will remain, and the other components in the increase will disappear. Given lower stock market results, the pension profits can turn into a –3% expense. These changes will be significant if they happen. We would return to a pre-1987 world where reported profits are meaningful in judging a company's success.

CORNERCAP OUTLOOK

Mood Of The Market

The people at CornerCap do not know what the market will do, but we do know a few things that guide our investment approach. We recognize that market psychology plays a role in stock prices. The efficient market isn't quite as efficient as the academics would have us believe. Just as prices went to extremes on the upside, they can go to extreme under-valuation.

A bull market climbs a psychological "wall of worry." Skeptics doubt that a rise in the market is justified in its early stages, but stocks continue to climb. Finally, at the peak, there is no more worry; investors are quite comfortable. They see only a rosy economic and market outlook. "Rosy Scenario" is one of the most provocative, deceptive, and dangerous ladies you will ever meet.

In a bear market, investors move through a reverse psychological pattern. As the market goes down, investors experience the "slope of hope." Market declines are punctuated with abrupt rallies that push stocks up temporarily. Investors continue to hope that the market has reached a bottom and will soon recover to its former highs. At some point, hope gives way to despair. Most investors sell, believing that stocks will never go up again. They just want to forget the market. Many will never again own stocks. The cycle is then complete.

Looking ahead, sooner or later stocks will probably fall to prices that are as ridiculously cheap as they were expensive at the market top. The only thing the market really tells me now is that stock prices are moving down toward a margin of safety for the first time in years. But I can assure you that when that margin of safety gets as big as it's going to get, most people will not want to own stocks. They will be sellers, finally believing that the stock market is a crooked game and no one can make money by investing in it. They will then wait patiently on the sidelines until the market moves up to a high level. They will find comfort that stocks again are doing well, and they will buy, near the top, just in time to lose money all over again. Remember, it is far more comfortable to lose money along with the crowd than to make money betting against the crowd.

CornerCap Investment Strategy

People naturally ask, "If you knew (or know) all this, why didn't you sell at the top, waiting to snap up bargains at the bottom?" The answer is the one we have always given. Nobody can time the market. Yes, broad patterns of market behavior repeat over and over, because human nature does not change. But, these cycles can take years. Each time is different enough to keep investors from capitalizing on them. Just as we didn't know "how high is too high" in the Bubble, we don't know "how low is too low" now. If market history is any indicator, then selling out at this point and buying back later will be a losing proposition. Getting out now is easy; knowing when to get back in, and doing it, is more difficult. The key is not calling the bottom; the key is continuing to commit funds to stocks that are at more favorable ratios than the market in general. CornerCap is constantly trying to find stocks that sell well below fair value, regardless of the market environment. Even if we find them, there are times when the market will carry them significantly lower. We can't control that.

Many people are losing confidence in their ability to invest. Most investors are licking their wounds and doubting whether they will ever recover their losses (some never will). We are confident that the world has not changed so much and that this is a time to continue to invest in good stocks. We are hopeful that the next few years will be like the years following the great bear market of 1973-74. We began our investing career in mid-1976, well after the initial rally from bear market lows. For the next six years, the broad market hardly advanced, taking time to close the great gap between economic reality and stock prices.

Timing The Market

Market timing is an issue CornerCap constantly wrestles with. What is the trend and how can I profit from identifying it? After all these years, we still conclude that the answer is - you can't identify the trend far enough ahead to change investment strategies and profit from those changes. The best that any investor can do is 1. Identify an asset mix that sets his risk where he wants it (usually done by the stock/bond/cash/real estate mix) 2. Stick with that because it made sense in the first place. 3. In each asset class, search for those investments that have the best probabilities of being undervalued at the time of purchase and sell them only when a much better prospect appears (which won't happen often.)

That is the short answer. But I want to give a more complete explanation. First we all frequently fool ourselves by looking at the recent past and saying, "That should have been so obvious. Next time, I will know better and I'll not get caught doing that again. Next time I will know where the market is headed - whether it is a new bull market or just a bear market rally; whether it is a new bear market or just a bull market dip." The fact is - it is never clear until after it's over.

We have no idea whether the market has now bottomed and we are starting a new bull market or whether the market has another 50% on the downside. Nor does anyone else. I'm not willing to bet any money on market timing because mine has been useless.

You can look back in history and find examples of bear markets that appear similar to the one that began in 2000 such as the great bear market of 1929-32 and the Japanese bear market of 1989-Present. It is convenient to believe the current bear market will end just like these two. But there are as many differences as there are similarities. In these two cases, the underlying economies were in very poor shape and the countries, U.S. in the first, Japan in the second, did not respond to the economic problems. As a result it took years to recover from the bear market because the economy (and profits that drive stock prices) did not recover. Proper economic response would not have prevented the bear markets, but it could have made them much less severe. In the Great Depression, government policies actually made things worse for several years. Japan refused to acknowledge the mess they were in and let their economy drift along. The U.S. economy today will probably not get so bad that it will drive the market down to the extremes of these major bear markets, though anything is possible.

Let's consider two other major drops that should be examined; 1972-74 the end of the nifty 50 and the go-go sixties, 1980-82 the end of the great inflation and oil stock mania.

The current market can be compared to either of these two. In each of these bull markets there was a favorite market sector, just as technology was in the latest Bubble. In 1972 it was the Nifty 50 and in 1980 it was energy stocks. In both cases the total market sold off from 35-45%. Each decline was led by the previously favorite group selling off from 50-90%, pretty close to what has happened so far in this bear market. If we continue that comparison, then the market here should have bottomed in October, 2002. There would be a sharp recovery for 12-18 months, and then the indexes will move sideways for several years, even as stocks with low P/E ratios do much better. This is a plausible outcome, but by no means a certainty.

The bear market in 1974 ended at an unbelievable 6 P/E. Again, it is dangerous to draw conclusions from these historic data. Bear markets frequently end when P/Es on trailing earnings are very low and future earnings are expected to recover sharply. So it matters whether you use trailing or year-ahead earnings. The P/E will also largely be determined by the outlook for inflation. The higher the expected inflation, the lower the P/E. When the market dropped in 1974 there was an outlook for high inflation, an outlook that proved very correct over the next six years. At this point, the best we can say is that the inflation outlook is for low inflation and the expectation is for a continued economic recovery. That doesn't tell us much about where the bottom price and P/E has been (or will be). A good guess would be that the S&P can earn $50 a share in 2005 and the P/E could bottom at 16.5 based on those earnings. This would put a floor at 825, about 32% below year end 2004.

The point is that investors can't call market tops or bottoms. If we liquidate all stocks, it raises a big question about when to get back in. Making two such right calls is almost impossible except by sheer luck. The better strategy is to do what we do with our methodology, look for stocks that appear to be selling below their real value.

Where Are We Going?

Tom Quinn wrote this in 2002, but it is timeless:

For long-term investors, it doesn't matter where the market is. Most investors should have a long-term allocation to the equity market, and they should stay with that allocation. In the shorter term (say, less than five years), the market will move up and down, cresting and bottoming at unpredictable points along the way. The peddlers of stocks or investment information will always be fueling the hope that they have the answers this time. Today's complexities include many critical matters - terrorism, Iraq/North Korea, oil risks, and a sluggish economy. You may be right predicting the outcome of these issues, but how they may affect the market is little more than a random walk.

Because of the various costs incurred (spreads, commissions, taxes), long-term investors will never win by trying to time an unpredictable market. And now, with the after tax yield on money market funds in the 1% range, why would a long-term investor give up the higher dividend yield on equities and assume a zero or negative growth rate for the coming five to ten years? This makes no sense to us.

How do you win? Many people believe that investing is very complicated today. We disagree. It has never been that complicated. As Warren Buffett said at a Berkshire Hathaway annual meeting, "the most important skills for successful investing are realism and discipline ... not intelligence or ability to work with numbers." There is no magic formula - you simply buy a diversified group of businesses that sell at a price that is reasonable when compared to current earnings and projected cash flows. Success is predicated on having patience; giving the process time to work.

Successful investors, even Buffett, have learned that all selections do not work out as planned. That's why we diversify – to limit the impact of those things that we cannot control. That's also why we look for stocks that are priced low enough to have a margin of safety. Market emotions are usually the tricky part. An ability to detach one's self from the crowd is invaluable, and this is the one skill that may be more innate than learned. It would be difficult to survive at CornerCap without this mindset.

What is truly interesting is how consistent the valuations of our holdings have been over the years. At the market peak in the spring of 2000, our stocks were still priced at 12 to 14 times earnings. So long as our clients are long-term and we are able to buy stocks in this range, we expect to win for them. What we had to do was stubbornly stay with the discipline. However, every sound bite from Wall Street argues for change, action, response, exception, complexity – "Just do something so we can feed this massive machine of brokers and traders that we've built," Wall Street says.

The principals of CornerCap have been managing client assets together for over twenty-five years. If you prefer the thrill of the roller coaster ride, you'll find the shows are better in Las Vegas. If you prefer to realize higher returns while on a smoother ride, you will need to block out the noise of Wall Street – just put on the headphones and turn up the Lawrence Welk.

A <u>REALLY</u> LONG VIEW

The 2004 presidential campaign has been one of the most conflicted, divisive for the country in my memory, although I may have forgotten the details of past elections. The conduct of the election and the behavior of the candidates afterward gave us some hope that the country truly can begin to come together. But what really will be the result of George Bush retaining the presidency? Perhaps, in the long run, not as much as you think.

Why do I say this? Because I remember an incident that occurred just before the presidential election in 1980. I attended a client seminar in Los Angeles hosted by Capital Guardian Trust. A speaker at that seminar was Will Durant. Mr. Durant was then ninety-five years old. He and his wife Ariel over a fifty year period wrote the acclaimed *The Story of Civilization*, a series of books that covered one hundred ten centuries of human history. I was privileged to sit next to him at dinner. He was asked who would win the Reagan-Carter election. He said that it really didn't matter because in the long span of history there are cycles that last for decades or more. He said that America was moving more toward a conservative posture, and neither candidate could change that tide very much as president. As it happened, Reagan was elected and the trend toward conservatism did continue for eight years and more. Who is to say whether Will Durant was correct and the same thing would have happened if Carter had been reelected? Republicans would of course say, "No." But I wouldn't dismiss Durant's view. He had studied, and lived, more history than perhaps anyone ever, and he may have been right.

There is a parallel today. In the next thirty years or so, I believe we are going see major changes in our country. They will come no matter which political party is in power. Change will be forced on us by outside events that are largely beyond the control of our leaders. Change is always difficult, and people will have trouble with it.

How Did We Get Here?

The Great Depression and World War II were major events that caused grand social shifts. The Depression brought the New Deal and World War II victory brought America superpower status that allowed us to make nearly everyone else in the world dance to our tune. It was probably natural that these two events led to fifty years or so of what I would call the "Entitlement Society."

At the end of World War II, America stood alone as the sole world power whose land had not been ravaged by war. August 15, 1945 <u>was</u> an historic day. And the 20th century was the American century. America made capitalism work for us in the last century – in the end it showed that communism was a vastly inferior system, and indeed really no system at all. Freedom for the individual and capitalism go hand in hand, regardless of those who think romantically about the equality and fraternity of a communist system. But spreading freedom and capitalism around the world is also causing us problems.[lxxii]

What Do We Want?

We have come to think that we are entitled, all of us, to so many things – a job, a retirement, health care, national security, and much more.

Jobs

We believe that we're entitled to a good job. As these people all around the globe make a claim on their piece of the economic pie, their part of the dream for a better life, the competition is going to be keen. All those lunch-bucket workers carting DVD recorders out of Wal-Mart know those low prices weren't delivered by the tooth fairy, or by a factory on the other side of town. Everybody in America is happy to buy all this low-priced stuff, just so long as it isn't their job that is being moved to another country. And try as we might, we can't have the jobs and the low prices too. If we put up trade barriers to keep the exports out and the jobs here, prices here will rise. No more cheap DVDs. So there will be heavy world competition for jobs no matter who is in the White House, and there's no stopping that.

Retirement

We believe that we are <u>entitled</u> to quit work somewhere between fifty and sixty-five and take it easy for a few decades. The sad news is that you can do that only if you've worked really hard or been really lucky.

When I was in the pension business in the early 1980s, corporations began to switch from pension plans to 401k plans. This switch moved the responsibility for a worker's retirement from the company to the worker. Corporations had already figured out that they couldn't afford to keep making generous retirement promises to all the workers. Well, many corporations figured it out. Some, like the airlines and the auto makers, tried to maintain the pretense that they could pay high benefits, and we see where that's gotten them twenty years later.

The facts were there, and the worst offender was, and still is, the Social Security system. No politician will address the truth straight out, and we have deluded ourselves into believing we are entitled to social security benefits. The real present cost today if we had to raise the money to pay for our promises is probably $12 trillion, nearly twice the debt reported on the books of the federal government. And it is going to get bigger and bigger as things now stand. And guess what! Someday, somebody is going to have to pay for it or somebody else isn't going to collect. We will not be able to make enough money as a nation to retire as we think we're entitled. And no matter who is in power in the government, they can't create that retirement for us.

Health Care

We think we're entitled to great health care if we need it. Many people believe, "A nation as rich as the U.S. ought to be able to give everybody the health care they need. We must reach out and be compassionate." Well, you can be as compassionate as you want, but if it takes all the money the country's got to provide that compassion, those warm feelings are going to cool rapidly. And that is what will happen. The politicians are offering cheap drugs, cheap doctors, affordable "this" and lots of "that" to all senior citizens and maybe everybody else as well. The present value of this bill could easily be $60 trillion, five times as much as social security, to give everybody what they think they're entitled to. And again, no government can do this for us.

National Security

We're entitled to feel safe. Indeed, the prime task of government is to keep the country safe. This too is going to be much more difficult and more expensive than it has been. Throughout history, world order has usually resulted from the existence of one superpower – Ancient Rome, Victorian England – that didn't mind throwing its weight around to keep everybody else in line. To act as the world's policeman or enforcer, if you will. This isn't a task for nice guys. And it isn't a task for committees; the more bureaucrats involved, the worse the results. There are many who are opposed on moral grounds to the U.S. playing such a role. It isn't in the nature of Americans to want to be the heavy, and that's all to our credit. But there are lots of people out there who want to kill us. It doesn't matter why. We'll be just as dead regardless of the righteousness or unrighteousness of their cause. 9-11 was not one of those events like the Depression or Pearl Harbor that "changed everything." Most people haven't really adjusted to the new reality. Terrorism is still only a bit of an "inconvenience" to our lives, and usually only if we're passing through an airport. But the next terrorist act on American soil, or the one after that, may be the big event. It would be best if it never happens. So we expect to be protected. That protection is going to be costly, if it is possible at all.

What's Going To Happen?

I think that we will inevitably move away from the "Entitlement" mentality because we have reached the point we are demanding more entitlements than we can ever deliver. We can never meet all the promises that we have made to ourselves. It might be possible for part of our society to get what it believes it's entitled, if another segment is willing to bear the tax burden to provide it to them. But we are making huge promises that no society in history has ever been able to keep. And we won't keep them this time either. There will be a struggle by various groups who will each demand that they are "entitled" to their share of the pie. But sadly, we run the risk that the pie is going to get smaller, or at least not expand fast enough to keep everyone happy with his or her piece of it. Why?

Other players on the world stage are limiting our ability to suspend reality. They are competing for our jobs. And they are financing our way of life by lending us money. When foreigners finally believe that we have extended our national balance sheet so far that we are a bad credit risk, they will impose a fiscal discipline on us even if we won't do it ourselves. They will demand that we repay them. No more rolling over the debt. So the 21st Century is likely to be a Brave New World for all of us. And it may well be the Asian Century. The people in places like China, India, and even Brazil are as entitled to share in the competition, risks, and rewards of capitalism as we are. And they are beginning to do so.

In the mid-1960s, about the time that LBJ cranked up the "Great Society" my grandfather said, "The government is going to try to spend its way out of debt, but it won't work." At face value, a facetious, even ridiculous, comment. But that fairly well described our attitude as a nation in the forty years that followed. We have borrowed from our future and pretended that it didn't matter. " If I don't have to pay, who cares. In the long run, we're all dead." The real inconvenience for that philosophy is that one day the Long Run may arrive and we'll find that unfortunately we're still alive.

Financial responsibility does matter. If deficits didn't matter, then why bother with taxes, just finance everything we want with deficits. My grandfather wasn't necessarily wrong, he may have only been early. And as we've said before, "early" looks just like "wrong." Especially if you are fifty or sixty years early. We've been able to push our day of reckoning into the future and borrow from that future for well over a half century. But time is running out. The world is shifting. My guess is that in another twenty or thirty years, all the "entitlement" seeds we have sown will yield a disappointing harvest. People will be bitter when they realize that they've been sold a bill of goods, that no amount of threats or complaining will get them what they have been led to expect. It just won't be there for them, and there won't be anybody for them to take it from because it won't exist.

We will move to a "responsible" society – the quality of people's lives will be determined by what they do for themselves – not what government can do for them. This will allow them to have some personal control and to compete in the world. The government cannot take care of them; it can't get the resources. Neither can the other institutions we have depended on for most of the last century. An individual who does not join the "responsible" class will become part of the "underclass." Hopefully, this class will include only a few Americans, but it could include most of us. That will depend on how soon we make the "paradigm" shift and how many are willing to sign on for it.

The train is leaving the station. We better be on board. The Asians and other parts of the third world already are, and they aren't waiting for us.

8:   REFLECTION ON MY "RETIREMENT"

BACKGROUND

From the day we started CornerCap, our competitors talked about Gene Hoots being near retirement. I was a few months shy of fifty years old. Retirement was not on my mind then and is not now. Leisure isn't a big part of my personal makeup. I might add that it is definitely not any part of Tom Quinn's makeup.

My family has never been good at retirement. They have nearly all been hard workers and retirement has never set well with them. My parents were born and raised two miles apart, so all my family came from the same neighborhood and the same culture of the rural South. My paternal family were farmers. My maternal grandfather was an entrepreneur. My parents, aunts, uncles, and cousins have always been supportive of our investment efforts. Like everybody who starts a business, we got help along the way. I was fortunate to marry into a family with the same values. Nobody was a bigger supporter of CornerCap than my father-in-law.

Hoots

I had no idea about the Hoots family origin until a few years ago when a cousin, Carl Hoots, published a history. The original Hoots was a German (Johann Huth) who settled in Yadkin County shortly after the American Revolution. Carl discovered that this original Hoots had eight children and our branch of the family descended from the youngest child. The other seven migrated west, in the early 1800s, so there are groups of distant Hoots relatives scattered across the country. A few years ago I learned that there is a Gene Hoots living in Mattoon, IL. Judy and I visited him in 1996. He is an accomplished songwriter and his wife is an artist. For years they were very successful restaurateurs, and he even waged a successful lawsuit against Burger King that made national news. When we met, the accomplishments of the "other" Gene Hoots were a bit humbling.

Jasper

Tom Quinn believes that each of us has a behavior tape programmed in our brain and that the programming has been completed when we are five or six years old. I'm coming around to that belief myself. Until the age of six, the man I spent more time with than anyone else was my grandfather, Jasper "Jap" Hoots. Until the end of World War II both my parents worked in defense plants, including the Glenn L. Martin aircraft plant in faraway Baltimore. (For rural North Carolinians, this was a mysterious city somewhere in "Yankee Land." Twenty years later I would marry "one of those Yankees" a few miles from there.)

Most of the War years, I lived with my grandparents on an isolated farm in North Carolina. For better or worse, I suspect that my grandfather programmed my tape. This was far from obvious until the last few years, but now I see that in many ways I have become him, with both his virtues and his faults. Most of us get a chance in life to thank our parents for the sacrifices they make for us, but unfortunately by the time we are grandparents ourselves and keenly aware of that special grandparent-grandchild relationship, it's much too late to tell our own grandparents how much we appreciate them. We wish that we could, but that's not one of life's options.

My grandfather never told me much about his life, but I learned a bit of it from his sisters, and other family members. He was born in Yadkin County, NC in 1886. Then Yadkin was a poor, rural county in the Piedmont region, and as a matter of historical interest, it is still the only one of the state's hundred counties without a foot of railroad track. That isn't important now, but a century ago it was very significant to the prosperity, or lack thereof, in that area.

Sometime late in the nineteenth century, both my grandfather's parents died. He was fourteen and his brother Otis was younger. They had invitations to move to the city and live with their older married sisters, but the boys declined. They wanted to stay on their farm and make it on their own. (An option that the welfare safety net would not allow today.) We've already said that adversity builds character, and I can imagine that these two youngsters had lots of opportunities for character building in their teenage years. And they did manage to raise themselves. When he was sixteen, Uncle Otis moved to Winston-Salem and joined the fire department where he rose to the rank of station chief, serving for almost fifty years.

Jap stayed on the farm. He was a self employed farmer all his life with the exception of a very short period when he worked in a local gold mine and later when moved to Indiana around 1910. There he worked in Newcastle at a foundry of the Maxwell automobile company (the car that Jack Benny made famous). He said the safety conditions were unthinkable and that there was a serious worker injury almost every week. He never mentioned any details of his move to Indiana to me, but years after his death my uncle Kenneth told me that his dad, Jap, had had "a little trouble" with the local law enforcement. It was something about distilling non-tax-paid spirits, not an uncommon business venture at that place and time. That had apparently prompted Jap to leave the area for a couple years until his transgressions were forgotten by the local authorities. Jap did mention to me once that at various times he had had several barrels of whiskey stored in the woods, but that he had never drunk alcohol.

Because of a very deprived youth and literally a struggle for survival, he was frugal almost to a fault. It does not surprise me that he never touched his whiskey inventory; alcohol was a way to make a living, not something to waste in personal consumption. In a similar vein, he was also a tobacco farmer, again very common in the area. Yet he never used tobacco, and was always critical of the foolish waste of money by all tobacco smokers and chewers.

My grandmother and he were married in 1915. They were from the same community. They raised four sons and farmed the rest of their lives. They made a modest hand-to-mouth living in the 1920s. The absence of a railroad played a part in the lives of farmers like Jap and Maude Hoots. They owned no car, and made few cash purchases of any kind. Once a year in the fall, Jap would take a three-day trip from their home in Deep Creek to Winston-Salem with a wagon load of tobacco to sell at auction – their main source of cash. It would take a day to make the twenty-five mile trip. There was no bridge and the river had to be forded. Jap's older sister, my Great Aunt Della, had moved to Indiana and she told me that in those days, when she made the trip home, it took longer for her to travel from Winston-Salem to Deep Creek than it did from Indianapolis to Winston-Salem on the train.

My grandfather continued to farm his not very productive land. And then he got a lucky break. In the late 1930s as part of President Roosevelt's massive federal works programs, a dam was proposed on the Yadkin River, the eastern boundary of Yadkin County. This was a flood control project and when the dam was built, the river would flood Jap's farm. The government bought his farm. (The dam was never built and the farmers were offered back their land, but by then Jap had moved on.) Jap's son Kenneth found a beautiful farm some miles south in adjoining Davie County along the Yadkin River. In 1943 they bought this new farm in the Advance community, and one of my earliest memories is moving to my new home. This farm had been recently owned by the Chairman of R. J. Reynolds Tobacco Company who had kept it in excellent condition and it was quite productive. (The farm is little changed to this day. The nearest neighbor is still almost a half mile away. It is bounded on three sides by the river and this greatly limits access to it. Suburbia is approaching, but it hasn't reached quite this far yet.)

So with the government payment and whatever other cash he had, Jap bought this new farm from a local man named Roby Patterson. I don't think my grandfather ever had a checking account, probably because he seldom had enough cash at one time to make it worthwhile to have one; also, getting to a bank from where he lived wouldn't have been easy. More than forty years later I heard a story about the day he bought the farm. In the 1980s when I was the trustee of the family farms, I met a man at the courthouse in Mocksville and sold him the farm's tobacco allotment for about $12,000. He said, "You know, I'm paying you about what your grandfather paid for that farm." He was right, and I asked him how he knew. He said, "I was there that day with Roby Patterson. And a funny thing, Mr. Hoots counted out the $12,000 in twenty dollar bills."

I once told this story to an investment banker in New York, and he said, "I suppose an investment means more to you when you earn the money $20 at a time." And I suspect that's the way Jap got that money. Today it is hard to imagine the work that went into earning and saving each of those $20 bills in the 1930s.

Gradually, quietly, one by one, the trees are falling – the trees that made up the forest of the Deep Creek community [Yadkin County, NC] when I grew up. The men – good men, honest men, hard working men – who lent solidarity and a sense of security to the spirit of the neighborhood, are passing from our midst. Men who believed in God, who trusted in one another – men who said what they meant and meant what they said. Humble men who realized that their days were numbered, and that they were ever subject to the will of the one who holds the reins of fate in His hands.

I am increasingly grateful that it was my good fortune to grow up in such surroundings. My earliest recollections include Mr. Jap Hoots and his family – my kinsman and my friend. I remember Mr. Hoots as a man respected and appreciated by his fellowman – working hard and long to provide well for his household. He had a great sense of humor, but he also had a sincere interest and concern in those he knew and loved. He recognized an obligation and debt of gratitude to those who shared with him along the way.

Rev. Clarence Shore, Eulogy, November 1969

Allen

The same work pattern was true in the Depression years of the 1930s for younger people in the area. Like most farmers, my Dad said he never knew when the Great Depression came. He was born in 1917 and he said every year had been a Depression for him until he was an adult. In the great boom of the 1920s wealth was largely confined to the industrial and commercial areas of America. Farmers did not participate in the general prosperity, and agricultural commodity prices fell. So in the mid 1930s most young men like my Dad turned to whatever non-farm work was available. For young men in Yadkin County it meant moving a few miles northwest and getting a job building the Blue Ridge Parkway. When my dad was sixteen, he took a job on the road building project as a truck driver hauling paving stone.

Dad, too, never had much extra time. Mostly he worked at two full time jobs. In 1957 he bought a four hundred acre farm and he worked evening shift as a supervisor at an AT&T plant and in the morning he would farm. He did this for several years.

Dad just celebrated his eighty-seventh birthday in November. Until two years ago, he continued to have a two acre garden, and even now he keeps a small garden beside his home. He still lives in the house where I grew up, a pine-paneled cabin Mom and he built in 1947.

Kenneth

My Uncle Kenneth was a cattle farmer his whole life. He was in my Mom's class in school and by all reports from his earliest days until his last he was known as a real "character" and genuinely liked by all who knew him. One of my great regrets is that nobody ever recorded the things he said. But to show how he felt about his fellow man and conflict, he once told me, "I never met a man I couldn't get along with or away from." He always had a clever turn of phrase, and George Martin, a noted local attorney, said that Ken had the ability with a few well-chosen humorous words to sway a crowd more than anyone George had ever seen.

He didn't go beyond middle school, but he always said he had a sixty year education and he had majored in "cowology." Because of the work projects in the Depression, the buyout of his Dad's farm and other experiences, Kenneth said, "Franklin Roosevelt is the only president who ever cared about people like me. He taxed the rich and made them spread their money around so that America could have a middle class. There wasn't a middle class in the South before FDR – there was only the rich and the poor."

He was a lifelong Democrat who believed in the value of taxing the rich. Toward the end of his life, I didn't have the heart to tell him that he had become one of the "rich." He, like many people who started with modest means, still thought of himself as poor, but when you counted the value of his farms, he had definitely shown up on the radar screen for estate tax. His attorney, his accountant, and I did some serious estate planning, something he never dreamed he'd have to do.

Baity

My mother's father, Isaac Baity, started a tobacco basket manufacturing business in the 1920's. The large, flat woven oak baskets were used to transport tobacco. The Baity Basket Shop was the biggest employer in the county (an agricultural area) for a few decades. He died before I was born, and his sons ran the business until industry changes made the baskets obsolete. Mother was the youngest of nine children. Her four brothers operated the company after their father's death. They were an unusual family, in that all the in-laws seemed to be a natural part of the family and they were much closer than most families.

My grandmother lived to be ninety-nine, and the basket business was shut down many years before she died. Her sons continued to support her. Despite the fact that there was no income from the business, they told her that she was being supported by her share of the "profits," which was typically generous of them.

The four Baity brothers were great racing enthusiasts. And their racing endeavors come under the heading "What Might Have Been." Until the last few years, I had not known the story of their work in stock car racing, but the High Point, NC City Museum had an exhibit about the early days of stock car racing, pre-NASCAR of course. My uncles played a prominent part in that history. They were early in the racing business. In 1940 they built the High Point Motor Speedway and held several stock car racing events, but World War II gas and tire rationing closed the enterprise and it never reopened after the War. Most of the early pioneer drivers raced at their track. One anecdote from that "ancient" history was that the young driver, Bill France, came up from Florida and raced. His car broke down, and he didn't have the necessary $50 to tow it back home. Bill France went on to found

NASCAR in the late 1940s, and today his children are billionaires. Naturally, I like to think that had the War not intervened, the Baitys, not the France family, would be the premier racing family in America. Probably wishful thinking on my part.

My first investor, Buck Baity, continued to race occasionally after the war. An early memory of mine is listening to the first Southern 500 at Darlington, SC on Labor Day 1951. Buck raced in that hallmark event. In those days, there were no racing teams or big money supporting the racers. Buck had to pay his own expenses and furnish the car. The economics changed dramatically over the years, and of course racing teams are now multi-million dollar enterprises.

The Baitys offered encouragement, and as I've said before, my Uncle Buck and three of my cousins were my first clients, investing seed money in 1969 that remains invested with us to this day. The three cousins are still involved in the automotive or tire businesses. Two of them are now well over seventy and they work every day at their retail tire stores.

I greatly admire and respect the Baitys, and I identify with their clan in a curiously Southern way. My mother, like many Southern girls at that time, always was called by her double given name, Sally Mae. And all my life, even now among her contemporaries I was and am known not as Gene Hoots, but as "Sally Mae Baity's boy." Old traditions die hard.

Sylvester

My father-in-law, Charles Sylvester, was one of CornerCap's most enthusiastic supporters. I could not have asked for a better father-in-law than Dad Sylvester. He and I were close from the time I met Judy in 1962 until his death in 1999. I admired him for his hard work, his concern for others, and his professional accomplishments.

He had a very difficult childhood. His father abandoned and divorced his mother. She raised Charles and his younger brother by working night shift at the cereal plant in Battle Creek, MI. Later she moved to Wilmington, DE, following a sister who found work there. Dad Sylvester was an excellent athlete and perhaps the most competitive person I've ever met. He played football at the University of Delaware a year or two, but early in the Depression he was forced to drop out of school to support his mother and his brother.

He went to work for DuPont in the early 1930s as a chemist's assistant in the research laboratory. Despite the fact that he had no college degree, he honed his technical skills and advanced within DuPont over the years. He became one of the world's foremost experts on colors in the dye industry, one of DuPont's major product lines when he worked there. He won a number of prestigious awards for his work to establish color standards worldwide in the international dye industry. He retired after forty-two years at DuPont, a record seldom equaled today in the transient business world. His hard work, thrift, and competitive spirit were certainly a great example.

RETIREMENT

This historical background on our family does have a point, beyond a rambling, irrelevant history. My family has been little different and no more distinguished than millions of others in this country. Work is what we do. As a child and as an adult, for better or for worse, words like "vacation,' "leisure," "hobbies," "retirement" weren't part of our vocabulary. As a result, work is about all I've ever known. That may not be good for me, but hopefully it's good for our clients.

Of course we must make certain allowances for our godparents, Mother Nature and Father Time. The two of them have a way of making us slow down whether we want to or not. But I've also remarked that this work, unlike some other work I've done, is "all indoors with no heavy lifting." I've often said that my first boss, Donald Bingham, taught me one valuable lesson well before I was eighteen. He taught me that I had better find another way to make a living besides stacking lumber in a lumberyard. There is certainly nothing inherently bad about that work; it is honest labor. But I saw too many men in their sixties working there all their lives. It was not a career path that I wanted.

It took me a long time to decide what I wanted to be when I grew up, in fact thirty or so years. I like to say that I spent four years getting an engineering degree, and to my disappointment found out that I still wasn't qualified to drive a train and had to move on to something else.

And I have noticed that people in the investment business who enjoy the work stay on the job into their seventies and eighties. I've known a couple people who were still working in their nineties. However, we are realists, and we know that actuarially we probably won't be working into our nineties. My associate Jim Carr, the president of CornerCap, has said, and I agree, "You really can't quit this job. Once you sign up to help clients with their finances, it becomes a lifetime commitment." And he is right. Fortunately for all of us, CornerCap has cultivated a staff of professionals who make my job much easier than it used to be.

I most enjoy reading and travel as diversions, "hobbies" if you will. And it is true in the last few years Judy and I have certainly increased the travel part. But much of that travel has been a real benefit in helping us understand the world around us, and I believe has also made me a better investor.

If you want to make God laugh, tell him your plans.
    Unknown

I am well aware of this adage and want to be careful about making too many promises. But I intend to work and serve CornerCap clients as long as my health will allow. A real "retirement" is not in my plans.

9:   PROFILES

Success usually comes to those who are too busy to be looking for it.
  Henry David Thoreau, naturalist and author (1817-1862)

Great friendships are one of the joys of our job. I like to think that "birds of a feather do flock together," and that our people associate with us because they think we are like them. It would be an honor if it were true. One thing is certain – I have learned far more from our friends than they have learned from me. Their collective wisdom and their example on how to conduct one's life, personal and financial, are priceless. They are great examples of entrepreneurship, thrift, and hard work. At the risk of offending many who should be recognized here, I have chosen only two. They are singled out because the first is a friend I have known the longest – my first boss. The second is our oldest friend (now deceased). She is recognized for her generosity. Doubtless we have many friends who will equal her generosity over the coming years, and we hope to write about them too.

DONALD BINGHAM

He has been my friend since 1947. I worked for him part time for four years, beginning at fourteen as a laborer in his wholesale lumberyard. I have often joked that he taught me a very valuable, early lesson – find some other way to make a living. As a part time job it was great, but he helped me figure out early that I didn't want a career stacking green 2x8s every day in the heat or cold. That job was a real incentive to get a further education and learn a skill.

November 17, 1999 - Three of us from CornerCap had breakfast with Donald. He told my two young associates something of his personal history, and I thought it might be interesting to pass it along. It is a story of entrepreneurship and how "EASY" it is to start and build a business.

Donald was a World War II army veteran, serving in the Pacific theater. He came to Clemmons from Farmer, NC, following his two older brothers. Like millions of other young veterans, he was eager to build a life. An excellent car and truck mechanic, he first opened a garage in Clemmons and repaired cars. Then for two years, he drove for Roadway Express, a major trucking company. Many weeks, he made four round trips to Atlanta with his rig. That was twelve hours each way (320 miles, no Interstate.) He was paid $.13 per mile so he grossed $332 a week, but paid his truck operating expenses from that amount. Net was probably about $125 a week for up to ninety-six hours driving. (Equivalent to annual income of about $46,000 in 2004).

He said he did this until he paid off the mortgage on his home. Then with his $5,000 cash and a truck from his partner, W. D. Parks, they started a wholesale lumber business. (Note that he not only paid his home mortgage in two years, but also accumulated $5,000, all from a gross income of about $13,000 over two years.) They borrowed $90,000 to start their business in 1952. They bought timber inventory and a small secondhand lumber planer. The diesel engine that powered the mill broke, and they needed $5,500 to buy a new one. They had no credit left. They finally convinced a helpful banker to advance them an additional $5,000 and they were able to stay in business.

Parks went each Friday to their customers in Winston-Salem and collected a check for that week's Accounts Receivable. They had to have the cash to meet the Friday afternoon payroll. (I worked there then, and it never occurred to any of us that Parks had to make his rounds and deposit the money in the bank early Friday afternoon so that our weekly paychecks handed out at 5:15 on Friday afternoon wouldn't bounce. Like most employees of a small firm, we assumed that the bosses had plenty of money and no worries; that only employees had worries. How little we knew!)

Postscript

I recalled an incident when I worked at the lumber company. I was seventeen at the time, and one afternoon Donald called me into the office. He said, "Take my car and go into Winston-Salem to the bank. Deposit this $600 check and this $1,100 in cash."

He handed me the money, equivalent to perhaps $20,000 today. When I walked to the cashier's window, looking like a beggar having come straight from the lumberyard, and presented the money for deposit, the bank teller had a very surprised look on his face. Of course, the significance of that event didn't strike me until about thirty-five years later. I realized that Donald had sent a kid off with that much money and his car. He had confidence in me then, and we hope clients have the same confidence in us today. This is the kind of trust that you appreciate, and that must never be violated. Incidents like that one build a young man's character, and I am grateful to him for it.

PAULINE CARTER

To date our friend Pauline has been most generous, giving nearly all her assets to various charities. From Pauline, and from the trustees of her charitable trust, I have seen first-hand the joy and the good that come from being generous – benefits for both the benefactor and the beneficiary. It is important to me to share Pauline's story, to explain where this money came from. It did not appear by chance or magic, but by a fine lady's lifetime of work and sacrifice.

October 23, 1998 - Pauline Carter will be 88 years old on November 25, 1998. I met with her and we talked about her life. She is a remarkable example of what a person can accomplish with the determination to sacrifice for long-term benefits.

She was born in Salem in 1910. She left school in the seventh grade to work. At sixteen, she joined Reynolds Tobacco, starting at $12.20 a week. When she was hired, RJR paid in cash; paychecks were not introduced until the late 1930's. Pay was initially in $5 bills with odd dollars paid in silver dollars. She was soon assigned to the lunchroom at one of the factories where she spent most of her career. This building had formerly served as the Reynolds Inn, a dormitory for young women who came to Winston-Salem from R. J. Reynolds' native Virginia to work in his tobacco factory. Mr. John Whitaker had created this dorm-like setting to assure that these young girls, straight from the country, had a good and protected living environment in the big city.

As the years went by, RJR had five factory cafeterias. While working there, Pauline got to know all the executives and everyone else in the company. She said they recognized that she had a head for figures, and in 1964 she helped with the analysis and conversion when the cafeteria operations were transferred to a food service company. Pauline then briefly worked in the filter room where Winston and Salem cigarette filters were attached to the tobacco part of the cigarette. This was a real engineering feat at that time. They probably were initially able to make about 400 cigarettes a minute on a machine. Today, after four new generations of equipment, a machine produces 14,000 cigarettes a minute.

Pauline retired in 1965 with 38.7 years of service at age 55. Once I estimated that she probably never made $6,000 pay in any year. Given her starting annual pay of $635, my estimate was probably high. She saved her "dimes and quarters" and when she got enough money she would buy two or three shares of Reynolds stock.

W. A. "Nab" Armfield had a small brokerage office on the mezzanine floor of the RJR Building when it was built in 1929. He later merged into Reynolds Securities that has become part of Morgan Stanley. At the time, Armfield promoted the local Reynolds stock. There was an unusual, and especially attractive, stock available only to employees, the "A" stock. It actually was a convertible preferred stock. Rather than a dividend, it paid a "bonus" which was treated as W-2 earnings so that it could be tax deductible to the company. The bonus consistently gave a yield in the 13-15% range at a time when interest rates were 1%. Any employee lucky enough to find "A" shares could borrow 100% of the purchase price from the broker. It was not unusual to find employees whose total W-2 earnings were many times their actual pay, due to the "bonus" they received. Later the IRS forced Reynolds to convert the "A" stock to common so that the dividend would not be tax deductible to the company.

Pauline kept investing. Her world was simple, revolving around her Methodist church, investing in stocks, and working in her yard. She married late in life and had no children. Pauline spent much of the last half of her long life in her modest home, making investments and jotting them down in careful script in a black-and-white composition book. She immediately reinvested her dividends. Then came the Reynolds buyout in late 1988.

Pauline continued to regularly invest in RJR even after the buyout offer. Like many people with RJR, she was most disturbed by the buyout. She did not understand it and felt that "her company and her stock" were being taken away. She had depended on the dividend which paid her $20,000 or so each quarter. She wondered how she would make ends meet without the dividend. Pauline had 42,500 shares that she sold for about $100 per share. Her cost basis was well below $2 per share, and she paid about $1 million in capital gains tax. She netted $3,000,000, but continued to live modestly. "I want to be just like I have always been," she told a reporter for *USA Today*. "Let me tell you, honey, I always drove a Chevrolet, and I'm not going to change." She allowed herself one luxury: wall-to-wall carpeting. But she continued to shop with coupons.

The next year she established a $500,000 Charitable Remainder Trust for her church. She also set up a Grantor Retained Income Trust (GRIT) that has since paid out $1 million to eight of her heirs. She continued to invest her money wisely - a $1 million thirty year treasury at a high coupon (which now has appreciated 30%) and blue chip stocks. Her total portfolio is worth more than $4.7 million, so taking into account the GRIT that has been disbursed, Pauline's portfolio from the RJR sale has more than doubled in the ten years or so since the buyout.

Pauline is proud of her years at RJR and takes great pride in her financial accomplishments. She is a living example of the work ethic and spirit that allow even people of modest means to become the "millionaire next door." She intends to leave a significant portion of her estate to the Winston-Salem Foundation as a perpetual trust to support local charities. I only hope that those who will be the beneficiaries of her work and generosity can appreciate what she has done.

February 24, 2000 - At her death, she had already given $1 million to her heirs and $500,000 to charity. The balance of her estate will go to heirs and to the Winston-Salem Foundation, with approximately $3 million going to the charitable foundation.

August 26, 2002 - Charlotte, NC, - Norma Charles and Charlie Hemrick, trustees of the Carter Foundation in Winston-Salem have made a $5,000 contribution to Carolinas Concert Association (CCA). They enjoy helping those in need, especially children. When they learned of CCA's work, they decided to make this gift. They are Winston-Salem oriented, so this gift in Charlotte is unusual. I would like you to know about these generous people, and their remarkable aunt, Pauline Carter.

"Her main thing in life was to save a dollar when she could," Charlie Hemrick said. "She always encouraged the family to save, save, save and to always watch their spending. I don't believe she had any concept of how much money she really had, although she had the figures right there in front of her." Still, Pauline was proud of her financial accomplishments. She had the work ethic and spirit that can turn people of modest means into the "millionaire next door."

Norma and Charlie shared a new story about Pauline recently: Charlie always took Pauline to the grocer for her shopping. On one trip, Charlie found Pauline in the fruit section. She was breaking off bananas and putting them in her basket one at a time. Charlie said, "Aunt Pauline, why don't you just buy a bunch of bananas?"

Pauline replied, "You don't think I'm going to pay 29 cents a pound for stems, do you?"

APPENDICES

[Appendix One]

SOME CONSIDERATIONS INVOLVED IN THE PURSUIT OF INNOVATIONS IN PENSION FUND MANAGEMENT - TOWARDS A BETTER UNDERSTANDING OF THE CORPORATE SYSTEM AND HOW TO GET THINGS DONE IN IT

For better or for worse, I have the assignment of discussing with you consultants – other players in the game. Consultants can be useful players only if we fully understand our game, its rules, the consultant's skills, and the instructions we should give him as he takes the field. Now, I am not going to discuss the merits of any particular consultant. We usually think of consultants for money manager searches, performance evaluation, or actuarial studies. As a generalization consultants are employed because they possess special skills that a corporation cannot or will not develop in its own organization. I hope that my comments will give a better appreciation for using consultants. And I want to address the area where consultants can probably be most valuable, the introduction of new ideas.

I believe that each of us will serve our respective employers best by being an innovator, and not simply a caretaker of an asset pool, trying to play a no-lose game. In fact, I suspect that each of you is an innovative type or you would not be here in the first place. However, there are certainly many times when you experience the agony of defeat rather than the thrill of victory, as management shoots down a proposal you were certain was a surefire winner. So let's discuss the forces at work to get management approval for new concepts. Along the way, we can examine how the consultant can help.

THE ENVIRONMENT

To succeed as innovators with the pension fund, we must understand the environment in which we work.

There is a basic rule in any long-lived institution – religious, business, or otherwise: when operating continuity is achieved for long periods of time, it is necessary within the institution to have both the prophet and the priest. An institution can be stabilized only by certain rigidity of thought and formalized action. This is how it became an institution in the first place. There is no other way to deal with large numbers of people to achieve a common purpose and survive year-in and year-out. For, if the system is too flexible, it leads to loss in leadership control and chaos. If it is too rigid, discontent eventually brings it down. If it gets too fat and happy, outside forces prevail in its destruction. The art of priesthood therefore is the ability to strike the correct balance among many forces, a balance of necessity heavily weighted on the side of rigidity because the major effort must be to maintain the "Status Quo." The priest must resist change in order not to gamble with the uncertain, and thus the life of the institution.

Since any institution has a large number of people, within its boundaries there will be prophets – men with acute vision about the environment and the future - men to whom the institutional cant is meaningless because it portrays neither the troubled times nor the boundless opportunities they see about them. To the prophet, the need for change is paramount - and he is constantly striving for it. But he is as obtuse about short-range survival as the average priest is about long-range survival: hence the need for both, and the need for the priest to be in command because short-range survival is always more important than long-range survival.

If the prophet rocks the boat too much, he must be crucified. For that matter, so must the priest by his peers if he ever digresses far from his priestly qualities. An institution doesn't put up with mistakes – it is geared to prevent them. The smart priest understands this: he tolerates the prophet because he realizes that gradual change prevents the institution from getting completely out of whack with the times. He permits as much innovation as he can afford without getting disrobed for errors in judgment, always appreciating that survival is his basic responsibility and that improvement is secondary. However, in any system most of the priests sit tight, and for good reason. The less smart they are, the more necessary it is that they should. They play an essential role, and survival of the system depends upon their predictable behavior.

But what does this philosophical discourse mean to our efforts as pension managers? Simply this: We work for some of the finest institutions in the world. And we can butt our heads against a stone wall repeatedly. We can sit on our bottoms and feel frustrated about a system that looks stupid. Or we can try to understand why it is essential for it to operate the way it does and put it to work for us. A prophet who understands the system can create change and particularly so in our companies where the priests we answer to are financial priests in a rapidly changing environment.

RECOGNITION OF THE OPPORTUNITY

Obviously, you have to recognize an opportunity to innovate as the first step in the process. Actually, you must recognize a number of them, cull them, and select a candidate to work on in detail.

It is at this stage that the consultant can begin to make a contribution to you – in searching out new ideas. He is a specialist who confines his efforts to becoming quite skillful at one of the many tasks you can only devote a small part of your time to learning. He is in contact with many of your counterparts in other companies.

He is aware of what is happening in a larger universe than you probably ever get to see. He should have good ideas and he deserves your audience – much of what he suggests may simply not fit your organization. He won't appreciate the subtleties of your corporate world as well as you should – timing, management preferences, etc. But you can't learn from him if you don't listen. He almost certainly will have a background that you can only develop much too late to do any good.

First, pick innovations that are compatible with your pension fund goals and your responsibilities. Do not waste time on ideas that are not your functional concern. The probability of success is small enough for the dedicated person in the right area. One must appreciate that it is a human failing to try to run everyone else's business but his own. We all do it more or less, and some of us more than less, and I more than most.

Second, the pension manager must know what is going on in the business world and have a sense of business history. The pension manager must keep up with the newest ideas and technology being presented in a vast amount of trade and business literature and intelligence in order to forecast future trends. Timing requires you to forecast the future, because it takes so long to get things moving. Furthermore, one forecasts the future in the hope of partially controlling it and to make sure that the steps being taken today keep your pension plan compatible with the future. To do this, you need to be conversant with the past and present since you don't fabricate opportunities in a vacuum. Hence, the basic requirement is that you know your assigned job, and know it well both internally and externally. This involves average brains, a lot of overtime reading, good imaginative ability, and mostly a consummate desire to get something accomplished in your lifetime.

HOW TO GET FROM HERE TO THERE

A lot of people with very good ideas strike out because their business plan is poorly conceived and executed. If you can't devise a good workable plan, then forget it. An opportunity that cannot be planned cannot be exploited. The plan should define the opportunity, the cost, the benefits, and the uncertainty.

Numbers used are, of course, judgment numbers, depending upon human accomplishment, and they have to relate to what you are trying to accomplish. This is the quantitative assessment of the venture dollarwise, peoplewise, and timewise. Until you have confidence in your plan and projections you don't have an idea worth selling to management. It takes a lot of thought and study to reach this stage. The power of positive thinking is essential to work your way out of foreseen difficulties. One should not gloss over difficulties, but one should weigh the strengths against the weaknesses. If there is a critical weakness, then there is no innovation. If it is an outright gamble, forget it. You don't gamble with your pension plan. Your ideas will always look good to you. After all, it is your own brilliance that got it this far along, so there must be very little wrong with it. Here your consultant is suited to the highly needed role of "Devil's advocate."

He will bring a fresh view. He can challenge your thought processes with the questions that have not occurred to you or that you have tried to ignore. And if he really is as good as his marketing brochure says, he will have had some similar experiences already at other companies. He should easily be able to point out what went wrong with those plans, and how you can avoid the same mistakes that are sure to result from inexperience. But remember that an innovation in the pension fund business can require a long time to establish its profitability. Management has a finite patience, and it's shorter than you think or they agree to. Management will not accept losses over an indefinite period of time.

OBTAINING MANAGEMENT APPROVAL AND SUPPORT

Probably more potential innovations fail at this step than at any other since it appears to be the least understood by those responsible for selling management on future courses of action. The natural tendency of the bright-eyed and bushy-tailed novice is to ride in on a big white horse with a battle plan to conquer the world. At a glance, the Treasurer or Vice President of Finance can see that the horse is neither sanitized nor castrated, and what the hell is it doing on his expensive carpet? Since it takes a long time for the business innovator to learn better, many have spent considerable years frustrated to the core by the lack of management understanding of their proposals. Now the problem is to sell the CFO. He is your customer. Like any other customer, you must understand what motivates him and what restricts him. Basically, he has full responsibility for the finances of a major corporation, with his areas pretty well staked out and answering to the finance committee. One can consider him a local tribal chief with local authority reporting to a committee of high priests who possess long sharp spears. Furthermore, the priests outnumber him about seven to one, and that's a lot of spears per fanny even if you are a chief. Each quarter he has to produce a report showing profits and losses by individual business, return on investment, and performance against forecast. He has to monitor the company's cash, debt, and dividends. He may also be concerned with a new acquisition. He is constantly under the microscope on all phases of the corporation's finances.

Unfortunately, his world only takes 365 days to go around the sun, the moon month is only 30 days, and the earth revolves in 24 hours. On a different planet with a 600-day year, a 60-day month, and a 30-hour day, the CFO might have time to run his business. Before we complain, remember: the poor SOBs on the planet Uranus have four moons and an 11-hour day. So, it could be worse. But given all the constraints of a going business, it is somewhat of a miracle that the CFO ever buys anything new.

Now, you are coming along with a new idea that is far from risk-less. He is going to have to tie up people and cash for a long time to come. If the idea succeeds, the pat on the back that he gets with the feathered frond is not equivalent to the jab in the fanny with the spear if he fails. The spear is there every quarter, and the pat only at the end of the line and possibly not at all, because success is always obvious and who should get credit for doing the obvious.

I have exaggerated these conditions deliberately for emphasis because we probably don't fully appreciate the CFO's problems. But you obviously better have something to sell and you must know how to sell it in the business environment in which you operate. You have now recognized the opportunity and devised a plan to exploit it. Here you must draw up your proposals for the first of many tries to meet management's yardsticks. Stay off the white horse, have a reasonable and well thought-out route, a strong ability to spell out early troubles, and most of all be able to retreat without loss of face if this becomes advisable.

Now at this stage of the game you have only synthesized the skeleton. Your audience will put the meat on its bones. Here one needs real humility. The artist in you will suffer when the comics redraw your pictures. But, as one gains experience, humility comes with the growing appreciation that you are much more stupid than you ever thought. Now, you are prepared to listen instead of defend, and as you give your story repeatedly in the lower echelons, you start to build from the many criticisms and suggestions received.

Thus, you end up with a group assessment and recommendations. When your story is in good shape because it is a group opinion, you are prepared for the sell that counts with a product worth selling. Now, it is the height of folly to give this story to top management without first working your way up in the organization. Initially you should sell middle management, preferably one at a time, and have them inform corporate management ahead of time what is coming so they understand it broadly before they see the story in detail. At the final presentation, every person in the room has to be for it before you even start insofar as possible. The reason is that only one person has to express strong doubt and the project will probably be sent back for further study. This is how paralysis by analysis results when the selling job isn't done properly. One has to appreciate that a business can be a democratic dictatorship: Everybody gets to vote but the vote has to be unanimous before something can happen. Thus, the necessity for the complete sale.

We must add that it is in this difficult process of obtaining management approval that the consultant can be worth his weight in gold – of course there are exceptions, depending on the price of gold and the girth of the consultant. To understand why he is so valuable, it is important to recognize that he is, in our former terminology, a true prophet. And we are all corporate creatures, and therefore almost surely a blend of priest and prophet because the dedicated prophet seldom survives long in a corporation except perhaps far back in the corner of a research laboratory. In contrast, the consultant chooses to live outside the confines of an institution. He works alone moving from the gates of one mighty enterprise to the next with some prophetic message such as "Repent, asset equilibrium time is at hand", or "Active management is the answer." In any event, he does not have the same awe of the mighty priests that members of the institution have, simply because he is not on their payroll. He believes the adage,

"He who controls my wages, that man is my master let me call him what I will." And he will acknowledge no master.

Now, if you are smart you can put this unusual talent to work for you. There are key advantages in his position: First he is objective. His motives will not be nearly so suspect as will your own, no matter how well intentioned your proposal. Second, he is an expert. Your own faults and shortcomings will be well known to your audience. They still remember the last time you rode that white horse into their office, and although you have long since learned better, the memory somehow lingers on. Also, there is your superior-subordinate relationship: though almost certainly unconsciously, it is only natural for your audience to think, "If this guy were any good, he'd be up here saying 'yes' or 'no' instead of down there going through a pleaful pitch for a favorable decision." Because of these credentials, the consultant is in a much better position than you to get management approval. This is not to suggest a devious distortion of fact or attempt at manipulation. It is simply to point out that the consultant can bring credibility to your story.

GETTING THE SHOW ON THE ROAD

While any organization has to be set up to operate with average people, you don't use average people to innovate. At this last stage, the consultant can offer additional counsel drawing on previous experience. It could be timely suggestions on organization, or what key problems to be alert for in a new project. The innovative fund manager has to be a gamesman. He has to know not only when to spend his blood but how to spend it well because he only has a finite amount. Also, keep your cards on top of the table. You can get a lot more freedom when people know what you are up to, even if they don't like it or have reservations. Don't hide your failures and mistakes. Bury them in full view with due humility and contrition. Who has the heart to castigate a repentant sinner? A good player doesn't win every inning; he wins the game. But, under no circumstances do you gamble with the sanctity of your fund or company image. If you aren't convinced of that, you will surely come to a poor end.

Don't make decisions and commitments ahead of time that you don't have to make. Every night you go to bed a little smarter, and under the circumstances you should defer decisions for maximum smartness. You do everything yourself that can be done at a reasonable cost. You spend your time finding out how naïve your initial assumptions were and doing something about it. You don't let an unexplainable isolated failure receive minor attention. It can be the first clue to a major catastrophe. And a considerable part of your effort should be in setting the stage to meet next year's plan. Don't start January 1. Tomorrow is yesterday in inventory and progress at best is agonizingly slow. And, while much has to be covered, hit or miss, this never applies to your basic facts. Inevitably, they catch you wanting some time, some place. Realize it, guard against it, and keep it to a minimum. They are the true bosses. You don't shove them around and you don't neglect them, except at your peril.[17]

---

[17] These comments were presented at a Bud Watnik Pension Fund Sponsor's Meeting, 6/27/79 at the Keltic Lodge, Cape Breton Island, Nova Scotia. They are not original – they paraphrase a speech given by Milton J. Roedel of the DuPont Company on 2/12/63 at the DuPont Development Managers Group Meeting. Mr. Roedel was responsible for several new ventures in forward integration at the giant chemical company. His observations on large, bureaucratic organizations are universally applicable. They are as timely today as they were nearly fifty years ago.

[Appendix Two]

HOLLYWOOD AND TERRORISM

In Hollywood we like to feel useful. And to be useful, we must first feel important. But it's hard to feel important when the biggest terrorist of them all, Osama bin Laden, hasn't had the common courtesy to so much as name us in a fatwa. "Of course the studios are next," a studio executive told me at lunch, in the days following September 11.

"They'll definitely hit one of the big talent agencies," a big talent agent told me on the phone a week or two later. "Probably not one of the smaller ones, but a big one. I'm sure they're next," he went on.

"Really?" I asked. "Do you really think al Qaeda reads Variety? Eyes were rolled in my direction. "Rob," an entertainment industry attorney said to me, "*everyone* reads Variety, okay? Don't be naïve."

So the studios barricaded themselves with concrete and bomb-sniffing dogs, mail was opened and checked for mysterious powder, and the town braced itself for what was surely going to be the next wave of attacks. We are, we told ourselves, the single most influential group of people in the nation. We are the exporters of the American way of life, the sellers of the American dream, and the picture postcard image of decadence for every nerdy, dateless Islamic extremist.

When people think of America, they think of blondes, "Baywatch", and the beach. On the great heap of American society, we're at the top; if American is a fashionable nightclub, we are very much at the front of the line. I mean, aren't we? Because with the war almost over and the wave of anthrax mailings last week's news, we're suddenly not so sure that we're on the A-list of people worth murdering. It's impossible to wrap your head around, I know, but maybe, just maybe, all of our music and television and movies – the collected work product of thousands of talented people – is, well, marginal. Irrelevant, even. Nice to have around, but a quiet-now-the-grownups-are-talking type thing.

"I miss Clinton," a development executive at a television network said to me last week. "First off, the guy was always in town. I mean, he must have spent half of his eight years in L.A. Second, he listened. Really listened. I remember back then we had a sitcom on the air and one of the actresses on it was really concerned about . . . I don't know, air quality or something . . . and she marched right up to him and started talking air quality policy stuff to him and he just listened for, like, half an hour."

It's true. When Bill Clinton was president, we were more than entertainers and campaign contributors. We were policy makers and deep thinkers. Our ideas on environmental protection and space exploration were sought after by the White House. Articles were written in important chronicles – well, Vanity Fair, but still – about the "New Establishment" and the "Powerful Media" and guess what? They were talking about us! We were the New Establishment, and we had the president in town to prove it. We slept over in the Lincoln Bedroom and had all-night snack and policy fests in the White House kitchen and got Important Briefings from Important Staffers. It was a glorious time, let me tell you. Even I miss it, and I'm a Republican.

Not long ago, Karl Rove convened a meeting of Hollywood's top executives to discuss how we could join the war effort. The days that preceded that event were a blur of furious jockeying for seat placement and wheedling invitations. Hollywood is prepared, the various executives promised, to support the president and the war effort. But when the meeting was over, the only concrete outcome was an agreement by the studios to supply first-run movies to our armed forces overseas. That's it. That's where we are on the food chain these days – something in the middle ranks of Defense Department suppliers.

In the wake of his masterful handling of Sept. 11, our president has been compared to Shakespeare's Prince Hal, the callow youth who transforms himself into a warrior king and into the leader of a great nation. In many ways, this comparison rings true. But what happens to Falstaff, Prince Hal's entertaining and pompous companion? What happens to the clown when the party hats are put aside for the real and grim business of war?

He sinks to his rightful place, is what happens. And after eight years of Bill Clinton, Hollywood is back where it belongs. At the great Thanksgiving dinner of American society, we are back eating at the kids' table. Among the not-so-terrible casualties of Sept. 11, along with Bill Maher's career and Susan Sontag's credibility, we must now add Hollywood's flatulent self-importance. Just my luck. Now that we've got a Republican in the White House, I've joined the ranks of the unimportant.[lxxiii]

[Appendix Three]

DAVE BARRY ON TOBACCO

In these troubled times, it's nice to know there is one thing that can always bring a smile to our faces, and maybe even cause us to laugh so hard that we cry. I am referring, of course, to the War On Tobacco. Rarely will you find a program so consistently hilarious as the campaign against the Evil Weed.

Before we get to the latest wacky hijinks, let's review how the War On Tobacco works. The underlying principle, of course, is: Tobacco Is Bad. It kills many people, and it causes many others to smell like ashtrays. So a while ago, politicians from a bunch of states were scratching their heads, trying to figure out what to do about the tobacco problem. One option was to simply make selling cigarettes illegal, just like other evil activities, such as selling heroin, or giving unlicensed manicures. But the politicians immediately saw a major flaw with this approach: It did not provide a way for money to be funneled to politicians. And so they went with option two, which was to file lawsuits against the tobacco companies. The underlying moral principle was: "You are knowingly selling a product that kills tens of thousands of our citizens each year. We want a piece of that action!"

The anti-tobacco lawsuits resulted in a humongous jackpot settlement under which the tobacco industry is paying hundreds of billions of dollars to forty-six states (and of course their lawyers). The tobacco companies are raising this money by mowing lawns. Ha ha! Seriously, they are raising the money by selling cigarettes as fast as they can. So *everybody* wins in the War On Tobacco:
- The smokers get to keep smoking tobacco.
- The tobacco companies get to keep selling tobacco.

The politicians get a big old ton of money, as physical proof of how much they are opposed to tobacco.

Originally, the states claimed that they would use the tobacco lawsuit money to … well, to do something about tobacco. But that of course makes no economic sense. To actually stop smokers from smoking would be to kill the goose that is coughing up the golden loogies. So the states, according to the Government Accounting Office, are using less than a tenth of the tobacco-settlement money on anti-smoking programs. Meanwhile, they are spending bales of it on all kinds of projects, such as highways, bridges and museums. Officials of Niagara County, New York, spent $700,000 of their anti-tobacco money to buy a sprinkler system for a golf course. Maybe they were thinking that a golfer, while teeing off, would get sprayed in the eyes, causing him to hit the ball into a foursome of tobacco executives. Take that, merchants of death!

But as comical as all this is, it is not the zaniest development in the War On Tobacco. For that, we must look to North Carolina. According to an article by Liz Chandler in *The Charlotte Observer*, NC officials have so far given $41 million of their tobacco settlement to – I swear I am not making this up – tobacco growers. Yes! The state gave this money – which, you may recall, was taken from tobacco companies to punish them for selling tobacco, which is evil - to these growers so they can buy machinery that will make them more competitive producers of … tobacco! This is like using War On Terrorism funds to buy flying lessons for al-Qaida.

So that's your update on the Wacky, Wonderful War On Tobacco. It's only a matter of time before some shrewd state cuts out the middleman and starts funding the War On Tobacco by making cigarettes and selling them directly to the public. No, wait, that would be completely insane. I give them two years.[lxxiv]

[Appendix Four]

BUFFETT ON PENSION FUNDS

In calculating the pension costs that directly affect their earnings, companies are today using assumptions about investment return rates as high as 11%. The rate chosen is important: in many cases, an upward change of a single percentage point will increase the annual earnings a company reports by more than $100 million. It's no surprise, therefore, that many chief executives opt for assumptions that are wildly optimistic, even as their pension assets perform miserably. These CEO's simply ignore this unpleasant reality, and their obliging actuaries and auditors bless whatever rate the company selects. How convenient: Client A, using a 6.5% rate, receives a clean audit opinion — and so does client B, which opts for an 11% rate.[lxxv]

Don't think for a moment that small investors are the only ones guilty of too much attention to the rear-view mirror. Let's look at the behavior of professionally managed pension funds in recent decades. In 1971 - this was Nifty Fifty time - pension managers, feeling great about the market, put more than 90% of their net cash flow into stocks, a record commitment at the time. And then, in a couple of years, the roof fell in and stocks got way cheaper. So what did the pension fund managers do? They quit buying because stocks got cheaper!

This is the one thing I can never understand. To refer to a personal taste of mine, I'm going to buy hamburgers the rest of my life. When hamburgers go down in price, we sing the "Hallelujah Chorus" in the Buffett household. When hamburgers go up, we weep. For most people, it's the same way with everything in life they will be buying--except stocks. When stocks go down and you can get more for your money, people don't like them anymore.

That behavior is especially puzzling when engaged in by pension fund managers, who by all rights should have the longest time horizon of any investors. So they have total freedom to sit back and relax. Since they are not operating with their own funds, moreover, raw greed should not distort their decisions. They should simply think about what makes the most sense. Yet they behave just like rank amateurs (getting paid, though, as if they had special expertise).

Consider the circumstances in 1972, when pension fund managers were still loading up on stocks: The Dow ended the year at 1020, had an average book value of 625, and earned 11% on book. Six years later, the Dow was 20% cheaper, its book value had gained nearly 40%, and it had earned 13% on book. Or as I wrote then, "Stocks were demonstrably cheaper in 1978 when pension fund managers wouldn't buy them than they were in 1972, when they bought them at record rates."

At the time, long-term corporate bonds were yielding about 9.5%. So I asked this obvious question: "Can better results be obtained, over twenty years, from a group of 9.5% bonds of leading American companies maturing in 1999 than from a group of Dow-type equities purchased around book value and likely to earn, about 13% on that book value?" The question answered itself.

Now, if you had read that article in 1979, you would have suffered for about three years. I was no good then at forecasting the near-term movements of stock prices, and I'm no good now. I never have the faintest idea what the stock market is going to do in the next six months, or the next year, or the next two. But I think it is very easy to see what is likely to happen over the long term. It was not hard to see that, over a twenty-year period, a 9.5% bond wasn't going to do as well as this disguised bond called the Dow that you could buy below par--that's book value-- and that was earning 13% on par. How could that not be better than a 9.5% bond? From that starting point, stocks had to outperform bonds over the long term. That, incidentally, has been true during most of my business lifetime. But as Keynes would remind us, the superiority of stocks isn't inevitable. They own the advantage only when certain conditions prevail.

Let me make another point about the herd mentality among pension funds - a point perhaps accentuated by a little self-interest on the part of those who oversee the funds. Companies set the expected returns on their pension fund assets that they used in calculating what charge (or credit) they should make annually for pensions. Now, the higher the expectation rate that a company uses for pensions, the higher its reported earnings will be. That's the way that pension accounting works - and I hope, for the sake of relative brevity, that you'll just take my word for it.

Expectations in 1975 were modest: 7% or less. The oddity is that investors could then buy long-term government bonds that paid 8%. In other words, these companies could have loaded up their entire portfolio with 8% no-risk bonds, but they nevertheless used lower assumptions. By 1982, they had moved up their assumptions a little bit, around 7%. But now you could buy long-term governments at 10.4%. You could in fact have locked in that yield for decades by buying so-called strips that guaranteed you a 10.4% reinvestment rate. Your idiot nephew could have managed the fund and achieved returns far higher than the investment assumptions corporations were using.

Why would a company assume 7.5% when it could get nearly 10.5% on government bonds? The answer is that rear-view mirror again: Investors who'd been through the collapse of the Nifty Fifty in the early 1970s were still feeling the pain of the period and were out of date in their thinking. They couldn't make the necessary mental adjustment.

Now fast-forward to 2000, when we had long-term governments at 5.4%. And what were companies' expectations for their pension funds? They were using assumptions of 9.5% and even 10%. I would love to make a bet with the chief financial officer of any one of those companies, or with their actuaries or auditors, that over the next fifteen years they will not average the rates they've postulated. Just look at the math. A fund's portfolio is very likely to be one-third bonds, on which the fund cannot expect to earn much more than 5%. It's simple to see then that the fund will need to average more than 11% on the two-thirds that's in stocks to earn about 9.5% overall. That's a pretty heroic assumption.

Heroic assumptions do wonders, however, for the bottom line. By embracing those high expected rates, these companies report much higher earnings than if they were using lower rates. And that's certainly not lost on the people who set the rates. The actuaries who have roles in this game know nothing special about future investment returns. What they do know is that their clients want rates that are high. And a happy client is a continuing client.

Are we talking big numbers here? Let's take a look at General Electric, the country's most valuable and most admired company. I'm a huge admirer myself. GE has run its pension fund extraordinarily well for decades, and its assumptions about returns are typical of the crowd. I use it as an example simply because of its prominence.

If we may retreat to 1982 again, GE recorded a pension charge of $570 million. That amount cost the company 20% of its pretax earnings. Last year GE recorded a $1.74 billion pension credit. That was 9% of the company's pretax earnings. And it was 2 1/2 times the appliance division's profit of $684 million. A $1.74 billion credit is a lot of money. Reduce that pension assumption enough and you wipe out most of the credit.

GE's pension credit, and that of others, owes its existence to a rule of the Financial Accounting Standards Board that went into effect in 1987. From that point on, companies equipped with the right assumptions and getting the fund performance they needed could start crediting pension income to their income statements. Last year, 35 companies in the S&P 500 got more than 10% of their earnings from pension credits, even as, in many cases, the value of their pension investments shrank.[lxxvi]

[Appendix Five]

BUFFETT'S STOCK MARKET HISTORY

FORTUNE ran an article, <u>Mr. Buffett on the Stock Market</u> (Nov. 22, 1999). His main points then concerned two consecutive and amazing periods for American investors, and his belief that returns from stocks were due to fall dramatically. Since the Dow Jones Industrial Average was 11,194 when he gave his speech and recently was about 9,900, no one yet has the goods to argue with him. So where do we stand now? Who better to supply perspective than Buffett? The thoughts that follow come from a second Buffett speech, given July 2001.

In 1999, I broke down the previous thirty-four years into two seventeen-year periods, which in the sense of lean years and fat were astonishingly

Dow Industrials	
Dec. 31, 1964:	874.12
Dec. 31, 1981:	875.00

symmetrical. Here's the first period. As you can see, over seventeen years the Dow gained exactly one-tenth of one percent.

And here's the second, marked by an incredible bull market that, as I laid out my thoughts, was about to end (though I didn't know that). Now, you couldn't explain this remarkable divergence in markets by, say, differences in the growth of gross national product. In the first period--that dismal time the

Dow Industrials	
Dec. 31, 1981:	875.00
Dec. 31, 1998:	9,181.43

market--GNP actually grew more than twice as fast as it did in the second period.

So what was the explanation? The market's contrasting moves were caused by extraordinary changes in two critical economic variables--and by a related psychological force that eventually came into

Gain in Gross National Product	
1964-1981:	373%
1981-1998:	177%

play. The definition of "investing," though simple, is often forgotten. Investing is laying out money today to receive more money tomorrow. That gets to the first of the economic variables that affected stock prices in the two periods - interest rates.

In economics, interest rates act as gravity behaves in the physical world. At all times, in all markets, in all parts of the world, the tiniest change in rates changes the value of every financial asset. You see that clearly with the

Interest Rates Year End	Long-Term Government Bonds
1964	4.20%
1981	13.65%
1988	5.09%

fluctuating prices of bonds. But the rule applies as well to farmland, oil reserves, stocks, and every other financial asset. And the effects can be huge. If interest rates are, say, 13%, the present value of a dollar that you're going to receive in the future from an investment is not nearly as high as the present value of a dollar if rates are

4%.

So here's the record on interest rates at key dates in our thirty-four-year span. They moved dramatically up--that was bad for investors--in the first half of that period and dramatically down--a boon for investors--in the second half.

The other critical variable here is how many dollars investors expected to get from the companies in which they invested. During the first period expectations fell significantly because corporate profits weren't looking good. By the early 1980s Fed Chairman Paul Volcker's economic sledgehammer had, in fact, driven corporate profitability to a level that people hadn't seen since the 1930s. Investors lost their confidence in the American economy: They were looking at a future they believed would be plagued by two negatives. First, they didn't see much good coming in the way of corporate profits. Second, the sky-high interest rates prevailing caused them to discount those meager profits further. These two factors, working together, caused stagnation in the stock market from 1964 to 1981, even though those years featured huge improvements in GNP. The business of the country grew while investors' valuation of that business shrank!

And then the reversal of those factors created a period during which much lower GNP gains were accompanied by a bonanza for the market. First, you got a major increase in the rate of profitability. Second, you got an enormous drop in interest rates, which made a dollar of future profit that much more valuable. Both phenomena were real and powerful fuels for a major bull market. And in time the psychological factor I mentioned was added to the equation: Speculative trading exploded, simply because of the market action that people had seen. Later, we'll look at the pathology of this dangerous and oft-recurring malady.

Two years ago I believed the favorable fundamental trends had largely run their course. For the market to go dramatically up from where it was then would have required long-term interest rates to drop much further (which is always possible) or for a major improvement in corporate profitability (which seemed, at the time, considerably less possible). If you look at a fifty-year chart of after-tax profits as a percent of gross domestic product, you find that the rate normally falls between 4% - that was its neighborhood in the bad year of 1981, for example--and 6.5%. For the rate to go above 6.5% is rare. In the very good profit years of 1999 and 2000, the rate was under 6% and this year it may well fall below 5%.

So there you have my explanation of those two wildly different seventeen-year periods. The question is, How much do those past periods for the market say about its future? To suggest an answer, I'd like to look back over the 20th century. As you know, this was really the American century. We had the advent of autos, aircraft, radio, TV, and computers. It was an incredible period. The per capita growth in U.S. output, measured in real dollars (that is, with no impact from inflation), was a breathtaking 700+%. The century included some very tough years, of course--like the Depression years of 1929-33. But a decade-by-decade look at per capita GNP shows something remarkable: As a nation, we made relatively consistent progress throughout the century. So you might think that the economic value of the U.S.- at least as measured by its securities markets - would have grown at a reasonably consistent pace as well.

That's not what happened. We know from our earlier examination of the 1964-98 period that parallelism broke down completely in that era. But the whole century makes this point as well. At its beginning, for example, between 1900 and 1920, the country was chugging ahead, explosively expanding its use of electricity, autos, and the telephone. Yet the market barely moved, recording a 0.4%

Dow Industrials
Dec. 31, 1899: 66.08
Dec. 31, 1920: 71.95

annual increase that was roughly analogous to the slim pickings between 1964 and 1981.

Then, we had the market boom of the '20s, when the Dow jumped 430% to 381 in September 1929. Then we go nineteen years - nineteen years--and there is the Dow at 177, half the level where it began. That's true even though the 1940s displayed by far the largest gain in per capita GDP (50%) of any 20th-century decade. Following that came a seventeen year period when stocks finally took off--making a great five-to-one gain. And then the past two periods discussed at the start: stagnation until 1981, and the roaring boom that wrapped up this amazing century.

To break things down another way, we had three huge bull markets that covered about forty-four years, during which the Dow gained more than 11,000 points. And we had three periods of stagnation, covering some fifty-six years. During those fifty-six years the country made major economic progress and yet the Dow actually lost 292 points.

How could this have happened? In a flourishing country in which people are focused on making money, how could you have had three extended and anguishing periods of stagnation that in aggregate--leaving aside dividends--would have lost you money? The answer lies in the mistake that investors repeatedly make--that psychological force I mentioned above: People are habitually guided by the rear-view mirror and, for the most part, by the vistas immediately behind them.

The first part of the century offers a vivid illustration of that myopia. In the century's first twenty years, stocks normally yielded more than high-grade bonds. That relationship now seems quaint, but it was then almost axiomatic. Stocks were known to be riskier, so why buy them unless you were paid a premium?

And then came along a 1924 book - slim and initially unheralded, but destined to move markets as never before--written by Edgar Lawrence Smith. The book, called Common Stocks as Long Term Investments, chronicled a study of security prices in the fifty-six years ended in 1922. Smith had started off his study with a hypothesis: Stocks would do better in times of inflation, and bonds would do better in times of deflation. It was perfectly reasonable.

But consider the first words in the book: "These studies are the record of a failure - the failure of facts to sustain a preconceived theory." Smith went on: "The facts assembled, however, seemed worthy of further examination. If they would not prove what we had hoped to have them prove, it seemed desirable to turn them loose and to follow them to whatever end they might lead."

To report what Edgar Lawrence Smith discovered, I will quote a legendary thinker--John Maynard Keynes, who in 1925 reviewed the book, thereby putting it on the map. In his review, Keynes described "perhaps Mr. Smith's most important point - and certainly his most novel point. Well-managed industrial companies do not, as a rule, distribute to the shareholders the whole of their earned profits. In good years, if not in all years, they retain a part of their profits and put them back in the business. Thus *there is an element of compound interest* (Keynes' italics) operating in favor of a sound industrial investment."

It was that simple. It wasn't even news. People certainly knew that companies were not paying out 100% of their earnings. But investors hadn't thought through the implications of the point. Here, though, was this guy Smith saying, "Why do stocks typically outperform bonds? A major reason is that businesses retain earnings, which generate still more earnings--and dividends, too."

That finding ignited an unprecedented bull market. Galvanized by Smith's insight, investors piled into stocks, anticipating a double dip: their higher initial yield over bonds, and growth to boot. For the American public, this new understanding was like the discovery of fire. But before long that same public was burned. Stocks were driven to prices that first pushed down their yield to that on bonds and ultimately drove their yield far lower. What happened then should strike readers as eerily familiar: The mere fact that share prices were rising so quickly became the main impetus for people to rush into stocks. What the <u>few</u> bought for the right reason in 1925, the <u>many</u> bought for the wrong reason in 1929.

Astutely, Keynes anticipated a perversity of this kind in his 1925 review. He wrote: "It is dangerous ... to apply to the future inductive arguments based on past experience, unless one can distinguish the broad reasons why past experience was what it was." If you can't do that, he said, you may fall into the trap of expecting results in the future that will materialize <u>only</u> if conditions are exactly the same as they were in the past. The special conditions he had in mind, of course, stemmed from the fact that Smith's study covered a half-century during which stocks generally yielded more than high-grade bonds. [A condition that disappeared as stocks rose in the 1920s – Gene Hoots]

The colossal miscalculation that investors made in the 1920s has recurred in one form or another several times since. The public's monumental hangover from its stock binge of the 1920s lasted, as we have seen, through 1948. The country was then intrinsically far more valuable than it had been 20 years before; dividend yields were more than double the yield on bonds; and yet stock prices were at less than half their 1929 peak. The conditions that had produced Smith's wondrous results had reappeared--in spades. But rather than seeing what was in plain sight in the late 1940s, investors were transfixed by the frightening market of the early 1930s and were avoiding re-exposure to pain.

[Appendix Six]

SOCIAL SECURITY

Introduction

Social Security is funded on a pay-as-you-go basis. The benefits of current retirees are paid by the taxes of current workers. When the baby boomers start to collect benefits, it will be tough to pay the bills because we have promised large benefits. Social Security has not eliminated poverty among the elderly. The program is so complex that the public is confused about its true nature.

What Is the Trust Fund?

The phrase "Social Security Trust Fund" suggests that it is an investment fund. The fund really only tracks the difference between Social Security tax collections and payments to current beneficiaries. In most years receipts have exceeded benefits, creating a "Social Security surplus." On paper, the surpluses are recorded as investments in special Treasury bonds and collect interest that is also recorded. However, those "investments" are transfers from one pocket of the government to another. Social Security is not separate from the government. Payroll taxes for Social Security are mixed with income taxes and other federal taxes. When other taxes fall short of non–Social Security spending—"surpluses" in Social Security automatically cover the gap. In most years the Social Security surplus was not large enough to cover the deficit in the non–Social Security side of the budget. Thus, of the past forty years, the unified federal budget was in deficit in all but five years: 1969 and 1998–2001.

The non–Social Security side of the budget is expected to run deficits through 2009 even with no new spending. The Social Security "Fund" has recorded assets of more than one trillion dollars. However, those so-called assets simply reflect all the money transferred from Social Security over the years to finance other government operations. What happens when Social Security taxes fall short of Social Security benefit payments? The federal government must get the money to make good on the commitment. The current pay-as-you-go system can get the money with a tax hike, a reduction in other government spending, or borrowing from the public. Social Security benefits can also be reduced in the short run by postponing a cost-of-living increase or in the longer run by cutting the benefits or increasing the retirement age.

The economy, the total budget, and the prevailing political winds obviously influence any decision. Social Security payments will begin to exceed Social

Security taxes around 2016 - as baby boomers retire in large numbers. Then the government must find the extra funds. At that time, the trust fund is projected to hold about $5 trillion in IOUs.

The surpluses are a source of current revenue for the government to use for whatever purpose seems most pressing at the time. It would be difficult, if not impossible, to determine whether the use made by the government of the surpluses has made it easier or harder to pay the benefits of future beneficiaries. Why then does the Social Security program have a trust fund? It was established by the 1939 amendments and, it was "a labeling device designed to provide political protection against the charge that the funds were being misspent." It is a misleading label and gives workers the false sense that they are contributing to an account held for them in a fund. The trust fund may help back up a promise that funds will be raised to pay benefits in the future when deficits occur. But keeping that promise may not be possible.

The Financial Outlook for the Current System

During the 1990s Social Security developed a sizable surplus partly due to a slowdown in the growth of new beneficiaries, as the low-birth group of the late 1920s and 1930s retired. A rise in the tax rate, low unemployment and rising wages also contributed to the surplus. But wage growth eventually will put added strain on Social Security as higher earnings cause higher benefits.

Social Security's financial status is expected to become increasingly unfavorable starting about 2010, when the leading edge of the baby boomers retire. The number of retirees will grow rapidly while growth in the number of workers slows. The surge in beneficiaries is tied both to the retiring baby boomers and to the longer life span of retirees. The slowdown in labor force growth is the result of baby boomers leaving the labor force. The worker-to-beneficiary ratio will fall from 3.30 workers per retiree now to about 2.00 workers per retiree in 2030, and will dip to 1.85 workers per beneficiary by 2075. Immigration and retirement age both could influence the growth in the labor force, but both are hard to predict.

Social Security benefits will use an increasing share of the nation's resources. Also, Medicare and Medicaid, two other large programs that serve the elderly, are likely to rise even faster than Social Security benefits. In 2030, Social Security, Medicare, and Medicaid will take 15% of all the wealth the country produces to support these programs.

Can a Near-Term Surplus Help Close the Post-2016 Deficits?

History suggests that if large surpluses return, they will not likely remain for long. In the late 1990s, the prospect of budget surpluses inspired proposals to invest the surplus in private assets. Proponents claim that this is particularly attractive because, if history is a guide, such investments would yield a high return. However, when government invests in private companies, numerous problems can easily arise to destabilize markets. The only way to reliably pre-fund retirement benefits is through individual accounts that are privately held and owned by the worker, a fundamental change in the system.

Can We Rely on Tax Increases Once Again?

Based on the actuarial estimates, increasingly large tax hikes will be required. Including the health program, which will almost double the size of the required tax increase by mid-century, the cost of the combined programs is projected to increase from its current level of 13.3% percent of taxable payroll to almost 25% by mid-century.

Fundamental Change

Shifting Social Security to a system of individual accounts would pre-fund benefits and avoid the problems of the pay-as-you go system. It would improve incentives to work and to save. Private retirement plans have made such changes, giving workers more flexibility and control over their money.

Social Security is now funded like most government programs; taxes of current workers pay the benefits of current recipients. In other government programs, however, either benefits can be adjusted to meet changing conditions, or the program is for only a small part of the population defined as needy. Social Security, by contrast, is broadly targeted on the elderly and disabled, not on need, and is to pay large benefits to a growing portion of the total population. Is the existing program really what we want? Originally, the goal of Social Security was to alleviate poverty among the elderly, but it grew much larger. The political wisdom, expressed by one of the major developers of the program, held that "a program that is only for the poor—one that has nothing for the middle income and upper income—is a program the public won't support."

So, from its early days, Social Security had a muddled mission. To support the program's welfare goals, the formula for calculating benefits at retirement was set to provide benefits that replaced a larger share of past earnings for low-wage workers than for high-wage workers. But to get the support of the majority, the program was given the trappings of an earned right, funded by worker "contributions"— actually a payroll tax that is somewhat regressive. And those with higher earnings still get higher benefits. How effective is Social Security as an antipoverty program? It has reduced poverty for the elderly, but in fact, only 20% of Social Security is required to eliminate poverty among those age sixty-five and over.

Most of the benefits are paid to those who would not be poor in any event. Moreover, Social Security provides no, or very low, benefits to those who did not earn enough to qualify. And such individuals are among the poorest elderly. That is why the current poverty rate of the elderly is 10% and not 0. As a transfer program, Social Security is not cost-effective.

Social Security has likely led individuals to reduce their own private savings. Substituting a system of individual accounts in which individuals pre-fund their own retirement may increase national saving and contribute to economic growth. It also is likely that by promising a relatively generous benefit at a specific age, Social Security contributed to the sharp decline in work over time among men age 62 and older. Work disincentives are greatest for low-wage workers whose benefits replace a high percentage of past earnings. Workers with shorter life expectancy, who are more likely to be low-wage workers, cannot receive a lump-sum withdrawal and therefore face a "use it or lose it" proposition. There is much more room for flexibility in an individual accounts system with no set "age of retirement" and with wealth accumulation.

Conclusion

We need to give serious thought to the type of system we want. Why do we need a government retirement program? From the start, the main goal of Social Security was to prevent destitution among the elderly, who are less able to fend for themselves. But that would call for a much smaller program, only for the poor. The coverage of everyone else is usually said to be necessary because the young will not see the need to save for their old age on their own. Compulsory saving can be attained more directly with a system of individual accounts and private investments. Most of the reform plans that have been proposed combine individual accounts with a pay-as-you-go component. That component varies in size from plan to plan.

The most significant issue is the overall size of the government program. We are now richer and better educated than our parents and grandparents. As a result, our ability to plan and direct our own savings should grow, particularly if changes in tax policy promote savings. Thus in time a reduced share of income might go to a compulsory individual account system, as voluntary savings grow. The generous pay-as-you-go system is important because its promise of a benefit is a very good reason not to save. Benefits for new retirees have been growing much faster than has inflation because they are indexed to wage growth. We should also seriously consider reducing the growth of benefits in the pay-as-you-go component in future years, particularly for those with average or higher earnings, by increasing the retirement age or by moving to a price-indexed system. It is time for Congress to stop playing games over accounting gimmicks and get down to serious work.[lxxvii]

[Appendix Seven]

INTELLIGENCE AGENCIES

There has been a deluge of stories about the failure of the American intelligence system to detect or prevent the September 11 massacre. Nearly all these accounts have expressed astonishment at the apparent incompetence of America's watchdogs. I'm astonished that anyone's astonished. The impairment of our spook houses has long been the least secret of their secrets. Their shortcomings go back fifty years. They failed to detect several million Chinese military "volunteers" heading south into Korea. We're paying between $30 and $50 billion a year for what is really a faith-based initiative. The intelligence system is broken beyond repair, self-protective, and fixated on a world that no longer exists.

In the world today, particularly the Internet world, much information is openly available. In the world of spies this is called, "open faced intelligence" and it is growing rapidly. But such information is not popular in organizations that pride themselves on a culture where "information is power" and they want to possess secret knowledge that makes them powerful. But today, power lies not in concealing information, but in distributing it. The Internet empowers small groups of zealots with the capacity to wage assaults on nation-states; young hackers can run circles around old spies.

As late as 1993, the CIA was still using Teletype machines, not computers. Somehow, over the last thirty-five years they missed the information revolution. Steve Jobs visited the CIA and suggested they put up a website. They didn't think it possible because they had an almost mystical superstition that wires leaving the CIA would also be wires entering it, a veritable superhighway for invading cyber crooks. They were told that they had to share information because information exchange is a barter system. This was an alien notion. They weren't even willing to share information among themselves, much less the world. In many ways, the CIA continues to operate as though they are fighting the USSR.

In 2000, the CIA and the NSA both had extensive systems to prevent the other from getting their information. The CIA and the NSA are much alike. They are secretive unto themselves, sullen, and grossly inefficient. The NSA was also technologically as maladroit as the CIA. There were thousands of unlinked, internally generated operating systems inside the NSA, incapable of exchanging information with one another.

There has been little adjustment to the new "enemies of the state." They have not yet gotten over the Cold War. One high-ranking intelligence officer says, "Our targets are no longer controlled by the technological limitations of the Soviet Union, a slow, primitive, underfunded foe. Now our enemies have access to state-of-the-art technology....In forty years the world went from 5,000 stand-alone computers, many of which we owned, to 420 million computers, many of which are better than ours.

But here is the bureaucratic paradox. The actual people in intelligence work are, in fact, intelligent. They are dedicated and thoughtful. How then, can an institutional sum add up to so much less than the parts? Because of something much larger: bureaucracy and secrecy. Bureaucracies naturally use secrecy to immunize themselves against hostile investigation. This leads to counter-productive information hoarding, technological backwardness, unaccountability, moral laxity, suspicion of public information, arrogance, xenophobia (and a resulting lack of cultural and linguistic sophistication), risk aversion, recruiting homogeneity, inward-directedness, preference for data acquisition over information dissemination, and uselessness of what is disseminated. These are all the natural whelps of bureaucracy. People who work in such organizations believe that job security and power are defined by the amount of information one can stop from moving. You become more powerful based on your capacity to know things that no one else does. Prior to September 11, none of the responsible agencies even shared the same definition of terrorism. It's hard to find something when you can't agree on what you're looking for.

Another sticky matter is budget accountability. The director of the CIA is supposed to be in charge of all its functions. In fact, he controls less than 15% of the total budget. With such hazy oversight, the intelligence agencies naturally become wasteful and redundant. Fewer than 10% of the millions of satellite photos taken have ever been seen by anybody. Only one-third of the employees at the CIA speak any language besides English. If they do, it's usually either Russian or a common European language.

There is also a systematic deficit in good old-fashioned spying. In the 70s, the congressional Church Committee had an unintentional devastating effect on this necessary part of intelligence work. The Committee caught the CIA in a number of dubious covert operations and took the guilty to task. Unfortunately, the leadership responded by pulling most of its agents out of the field, aside from a few hired traitors.

If things are to get better, what is to be done? First we might ask, what should intelligence do? The answer is simple: Intelligence exists to provide decision makers with an accurate, comprehensive, and unbiased understanding of what's going on in the world. In other words, intelligence defines reality for those whose actions could alter it. A suggested new approach is to have an Open Intelligence Office that gathers information from all available public sources, relying heavily on the Internet, public media, the academic press and an informal worldwide network of volunteers - a kind of global Neighborhood Watch. This OIO could work closely with a Clandestine Intelligence Bureau, also separate from traditional agencies, to direct infiltrators and moles who would report their observations to the OIO.

There is a problem with even this approach. Once this new group becomes effective in providing good information, the traditional bureaucrats will try to haul it back into themselves and kill it. It's the nature of bureaucracies to crush the competition. No one at the CIA would be happy to hear that the only thing the President read every morning is the OIO report. Preserving the OIO would be a nice problem to have. First it would have to be created, and the bigger problem would be to keep existing agencies from aborting it as soon as someone with the power to create it started thinking it might be a good idea. But we have to start doing something. Our existing systems for understanding the world are designed to understand a world that no longer exists.[lxxviii]

[Appendix Eight]

TAXES OVER LUNCH

I was having lunch with one of my favorite clients last week and the conversation turned to the government's recent round of tax cuts. "I'm opposed to those tax cuts," the retired college instructor declared, "because they benefit the rich. The rich get much more money back than ordinary taxpayers like you and me and that's not fair." "But the rich pay more in the first place," I argued, "so it stands to reason that they'd get more money back." I could tell that my friend was unimpressed by this meager argument. Even college instructors are prisoners of the myth that the "rich" somehow get a free ride in America.

Nothing could be further from the truth. Let's put tax cuts in terms everyone can understand. Suppose that every day ten men go to a restaurant for dinner. The bill for all ten comes to $100. If it were paid the way we pay our taxes, the first four men would pay nothing; the fifth would pay $1; the sixth would pay $3; the seventh $7; the eighth $12; the ninth $18. The tenth man (the richest) would pay $59. The ten men ate dinner in the restaurant every day and seemed quite happy with the arrangement until the owner threw them a curve. ":Since you are all such good customers," he said, "I'm going to reduce the cost of your daily meal by $20." Now dinner for the ten only costs $80. The first four are unaffected. They still eat for free. Can you figure out how to divvy up the $20 savings among the remaining six so that everyone gets his fair share? The men realize that $20 divided by 6 is $3.33, but if they subtract that from everybody's share, then the fifth man and the sixth man would end up being paid to eat their meal.

The restaurant owner suggested that it would be fair to reduce each man's bill by roughly the same amount and he proceeded to work out the amounts each should pay. And so the fifth man paid nothing, the sixth pitched in $2, the seventh paid $5, the eighth paid $9, the ninth paid $12, leaving the tenth man with a bill of $52 instead of $59. Outside the restaurant, the men began to compare their savings.

"I only got a dollar out of the $20," declared the sixth man pointing to the tenth, "and he got $7!"

"Yeah, that's right," exclaimed the fifth man. I only saved a dollar, too. It's unfair that he got seven times more than me!"

"That's true," shouted the seventh man. "Why should he get $7 back when I got only $2? The wealthy get all the breaks."

"Wait a minute," yelled the first four men in unison. "We didn't get anything at all. The system exploits the poor."

The nine men surrounded the tenth and beat him up. The next night he didn't show up for dinner, so the nine sat down and ate without him. But when it came time to pay the bill, they discovered something important. They were $52 short! And that, boys and girls and college instructors, is how America's tax system works. The people who pay the highest taxes get the most benefit from a tax reduction. Tax them too much, attack them for being wealthy, and they just may not show up at the table anymore. There are lots of good restaurants in Switzerland and the Caribbean. -Author Unknown

Politics, being a form of continual speculation on the economy and the mood of the people, resonates closely with the unpredictable tides on Wall Street. In fact, politics provides an essential third element of the boom-and-bust cycle: first boom, then, bust, then endless government investigations that convince the mass of speculators they never should have played the market in the first place.

Government action is now reminiscent of those that sought to explain and outlaw the energy crisis, the Great Depression, and the Panic of 1907. Hardly a day goes by without a resolute declaration from Washington that the current misery on Wall Street won't come to an end until some malefactors are put in jail. That's supposed to encourage others to right actions and clean accounting.

This is ironic because the accounting system that Washington works with daily is duplicitous from front to back, designed to inflate revenues, hide expenditures and cover up borrowing. The average businessman really would go to jail if he used federal accounting. Congress this year, for example, has entirely dodged the creation of a budget resolution, so as to avoid putting limits on its spending impulses.[lxxix]

II: THE TECHNOLOGY BUBBLE

LESSONS FROM THE TECHNOLOGY BUBBLE

1999-2000

January 1, 2001

To the Clients and Friends of CornerCap:

2001 is my twelfth year at CornerCap, my twenty-first year in partnership with Tom Quinn, and my thirty-seventh year as a serious market student/investor. These milestones are a good excuse to write some personal reflections. A greater motivation is the market movement over the last few years.

I work because I enjoy helping clients. There is satisfaction in knowing that over the last twenty-five years several people are richer because they have associated with CornerCap and me. I expect this relationship with clients to continue for years to come.

The year 2000 challenged me. As many of my associates know, it was a difficult year personally because my wife Judith faced a health crisis. It was also my most difficult year as an investment adviser. This might seem strange when you consider that CornerCap's value equity portfolios were up nicely while all the market indices were down. But I do not measure success only in terms of percentage gains, neither absolute nor relative.

Success depends on whether we convince our clients that we know what we are doing and that our advice is in their best interest. And on how they act on it. That is why 2000 was so difficult professionally. During the early part of that year, a few long-term clients dismissed CornerCap. At that point, I believed the advice we had given people was fundamentally sound; market events since have generally justified that advice. Unfortunately, some people chose to take a shorter view. This was disappointing and difficult for me because I care about our clients' financial health. That disappointment has led me to revisit some investment principles in this report.

Only a few people are willing to learn the business of creating wealth. Only a few others will admit that they need professional help. Investing is very hard work, like anything else that is worthwhile.

Some readers will find the report too long, too dull, or too technical. If this document is of limited value to you now, you may find it helpful to reread in the future. We notice that occasionally clients quote something about investing, accepting it as truth, but obviously forgetting that they heard it from us years ago.

Like everyone at CornerCap, I encourage you to maintain a dialogue with us. Only by addressing our clients' questions can we be responsible advisers.

Best wishes for a Happy New Year and successful investing in the new millennium.

Gene Hoots

INTRODUCTION

There are three kinds of men. The ones who learn by reading. The few who learn by observation. The rest of them just have to touch an electric fence for themselves.
   Attributed to Will Rogers

We all want others to learn from our mistakes. We want them to be spared the pain that we are sure will come from bad decisions. Our children frustrate us so much because we see them making our worst mistakes when we were their age. It is human nature to make errors. Most of the really valuable lessons in life come with some pain. Yet despite the obvious benefits of letting others make their own mistakes, most of us never tire of trying to pass on our "wisdom"—usually by lecturing to people who do not want to listen anyway.

At the risk of having your eyes glaze over at yet another "lecture," let's revisit some of the investing fundamentals that we have discussed over the last twenty-one years. We will reinforce these principles with some recent examples and compare them to similar periods in investing history. These comments may not keep you from making your own mistakes, but they may give you a new perspective on investing.

CONTRARIANISM

When people don't want to talk with me about stocks, it's time to buy. When people ask about what stocks they should buy, it's time to hold. And when people tell me what stocks I should be buying, it's time to sell.
   Attributed to Peter Lynch

Crowd Psychology

   Our first investment principle is very cynical — <u>most people will be wrong in the market most of the time</u>. To follow the crowd is dangerous. Time after time, the market does whatever it has to do to prove the majority wrong. Yet human nature never changes; people always seek comfort in doing what everyone else is doing. They feel it is much better to fail along with the majority than to succeed independently.

Experts
The same mistakes, made in almost the same fashion, crop up again and again. Most people are not aware that their perceptions are being manipulated by the estimates of others. This influence is subtle. People who are well liked, who have a high status, who are reputed to be competent, who are "experts," or who merely exude self-confidence, are especially effective in influencing the opinions of others.
   David Dreman[lxxx]

At times of great uncertainty, the crowd welcomes seers of the future. Yet again and again, we see that the experts do not really know any more than the rest of us. People have always been moved to extreme action by crowd psychology. Probably the most important book an investor can read is *Extraordinary Popular Delusions and the Madness of Crowds* by Charles McKay,[lxxxi] written in 1841. It's a bit dated, but its lessons are ageless. Later we will examine the accuracy of some of the "expert" advice on the current market.

The search for a super-hero with all the answers is part of human nature, as is following that individual's lead.

The Efficient Market

For many years, I believed in a more or less "efficient" market. Academics in the 1950s developed the "efficient market" theory - that at any given moment stocks are correctly (efficiently) priced and reflect all the information that everyone knows. And since the market is efficient, investors need not try to outguess other investors by trying to predict whether stocks, will go up or down.

It is admittedly very hard to select a portfolio of stocks that will outperform the general market. However, there are times when the market does appear to be not just inefficient but absolutely insane. No one can really say to what extremes such market trends will go or for how long. But there are periods like the year 2000, at least in hindsight, when the market does appear more or less irrational, ruled by crowd psychology. To cite two well-known examples: (a) October 19, 1987, the Dow Jones Industrial Average fell a record 23% that day and (b) more recently, the .com stocks' rise and fall. Such dramatic moves raise the question: When was the market efficiently priced—in the morning of October 19 or in the afternoon when the value of all U.S. stocks had been marked down 23%? Was the market efficient on March 10, 2000, with .com stocks selling at enormous multiples of sales (not earnings, there were no earnings) or ten months later at 98%-99% below their highest price?

Bubbles

The efficient market theory has no place for bubbles. If the market is correctly priced at all times, then only new information can move stock prices, and there is no such thing as a "bubble." The market is correctly priced at a high level and is also correctly priced at a lower level, based on new information that investors receive. This is a questionable premise.

So, academics and investors will debate whether we have had a bubble. Until the last year, I was not really convinced that stock market bubbles existed. But if a bubble is an irrational period when stocks are pushed steadily upward to unreasonable valuations, we have had a market bubble, beginning in early 1998 and ending March 10, 2000.

To understand the nature of a bubble or a mania, we can review some past investment bubbles. These will help explain what a bubble looks like. Manias are a basic part of human nature. Whether it is a mania for the latest hot pop star or a sure thing financial asset, manias have exerted their influence for centuries. Some are harmless, but a financial mania can often have devastating effects.

Tulip Mania

Tulip Mania is a term often used to describe any enthusiasm taking place in the market at a given moment. Few people know the term's origin. Tulips were first imported into Europe from Turkey in the mid 1500s. The flowers soon gained in popularity, and a demand sprang up for different varieties of the bulbs. The supply (and increasing popularity) of rare varieties of bulbs could not keep up with the demand, and prices began to rise sharply. By 1610, one rare bulb was considered an acceptable dowry for a bride. A flourishing brewery in France was actually sold for one particularly desirable bulb. Ordinary citizens soon began to view tulip bulb speculation as a sure-fire way to get rich. Holland, the largest producer of the bulbs, became the epicenter of the mania. The prices for many rare bulb types reached several hundred dollars each. One bulb of a very rare variety changed hands at over $20,000. Sales and resales were made many times over without the bulbs ever leaving the ground. The craze reached its height during 1633-37.

Before 1633, Holland's tulip trade had been restricted to professional growers, but the steadily rising prices tempted many ordinary middle-class and poor families to speculate in the tulip market. They mortgaged homes, estates, and industries to buy bulbs for resale at higher prices. By 1637, people began to see that prices had reached an outlandish level. Almost overnight, the price for tulips collapsed, sweeping away fortunes and leaving behind financial ruin for many ordinary Dutch families. They knew absolutely nothing about tulips except that prices were going up rapidly, and they suffered severe consequences for their speculation.

Ghosts of Bubbles (Recently) Past

This type of emotional investment outburst still happens periodically. Below are brief descriptions of three other periods of misplaced enthusiasm for a segment of the market. These took place during my life and have made a lasting impression.

Conglomerates [2+2=5]

In the mid-60s, conglomerates were the hot item for investors. The stocks included LTV, Litton Industries, Northwest Industries, Gulf + Western, Beatrice Foods, ITT, and many more. Investors believed that a good manager could manage any business in any industry, and that there was great "synergy" in collecting these diverse businesses under one great CEO. These great leaders were like alchemists who could turn lead to gold—hence they could make 2+2=5. The concept caught the fancy of investors. The value mostly lay in the accounting for acquisitions. The acquiring company would look around for virtually any company whose stock (1) could be bought in an exchange of shares and (2) at a lower P/E ratio than the buyer's stock. Accounting magic delivered an instant increase in Earnings Per Share for the acquiring company. And with these earnings growing steadily, Wall Street thought the game could go on forever. But a funny thing happened on the way to riches—somebody had to run those companies. Too late, investors learned that 2+2 really only equals 4, and the conglomerates lost their lofty multiples. Today, most readers have probably never heard of these companies, yet they were as popular with investors thirty years ago as tech stocks are now. One by one, they sank into oblivion or were dismantled. One brash young man named Saul Steinberg put together a conglomerate. Twenty-eight years old, he proposed to acquire Chemical Bank, one of the nation's largest. The hostile takeover failed, but Steinberg made many other acquisitions and built Reliance Group. In the last year, it has fallen on hard times and declared bankruptcy. And even more timely, on December 29, LTV declared bankruptcy. It is the sole remnant of the empire built by Jimmy Ling. Starting in the mid-'50s he assembled a group of major corporations including Jones & Laughlin Steel. It reached its peak about 1969 and now only a shell is left, the victim of poor management and a bad business idea from the beginning. Yet, it was an idea that investors were once willing to buy at an enormous price.

The Nifty Fifty [4/1=5]

In 1971-72, the Nifty Fifty, another "concept" captured the public's imagination. There were many proponents of this investing approach, but its creation was widely attributed to the Morgan Bank. Certainly, the Morgan was a strong disciple of Nifty-Fifty investing, if not its originator. Even other professional investors stood in awe as this investing fad gathered steam. One portfolio manager told me that during those years, whenever a Morgan person entered a room of peers, conversation would literally stop, and people would whisper, "He's from the Morgan."

The Nifty-Fifty concept was simple: about fifty great companies had leadership, marketing, technical skill, or some other attribute that made them totally invulnerable to the economic problems of other companies. Therefore, these were one-decision stocks; they should be purchased and never sold. Their earnings would continue to grow for decades. This group included Xerox, Polaroid, IBM, and Avon. At their peak in late 1972, they sold well above a 50 P/E, and some of them exceeded 100. Then they declined for ten years. As a footnote, in just the last three months, the once mighty Xerox is teetering on the brink of bankruptcy. Its technical and patent position with xerography has eroded over the years, and it had great difficulty coping in a highly competitive environment.

Energy [4^(1)= 5]

In 1979-80, energy stocks were another investor mania. Lines of irate motorists at gas stations are mostly a distant memory now. But in 1974 and again in 1979, this crisis led to a great speculative bubble. Oil had always been subject to boom and bust pricing, like most commodities. But in late 1974, the Organization of Petroleum Exporting Countries (OPEC) finally got the upper hand in controlling world oil supplies. OPEC increased the price overnight from $2.50 a barrel to $12.50 a barrel, sending shock waves through the world economy. Energy stocks began to rise. Then in 1979, the Iran-Iraq war shut down oil production in those two countries, leading to a second shock in oil prices. In late 1980, oil rose to $37 a barrel. Leading "experts" said that oil would be $100 a barrel by spring 1981. It was generally accepted that the world was running out of oil and natural gas. There would not be enough alternative fuels—coal, nuclear, solar—to replace them

Oil stocks, already at comparatively rich prices, moved up steadily in 1979, and continued to climb through most of 1980. Finally in November, energy stocks crested; they represented 35% of the S&P 500 value. Investors believed there would never be enough oil, that people would willingly go without food in order to buy gas for their cars. The justifications for the prices of energy stocks were endless, and in hindsight, it was nothing more than panic. The stocks started to decline sharply in 1981. It took six years for energy stocks to return to their pre-1980 levels. It became apparent as the years went by that there was indeed no real shortage of energy. The law of supply and demand worked its magic, after the politicians had their try at artificially manipulating economic laws and only making the situation worse. The higher prices did reduce demand. As one economist friend of mine summarized the cure for the crises, "There were all these elaborate energy conservation plans put forth, and all we needed to do was cut off the lights when we left a room." Many of the smaller, less seasoned oil exploration companies never returned to favor, actually going broke.

This was the first mania in which Tom Quinn and I were directly involved. In my annual meeting with the Finance Committee of the RJR board in 1980, I mentioned that value managers thought that there were better investment opportunities than in oil stocks. Some of the committee members were more than a little perturbed at me. They were obviously no better informed than the average investor about the energy situation and the value of energy stocks. Their reaction was pretty much the same as the average person in the market—they did not want to hear any bad news. They would have been well advised to be contrarian.

But they were far from alone. That is the nature of a bubble or buyers' panic. Major companies made ill-timed moves into energy. Most chemical companies found themselves in a profit squeeze because their raw materials were petroleum based. Costs were rising much faster than selling prices. DuPont wanted to secure supply of its raw materials. DuPont bought Conoco (Continental Oil) at virtually the peak in energy prices, and it proved to be a poor investment. In the last couple years, DuPont spun off Conoco to the shareholders, removing itself from the oil business.

Even the professional managers of giant funds are not immune to following the crowd. Many pension funds suffered through two years of underperformance in 1979-80 because they were underweighted in energy stocks. Literally at the peak, they moved billions of dollars from conservative value managers to energy specialist managers. This was horrible timing. They missed all the appreciation on the way up, but got all the downside as oil prices and energy stocks collapsed in 1981. In December 1980, many top investment analysts agreed that despite the lofty prices and two great years of gains, energy stocks would be the big winner again in 1981. These industry gurus were not just part of the herd, they were leading it.

In contrast to the "experts," I remember clearly the comments of my uncle "Buck" Baity, my first investor. He was not highly educated, but he had successfully built and run a retail tire and recapping business. He had been around long enough to be a healthy skeptic about experts. He said, "There is no oil shortage. It's a trick." It may not have been a "trick" by the big oil companies in the sense he meant, but there was no shortage in which fossil fuels would disappear in a few years. Oil companies have developed new techniques to find more oil and remove more oil from a field once they find it, and oil supplies are probably sufficient for the world economy for decades.

Technology—And Now We Give You [2x2=7]

The great propaganda machinery that led them into believing that this was real, that there must be some smart people knowing what they're doing, is the curse of a bull market. Of course, the market is crazier than the Mad Hatter every 30 or 40 years. And, of course, some investors will be badly damaged.
Jeremy Grantham of Grantham, Mayo, Van Otterloo & Co.[lxxxii]

So we come to 1999-2000. The tech stock bubble has undoubtedly been the zaniest in fifty years. It has carried stocks to levels never before seen. The Nasdaq, home to many of the technology stocks, soared at its peak in March to over three times the "headiest" valuation given to a group of market favorites in past bubbles.

Following are some anecdotes that left me shaking my head, dismayed and frustrated because no one would listen. (How could they possibly ignore me when I obviously had this thing pegged right, at least in my own mind?):

The public developed a great interest in stocks. Not many years ago, at the end of the day, I found it almost impossible to find out "what the market did today," meaning—the Dow Jones Industrials. There was nothing about the market on radio or television, and even the local morning paper did not carry quotes from the Nasdaq. Today, every news show carries a market report. As a contrarian, it bothers me that so many people are interested in stocks, and so many of them have a very distorted view of how much money they can make in the stock market.

New experts abound. In late 1999, one person told me, "I've invested on line now for a year. I'm retired and managing my own IRA." Such people then almost visibly recoil in disbelief when they learn that I am an "investment adviser" who knows nothing about Internet stocks. This sort of encounter is frightening because it gives some insight into what is probably coming. The last three years has hardly been the environment to give an investor a good perspective on the ups and downs of the market. Too many people have projected forward the results of 1997-99, 20%+ a year. That is not the way markets work. The television ads for online brokerage accounts and day trading ought to carry the warning. "Kids, what you're seeing is a professional demonstration. Do not try this at home." I am afraid that newcomers will reap a disastrous harvest from all this.

At a dinner party in early 2000, a lady in her 70's sat next to me. She learned that I was in the investment business and then she only wanted to discuss which hot stock I followed. I explained that the hot Internet stocks were very risky (thinking of her age and possible risk profile). Her response was, "Oh, I know they're risky. I just want to buy one and as soon as it doubles, I'll sell it." Actually she had about six weeks left to use that strategy. She might well have found several Internet stocks that doubled between that dinner and March 10. I only hope she got in <u>and out</u>.

Professionals have acted like amateurs, perfectly willing to promise outlandish returns. Many advisers and brokers told clients and potential clients what they wanted to hear - implying that they could get fantastic returns for years to come.

The media played a role in capturing the imagination of the investing public. Television ads for day trading suggested that you only had to sit at a computer, make short-term trades, and the profits would roll in. Day trading became a national pastime. Studies have revealed that during the last five and a half years, frequent traders have earned 5.3% a year less than the average investor. Yet stories abound of day traders who have made fortunes in a short while. People confused a bull market with brains. If the market is rising steadily and dramatically, does it not stand to reason that on average whatever you buy will be higher at some point during the day, and you can sell it at a profit? But in a level or declining market, the opposite will be true, and the success of the day traders will end.

New books raise expectations and faith in ever-rising stock prices. My favorite is Dow 36,000.[lxxxiii] This book said that the Dow Jones Industrials should be priced at 36,000, over three times the current level. And it should be priced there <u>now</u>, not years in the future. The author believed that the market was enormously undervalued. He based this on some very optimistic economic projections. You can make a mathematical case for any price for a stock. The value is determined by factors like earning power of the company and interest rates. Prices are very sensitive to even small changes in these factors. For example, you can justify a price of three or four times the current level for the market, if you assume that long-term interest rates and inflation will fall dramatically from current levels. Whether it is realistic to assume they will is a very big question.

Security analysts did not meet their responsibility to really analyze companies and tell buyers they were wrong about optimistic expectations. Analysts would announce their own valuation, and when the stock burst through that price level, they would tell the public, "Hey, the price obviously should be much higher, because that is where you have pegged it." They did not say, "You are wrong." The investment community crucifies any analyst who is bearish. They know that the individual investor just does not want to hear any bad news. And the result is that stock prices go up just because they have been going up.

Investors disregarded the risks that are always inherent in stocks. Lots of people made the comment to me, "I'm not afraid, long term." And indeed, they probably should not be. The problem is that they actually have little feeling for what the long term will be like. The long term is not straight up. Most investors today have seen only the 1990s. They did not experience 1987, and many were not even in the market in 1990 when the Gulf War caused a significant sell off. The only lesson they have learned so far is buy on dips because the market always comes back. Of course they are not afraid! They haven't been around long enough to understand what bear markets are like.

Main Street Meets Wall Street

We have a very savvy friend in Houston, Rodney Mitchell. He has run money management firms for at least 35 years. In early March, he made some observations on the market. In 1987, the bear market did not affect Main Street, only Wall Street. When the market crashed then, the folks on Main Street could not have cared less. In fact they were a bit happy that the rich money crowd finally got what they deserved. Now everyone is in on the game. Cattle ranchers in West Texas do not have time to feed their cows; they are glued to CNBC. Tennis pros at resorts in Mexico do not have time to teach lessons; they are busy running to the pro shop to check out how their Internet stocks are doing.

Rodney is right on the money about Main Street and the market. On Monday October 19, 1987, I left the office in Midtown Manhattan and walked up 5th Avenue toward home on West 57th Street. The Dow Jones Industrials had just dropped 23%. Like a few million other "Wall Street" types, I was in shock. At our apartment, Judy and our friends, Sammie and John McPherson, were waiting for me. We had planned to go to dinner together. John says that I ate a pound of salted peanuts without even knowing it. (It has always been a tradition of mine—Have a big problem? Eat something!) For professional investors, the world had just come crashing down. This had been worse than Black Tuesday in 1929, and who knew what tomorrow would be like. It was easy to imagine many scenarios, none of them good.

Early the next morning I had to be in Madison, New Jersey. At about 6:30 a.m., I found myself in a little coffee shop on Main Street having breakfast at the counter with a lot of guys getting ready to go to the factory. The two next to me were talking about the market. One of them said, "Did you hear the news about the stocks dropping?" His buddy, excitedly, "What did you say?" "I said that your stocks have dropped." His buddy again, "Thank God! I don't own any stocks. I thought you said, 'Your socks have dropped.' That would have been important."

Next time however, the public may be a great deal more interested in what the market does. That guy at the counter by now probably has a portfolio of growth mutual funds and may even have retired from the factory to be a day trader.

Does P/E Matter?

The change in the Nasdaq Price/Earnings ratio shows dramatically how the market has revalued stocks in general and technology in particular. [lxxxiv] The P/E ratio of the Nasdaq tracked the general market P/E for most of the early 1990s, rising slowly. But in 1998, it began to accelerate. It peaked in early 2000 at the unheard of level of 240. At that P/E, investors were expecting exceptional earnings growth not just for years, but for decades.

The P/E has fallen sharply since the spring. But it still stands at over 100. If you consider only the companies in the Nasdaq that <u>actually have earnings</u>, their P/E ratio is still well over 50. To be reasonably valued by any historical measure, the Nasdaq would be priced at only about half its current level. This is not to say that it will actually drop another 50%. At year-end 2000, the Nasdaq at 2471was already off its high by 51% and down 38% for the year. But the Nasdaq, by historical standards, is still far from a bargain.

So, does P/E still matter? The answer, until the last few weeks, has been, "Not much." The number of investors who say that they own only "conservative" technology stocks is surprising. By this, they usually mean Microsoft, Cisco, Dell, and AOL, as opposed to Priceline.com and PSINet. Again, defining these as conservative stocks is based on the idea that they are companies with giant market capitalizations and they have been in business at least a few years. This is another way of saying, "A lot of people have been willing to pay a lot of money to own this stock, so it must be conservative; else why would so many people be willing to do that?" They are clueless that they are buying a <u>business</u> that is returning them 1% or less on their capital and with very speculative prospects of ever returning them more than that. [lxxxv]

The number of irrational arguments around must be approaching a world record. The moral is simple: If you want to invest, don't be rational, and if you want to be rational, don't invest.

Jeremy Grantham, Grantham, Mayo, Van Otterloo & Co., June 12, 2000[lxxxvi]

Security Analysts—The Anti-Contrarians

Any time people in large numbers agree on the market, it is a bad sign. Time after time, unanimous agreement on some forecast turns out to be completely wrong. This is seldom truer than in the forecasts of security analysts. When they all agree on a buy, who else is left to supply the cash for another buy? And when they have all agreed on a sell, who is left yet to sell?

> **Analysts' Pick: Cisco Systems Inc.,** CNBC.com *Technology Reporter*, Nov 4, 2000
>
> CURRENT PRICE: $56.75
> 12-MONTH PRICE TARGET: $80
> REASON TO BUY: It's one of the best pure plays in the growth of the Internet. Cisco also boasts an order backlog of $3.8 billion and has the highest gross margin of any company this analyst follows.
>
> **Most analysts remain confident that Cisco still has the juice. This is the Company that has been exceeding analysts' expectations for the past 10 years or so and has racked up 11 consecutive quarters of year-over-year growth acceleration.**

Consider this report on one of the most successful companies and one of the best performing stocks in the technology group, Cisco.[lxxxvii] After this forecast, Cisco did not go significantly higher. It bottomed in late 2000 at about $10.50.

Another dramatic example of security analysts' herd mentality appeared in *The Wall Street Journal* on December 18, 2000.[lxxxviii] The following table shows the results of forecasts by six respected Wall Street investment house analysts. Each recommended a technology stock. They gave clients these reports in early to mid-2000. The average stock was predicted to rise 79% over the next 12-18 months. On average, at year-end, they have <u>declined</u> 91% in the months since the forecast. After the forecast was made, the average stock achieved only a 27% gain at its highest price, and none even came close to its predicted rise. Yet analysts are paid enormous amounts of money to produce these reports. Why? Because they wanted to give the firm's clients information that the clients wanted to hear, something that would generate commission business for the firm. Analysts' reports should be labeled: "Caution, use of this product could be hazardous to your economic health."

		Predicted	Price at	Highest		Since Prediction		Highest	Highest	
	Year 2000	Price In	Time of	Price since	12/31/00	%Change in Price		% Gain	As % Of	
Company	Date	12-18 Mo	Prediction	Prediction	Price	Actual	Predicted	Actual	Prediction	Firm
Lucent	May 15	$120.00	$56.50	$67.19	$13.50	-76%	112%	19%	56%	Dres. Klein.
Priceline	Mar 1	$150.00	$55.94	$104.25	$1.31	-98%	168%	86%	70%	Gold. Sachs
PSI Net	Jan 18	$86.00	$42.56	$60.94	$ .72	-98%	102%	43%	71%	Rob.Stephens
Red Hat	Feb 8	$115.00	$88.94	$94.38	$6.25	-93%	29%	6%	82%	J. P. Morgan
Linux	Jan 4	$260.00	$192.00	$199.44	$8.13	-96%	35%	4%	77%	Alex. Brown
Yahoo!	Jan 4	$300.00	$237.50	$250.06	$30.06	-87%	26%	5%	83%	Schroder Co.
					Average	-91%	79%	27%	73%	

Others in the Herd

Lest we appear to be pointing a finger only at security firms for herding, we hasten to add that there is plenty of rash action to go around. This table shows that very bright people beyond the analyst community are prone to participate in manias. The same *Wall Street Journal* story described five top executives at "old" economy firms who left to join "new" economy firms. They wanted to be, as the Priceline.com executive put it, "part of a growing business." Presumably, each was lured into the new economy by promises of riches from stock options. They have now averaged fifteen months tenure at their new employer, and the average stock has declined 91%. The Priceline.com executive has already quit, announcing that she still wanted to be "part of a growing business." By inference, this executive believes Priceline is no longer a growth company.

Old Economy Company	Position	New Economy Company	Tenure- Mo.	Stock Performance
Bessemer Venture	Partner	MotherNature.com	25	-91%
ITT	President	Cyberian Outpost	14	-78%
Citigroup	CFO	Priceline.com	9	-96%
Anderson Consulting	CEO	Webvan	15	-97%
Cardinal Health	EVP	Neoforma.com	18	-92%
12/31/2000		Average		-91%

The Customers Demand It

At times of such great enthusiasm, or "irrational exuberance," the sellers of investment services give the buyers what they want. There is tremendous pressure on investment managers and mutual funds to perform, even in the short term. Clients' patience is always shorter than the manager thinks, or the client agrees to. But patience shortens even more in times like these. One client told me, "I know you have been saying that value stocks will return to favor and will outperform technology, but you've been saying that for two years." That happened to be exactly one week before the decline started for the Nasdaq. The timing of my remark was sheer chance; it might have been another year before the market turned down. There is no way to know how far a market trend will carry. This market moved about twice as high as any seasoned market watcher would have expected.

But in a world that wants quick returns, two years is forever, and for a money manager "early" looks the same as "wrong." Any under-performing mutual fund or investment manager will quickly find himself in the cross-hairs of disturbed investors. He is given very little time, maybe a quarter or two, to "turn things around." Otherwise, he is taken out and shot.

DISCIPLINE

Human nature desires quick results. There is a peculiar zest in making money quickly. It is the long-term investor who will, in practice, come in for the most criticism. If in the short-run he is unsuccessful—which, of course, is very likely—he will not receive much mercy.

The common characteristic of really great investors is discipline. Investment philosophy matters far less than whether you have the courage to stick to it in good markets and bad. It is important that you do not cut and run when it is not working. No approach to investing works all the time. There will be long periods when a very sound investment approach will be out of favor. The disciplined investor does not abandon his approach for another one that seems to be working well at the moment.

There is no greater recipe for disaster in the market than chasing performance by constantly switching to the stocks that have been performing well. It is common sense that a stock that has risen sharply in price is not nearly as good a bargain as one that has not yet risen. Why do investors chase the "hot" market favorites to their long-term detriment? Most people cannot conquer their emotions and so they make irrational decisions. Also, many investors do not understand the role that diversification should play in their investments. And finally, many investors do not have a long-term view.

Greed and Fear

Investor emotion has a somewhat predictable cycle. As bull markets build to a peak, greed seems to seize investors. Part of this is because as markets rise, investors delude themselves that it is very easy to make money. People begin to believe that it is their right to be rich, and that it really is not all that difficult. In addition, investors grow to envy others who have been doing better in the market It matters little the amount of risk that others are taking; risk is a forgotten concept at market peaks. (A subject we will address later.) I have seen, in the last year, normally sensible investors behaving quite irrationally. Anecdotal examples include:

The investor who plays tennis with a friend. The friend has doubled his money in the last sixty days, while the conservative investor has made hardly any return in the last year and he is thoroughly embarrassed not to be able to match stories of stock market success. Cocktail parties are an equally great forum for bragging about successful investing. A wise old man said, "You get about as much useful information from people at cocktail parties and tape watchers at stock brokers as you get any place where loafers gather." The people who talk most about their stocks usually have a very selective memory about their winners and losers. Unlike an investment adviser who <u>must</u> own up to his actual performance, no matter how bad, individuals can choose to talk only about their winners. The average person has absolutely no idea what his actual return has been for the last year, two years, or ten years. This is commonly exhibited when an investor holds one stock for a very long time, and it rises several fold. We have had investors tell us how good a given stock has been. For example, it might have risen to eight times its purchase price. On questioning, we discover that they bought the stock in 1963. The compounded return over that thirty-seven years is a mere 5.7%, but they believe it is much higher.

A retired man in his mid-60s depends on his IRA as a major source of retirement income. In the mid-1990s, his consultant moves him from a mix of 60/40 stocks/bonds to a mix of 80/20, which is normally a pretty aggressive strategy. However, stocks continue to rise sharply, and his value-type stocks do not keep up. Then the consultant suggests moving from value stocks into more growth stocks. The man might have chosen a more appropriate adjustment if he had said to himself, "I gambled and won, so let's cut back to 60/40." But the lesson he learns is: Be greedy, it pays. Early in 2000, he is not worried about downside. The consultant projects the 80/20 mix will return 20% for stocks, 6% for bonds, a total of 17%. But what if the return is –25% stocks and 6% bonds, for a -19% total return? His income is constrained severely, and in a retirement mode, there is no opportunity to dollar average in at lower prices. A retiree dollar averages <u>out</u> at lower prices in a declining market. That is why it is so important to protect retirement funds.

An investor who had a retirement plan that earned 19% a year with value stocks from 1991-99, including the two "bad" years of 1998-99. In early 2000, he decides that the last two years will be the norm. His friends doubled their money. He doesn't consider how they did in the preceding seven years, 1991-97. He knows only that they are doing much better <u>right now</u>. So very near the peak, he switches strategies to get into growth stocks.

A young man works for a rapidly growing Internet company. In autumn 1999, since he has been with his employer, the stock has doubled three times. He declares that it only needs to double once more and he can retire, still on the sunny side of 40—quite an accomplishment. He may put his retirement plans on hold a bit longer. His stock now needs to double not one more time but <u>two more times,</u> having fallen by more than 50% in a few weeks.

As markets decline, investor greed and a sense of well being give way first to complacency, then apprehension, then as markets approach bottom, fear becomes dominant. And finally fear turns to disillusionment—"Everyone knows you cannot make a dime in the stock market." Usually at this stage, some major newsmagazine has a story on the stock market and a picture of a bear on its cover. Or even worse, a negative cover article appears on a major business magazine, asking something like, "Are Stocks Dead?" Such "news" fuels investor doubt. For example in mid-1982, the Dow Jones Industrial Average was 200 points lower than it had been in 1966. Think of that! Sixteen years with a return of –20%. Of course the average investor was disillusioned and discouraged. This was just before the greatest bull market of our lifetime.

We have an entire generation of investors that has not experienced the dark side of the stock market. They will surely get that experience. We have no idea when— we only know that they <u>will.</u> Bear markets are not pretty. By most definitions, we are experiencing one now at least in the dot-coms.

With the exception of some technology CEOs who borrowed against their zillions of dollars of stock and options, much of the recent market investment does not appear to be financed with debt. If there is little debt, this is indeed a blessing. Even the very rich are not immune to greed. (How much is ever enough? Always, just a little bit more than we have now.) We discussed the Hunt brothers' silver fiasco in early 1981. Two of the Hunt brothers had inherited about a billion dollars from their late father the famous oil wildcatter, H. L. Hunt. He was, then, one of only three billionaires in the world; oh, how times have changed. In any event, the sons who inherited his wealth leveraged their billion dollars and bought silver in an attempt to corner the world market. They borrowed about seven billion dollars, drove the price of silver to $50 an ounce, buying all the way up, and ran out of capital. Silver collapsed to about $5 an ounce, bankrupting them. Even billionaires can be made to respect the downside power of leverage.

Diversification

A key to all sound investing is diversification. No single asset class – stocks, bonds, real estate, cash, or tangibles will consistently outperform all others. While no other class of assets has come even close to providing the return that stocks have given, to get that return requires patience, and an extremely long investment horizon. For most people, stocks should be only a portion of their investments.

The market since 1982 is not the norm. The environment has been exceptionally friendly - a growing economy with declining inflation. These near perfect conditions cannot last forever. A prudent investor will always have a portion of his assets in bonds, real estate, and perhaps other types of investments. Three possible economic scenarios include price stability, inflation, and deflation. We have been in the stable scenario for a very long time. Someday we may get one or both of the other two.

It is impossible to know which stock group will perform best in the future, and a broad diversification of industry groups is always a good idea. Of course, the investor is tempted to overweight whatever has been doing best in his portfolio, because that is naturally what he is most comfortable owning.

Over the long run an investor is well advised to stay diversified. No one asset class or sector leads the market forever. And those that charge into the lead often become far overvalued and come down hard when they fall. Unfortunately the temptation to chase hot stocks is great. Investors are influenced by news reports and by stories of friends making big gains. Others want some of the action and pay little attention to whether the stocks are overpriced. In addition they are further tempted to be heavily invested in only the hottest sectors of the moment. Now that the Internet and technology stocks are stumbling, many investors may be disappointed with their losses in the market and rush for the exit, vowing to stay away from stocks in the future. And again, investment advisers will be called upon to prevent clients from overreacting to disappointments and making poor long-term decisions based on short-term developments.

The current market turmoil, with value stocks replacing growth stocks as leaders and blue chips replacing technology stocks, has reestablished the credibility of diversification.

Perspective

In the last year, many people who had professed to be long-term investors had a sudden, miraculous conversion to growth/technology companies. Why is this? They did not have the discipline to reexamine their actions in light of their investing time horizon. It is important never to lose sight of the length of the race you are running, investing is not a hundred-yard dash; it is a marathon.

Focus on the long run. But this does not mean <u>never</u> sell stocks. Any stock can get so high that it is a "sell," even with capital gains tax to be paid. While we at CornerCap perhaps err on the side of low turnover, it is not a good idea to buy and <u>never</u> sell. Consider this - of the thirty-four leading growth companies of 1980, only one of them remains a winner. Twenty-two are gone—merged, bought, or bankrupt. Eleven have trailed the S&P 500. In business, a lot can happen in a short time. This is true for any market sector. Where will Cisco, Intel, and Oracle be in 2010 compared to the S&P? "Hold for the long-term" does not apply to any one stock, it means the total market. Try to own today's best stocks, with the certainty that they all will not be tomorrow's best stocks.

Sir John and the Nikkei

Great patience is required to allow the market to move to what you determine is fair value. Results are not always measured in months or years, but sometime in decades. Sir John Templeton has been investing for over sixty years. He is one of the great investors of this era. He bought international stocks very early; beginning with Japan shortly after World War II. He has said that when he began his investing career, there was exactly one mutual fund in existence, run by Scudder Stevens & Clark in Boston. So he has seen a thing or two in his time.

In 1987, when the Nikkei Index stood around 25,000, Sir John said, "We haven't found a bargain in Japan in over a year. At 70 times earnings, there aren't any bargains."[lxxxix] The Japanese market had been rising rapidly, having gained about 125% in less than three years. After his comment, the Nikkei Index advanced to about 38,000 in late 1989, an additional gain of 52%, and a total five year gain of 242%. But over the next decade, the Nikkei has fallen to slightly above 12,000. Those who sold when Sir John cautioned that stocks were too high made 125% in three years. They would have missed the rest of the Japanese "bubble", but if they still hold Japanese stocks there total return since his caution is –50%, over a decade.

Conversely, he also said in January, 1983,[xc] "Odds are better than even that the Dow will hit 3,000 by the end of the decade." He was certainly within a reasonable margin of error. At that time the Dow was about 1050 and he was predicting a 185% increase in seven years. Sir John Templeton's message is always the same, and is always boringly simple - Buy good, cheap stocks and hold them until they are not cheap anymore. Then replace them with other cheap stocks – it matters not where in the world you find them.

Why has he been so successful for over sixty years? Because John Templeton is what John Bogle, founder of the Vanguard funds, calls an investing hedgehog.[xci] There are foxes and hedgehogs. "The fox knows many things, but the hedgehog knows one *great* thing." Sir John Templeton knows one *great* thing. He does not get sidetracked from his long-term objective with short-term market movements.

Your Time Horizon

It is very important to define your time horizon - the length of time before you will need to spend the money you are investing. The longer you can keep the funds at work, the more you can afford to invest in stocks. Stocks are very volatile in short periods, but over the longer run, time is on your side. In any one year, you might make or lose a great percentage on your investment, but over a five-year period the probability of loss is much less. The probability of losing diminishes the longer you keep your money invested in the market. This is <u>not</u> the same thing as saying you are sure to make a good return if you stay invested for twenty years. There is no sure thing in the stock market, only that the probabilities <u>favor</u> your making money.

Let us share two extreme examples of choosing the wrong time horizon. First is the person who is nearing retirement, but still insists in keeping his "nest egg" all in stocks. The danger is that he may need to sell his stocks for living expenses when they are at a very low point. He definitely needs the anchor to windward that bonds provide. The second extreme is the person who is overly cautious about stocks. Perhaps he is very young, has a good income, and is many years from retirement. He definitely can keep a large portion of his funds in stocks for many years. A similar case is the older person who has significant cash and bonds to support his lifestyle in retirement, but insists on keeping very little in stocks. Such a person really is investing not for himself, but for his heirs who have a much longer time horizon. But he is very cautious, and does not recognize that he can put a much larger percent of his assets into stocks.

What Are Your Goals?

It is also important to set an investing goal. Some people's goal is to create enough assets to retire comfortably. For others, the goal is to educate children or grandchildren. It could be to create wealth for charities. Whatever the goal, it is important to define it. You cannot know whether you are investing properly if you do not know what you are trying to achieve. You need a good financial roadmap, and if you do not know where you are headed, the road taken by chance might turn out to be a bumpy one.

What is Important?

You must define the important elements in your financial program. Sometimes, maximizing <u>investment</u> return is far from the most important element. Take the rather common case of family planning for estate and income taxes. Many investors now face an onerous estate tax bill, and they have little or no idea of its magnitude and impact. Some families face a combined income and estate tax, spread over two generations, at an 82% rate. By far the greatest threat to their financial security is the tax system that confiscates their income and capital. Yet many of these people continue to invest as though there were no taxes. They have set investment goals to maximize their pretax return, when their after-tax return will be miniscule once all the taxes are paid. They would be much better served if they emphasized minimizing taxes rather than trying to squeeze out another one or two percent of pretax return each year. It matters little if you make 9% or 13% pretax if the return after tax is only 2.5% to 3.5%. Your efforts should be focused on planning to reduce your tax bite.

There is some hope that the government will offer a tax reduction package, perhaps for both income and estate taxes. Personally, I think it unwise to build an investment and tax plan on "hope." Hope, especially hope based on the actions of politicians, is not a very acceptable planning technique. I used to work for a man who was fond of saying, "You can always count on politicians to do the right thing, when there is nothing else left for them to do."

REALISM

If you don't know who you are, the market is an expensive place to find out.

Investment Temperament

Many people never ask themselves if they are suited by temperament, or prepared by experience, to be a successful investor. The market can provide a great opportunity for introspection and analysis, but it can also be much more expensive than going to a psychoanalyst.

To be successful in the market, it helps to have a healthy dose of realism. The best security analysts/investors tend to be rather negative people. Most of us hold our own abilities in very high regard (whether we openly admit it or not). Investors generally suffer from overconfidence, and they believe they are better than they actually are at picking stocks or timing the market. You should be very realistic about the returns that you can expect from the market in the long run. It also helps to be realistic about the prospects of individual stocks, and never to fall in love with them. A good investor also understands the limits of what he can know.

But what we're going to have is so many broken hearts because the expectations for individuals now are 15%-plus growth rates. And even if we have 5%- let alone our projected minus 2% returns for the next ten years, all owners and investors in 401(k) plans - let along the day traders - are going to feel betrayed by the system.
Jeremy Grantham, June 12, 2000[18] [xcii]

Market Expectations

Controlling market expectations is an investment adviser's most difficult job.

---

[18] Jeremy Grantham was almost exactly right. For the 10 years ending 6/30/2010, the S&P 500 returned -1.5% a year.

This is really a matter of controlling two emotions, greed and fear. But it helps to have some understanding of what return the market should give. You are actually buying a piece of an ongoing operating business. That business has the capability to deliver a certain amount of profits to be used as dividends paid to you and as capital to be reinvested to make the business grow. In the long run it can deliver no more and no less. Someone may be willing to pay you more for your title of ownership – but do not count on it; they might only be willing to pay you less, especially just when you need cash the most.

What Can The Market Deliver
All expectation outruns performance.
    Attributed to Ralph Waldo Emerson

We must be realistic about the returns the market is likely to deliver. We have already pointed out that now expectations are extraordinarily high for stockholders. We want to examine in two somewhat different ways the returns that we might expect from the market.

More articulate investors, Warren Buffett for one, have given a better explanation than I can about what the market can reasonably return to shareholders. But the analyses below give a perspective that I can understand as a market analyst.

In the first one, I have borrowed from John Bogle of the Vanguard funds.[xciii] It shows what has happened, and what reasonably can be expected to happen in the market. Like all security analysis – this is not a forecast. It is a calculation based on a specific set of assumptions about the economy and market behavior. At best it can be described as having a fair probability of occurring. But there are so many possible outcomes that even a highly probable one can be far off the mark.

This table shows market performance data. From 1969-79, investors received an annual dividend of 3.4% and the profits in their companies grew 9.9% a year. This is a total investment return of 13.3%. However, during this ten-year period, the P/E ratio on stocks (the amount a buyer was willing to pay for $1 of earnings) dropped from 15.9 to 7.3, and this P/E shrinkage produced a return of

Annual Rates of Return on U.S.				
	Actual	Actual	Bogle	Our Projections
Stocks	1969-79	1979-99	1999-09	1999-09
Initial Dividend Yield	3.4%	4.5%	1.2%	1.2%
Earnings Growth	9.9%	5.9%	8.0%	15.0%
Investment Return	13.3%	10.4%	9.2%	16.2%
Speculative Return*	-7.5%	7.3%	-4.0%	-6.7%
Total Return	5.8%	17.7%	5.2%	9.5%
Initial Earnings	$5.78	$14.90	$47.00	$47.00
Initial P/E Ratio	15.9	7.3	30	30
Final Earnings	$14.90	$47.00	$101.50	$190.14
Final P/E Ratio	7.3	30	20	15
*P/E Change Impact				

–7.5%, what John Bogle calls "speculative" return in contrast to investment or business return.

In the 20 years, 1979-99, the picture changes. The dividend income is 4.5% and the profit growth is 5.9% for a total of 10.4%. However, the "speculative" return is

7.3% because the P/E ratio increased from 7.3 to 30.

Bogle gives his projection for the ten years 1999-09. He sees the current dividend at 1.2% (which is easily measured) and the profit growth at 8.0%, a pretty moderate rate. However he believes that the P/E cannot be sustained at more than 20, which is still well above the historical price the market has paid for a $1 of earnings. This shrinking P/E gives a "speculative" return of –4.0% for a total market return of 5.2%.

The fourth column shows our projections. We assume that the market can grow earnings at the very high rate of 15% a year. This is not necessarily what we believe, but what investors seem to be expecting. We go on to assume that the P/E investors will pay is equal to the growth rate, again 15. This would give a "speculative" return of –6.7% a year as the P/E gets cut in half. The total result is a 9.5% return. This is what stocks have averaged over the years. Either estimate, 5.2% or 9.5% is a far cry from the 15-25% a year that investors said in the summer of 2000 that they expect over the next decade. Again, the probabilities suggest many disappointed investors in the years ahead.

We also examined the market from a different perspective, still using dividends and earnings. This table has year-end data on the Dow Jones Industrials, the S&P 500, and the Nasdaq Index: Book Value, Market Value, Dividends, and Earnings Per Share. From this basic information we can calculate an estimated total investment return which is the growth of the company (or index) plus the dividend.

	DJI	S&P	Nasdaq
Book Value	$1,638.10	$200.35	$62.50
Dividend	$179.44	$15.71	$4.80
EPS	$525.65	$53.73	$24.00
Market Value	$10,787	$1,320	$2,471
Return on Equity	32.1%	26.8%	38.4%
Price/Book	6.6	6.6	39.5
Operating Growth	21.1%	19.0%	30.7%
Yield	1.6%	1.2%	0.2%
Total Return	23.7%	20.2%	30.9%
P/E Ratio	20.5	24.6	103.0
Total Return/PE	1.2	.8	.3

We can also calculate a P/E ratio. A measure of "fair value" is the Total Return/PE Index. This indicates how much total return an investor is getting for a unit of P/E.

The larger the number the better. The Dow Jones Industrials and the S&P 500 are now priced at an Index value of 1.2 and .8 respectively. However, the Nasdaq is priced about three times as richly as these other two market measures.

This table makes adjustments for return on book value for the DJI and S&P. We assume that their Return on Equity will drop to a more historical level of 25% and that the very high return on the Nasdaq at 40% will continue, taking into account the technology industry's ability to generate high returns. In this scenario, the ratio for the DJI and S&P would decline to .6, indicating that they are not such a bargain. But this tells nothing about the price at which they will actually sell. However, we have posed the question: At what price would the Nasdaq be comparably valued to the other two indices? The answer is 1,350. In other words, the Nasdaq would need to fall 45% in this scenario to be fairly competitive with

other "old economy" stocks. While
this appears to be such a low number
as to be ridiculous, remember that
market drops of this magnitude are
possible. The Nasdaq is already off its
high by 51%, and there is no law that
says it cannot drop further.[19]

What Can We "Know"?

*In the market, what everyone knows
isn't worth knowing.*

	DJI	S&P	Nasdaq
Book Value	$1,638.10	$189.54	$62.50
Dividend	$179.44	$15.71	$5.00
EPS	$409.53	$47.39	$25.00
Market Value	$10,788	$1,320	$1,350
Return on Equity	25.0%	25.0%	40.0%
Price/Book	6.6	7.0	21.6
Operating Growth	14.0%	16.7%	32.0%
Yield	1.6%	1.2%	0.2%
Total Return	15.6%	17.9%	32.2%
P/E Ratio	26.3	27.9	54.0
Total Return/PE	.6	.6	.6
December 31, 2000[xciv]			

Investors tend to suffer from information overload. Only a few basics about
any stock really make a difference. More information does not make for better
decisions; information is not necessarily knowledge. Warren Buffett says he can
give you an answer in five minutes on whether he will buy your company. That's
because he carries a few key "yardsticks" of value in his head. And when he gets
answers that allow him to measure with those yardsticks, he can very quickly make
up his mind. Many believe that the more research and analysis you do, the more
profitable your investment experience will be. This is wrong. The mental leap
between understanding and doing takes more than a keystroke. The missing
ingredient is experience or training. [xcv]

Risk

*Volatility is a symptom that people have no idea of the underlying value. They're
not buying because it's a company with certain attributes. They're buying because
the price is rising. People are playing games not related at all to what the long-
term value of the enterprise is.*

*It is a mistake to be too conservative in projecting future performance. The real
risk is not losing money—it is missing the upside.*

These quotes contrast the old and the new idea of risk in this bull market.
People now believe risk means not being in the market, concerned only about how
much profit they are going to leave on the table if they do not own stocks. It is hard
to imagine a concept of risk that is farther from what it has traditionally been. Risk
is usually defined as the volatility of an asset – how much it goes up or down in a
short period compared to other asset prices. But investors now believe that stocks
only go up. They do not even think about the traditional measure of risk, although
downside volatility certainly still exists. I have talked to any number of investors

---

[19] The NASDAQ actually bottomed at 1250, 75% off its 2000 high.

who clearly reject the entire concept of risk. None of them is old enough to have seen a bear market, and when they do, their idea of risk will change. The change will be dramatic and <u>permanent</u>.

A more easily understood measure of risk is the likelihood that your assets will have dropped in price at the very time you <u>need to</u> sell them. Investors have evidently discarded any such definition. It is obvious that at best they pay only lip service to the concept that stocks can actually drop for more than a few days. This notion of risk is now totally outdated. In 1999 stocks with no earnings did better than stocks with earnings. That should indicate how oblivious to risk investors were. They were willing to invest money in enterprises with no profits, but were unwilling to own enterprises that did deliver profits. At some point, after they lose a great deal of money, investors will again embrace the concept of market risk.

What Can We Manage?

There are several elements in investing: return, risk, timing, and costs. Most investors want to manage return. But investors will get from the market whatever it decides to give them. People who run their own businesses, or who simply like to be in charge, have a hard time accepting this idea. We have had people demand that we take <u>immediate </u>action to make their performance improve. They think the market is a machine that we operate, and if they demand action and put enough pressure on us, then we can make the machine run faster.

All investors get just what the market delivers. We might be cleverer at picking the right segment, but such cleverness is not a lasting trait. Investors cannot manage return. One potential client gave us feedback on why he did not choose us as an adviser. We had explained that over time the market tends to give a return of about 10% year. The prospect said he had decided to use another manager who had "promised" 15% a year. Now, we never said what our performance would be. Only a fool or a crook would promise high performance. And the other adviser probably did not promise a specific performance either; that manager most likely assumed a higher rate of return from the market going forward than we are comfortable assuming. We think we are closer to the mark, but could easily be wrong. The point is that no manager can manage performance.

So if the investor cannot manage return, what can he manage? He can manage the other three elements. Choosing an asset mix that is diversified manages risk. A good portfolio contains the proper weighting of risky and non-risky investments. Usually this means the proportion of stocks and bonds in the portfolio, but it can also mean adding other classes of assets such as gold, real estate, money market funds, and venture capital.

Timing is about adding and taking funds from an investment program. The best method has proven to be simply dollar averaging – that is, putting in a fixed dollar amount each period. This assumes that the investor is not capable of "timing" markets. He will not try to choose the most advantageous time to add money – that is, he will not wait to invest until he thinks the market is going up. Timing has proven futile for most investors; they nearly always get it wrong.

Finally, he can manage costs. It is not cheap to run a portfolio. The wise investor will look at trading, trustee, custodian, and investment adviser fees. When the market is rising at double digit rates, costs do not seem significant, but over the long run cost management helps a great deal in building wealth.

Reversion to the Mean

If something cannot go on forever, it will stop.
Stein's Law

The powerful concept of reversion to the mean is very useful in investing. Reversion cautions us that whatever goes up longest and strongest is mostly likely to lag in the future, and whatever has done poorly the longest is likely to perform better in the future. While this does work in the market, there are no yardsticks to tell us how long a trend will continue before it reverts to the mean.

To illustrate how reversion to the mean has worked for broad economic sectors over the last thirty-two years, consider this.[xcvi] Major economic sectors change in importance over time, partly because their underlying fundamentals change. For example, over the last thirty-two years, health care has grown in importance as our population has aged. Likewise, basic materials have become steadily less important in a service economy. Major changes reflect not only the economic importance of a segment, but also the economic importance that <u>investors place</u> on it.

If we examine the history of the eleven economic sectors of the S&P 500 from 1968 to 2000, we find two extreme shifts. First, energy in 1980 moved up sharply from 14% to 27%. At its peak, it was 35% of the S&P. Energy stocks fell steadily for six years before stabilizing. In 1999, technology shifted from 19% (already up sharply from a few years earlier) to 30%. At its peak in early 2000, technology had also risen to 35% of the S&P value.

Drill-Bit Dilemma[xcvii]

Company	IPO (1999)	First Day High	Date First Hit $1 (2000)	Dec. 31 Close
AutoWeb	Mar 23	$41.00	Oct 18	$0.25
Beyond.com	June 17	$13.88	Aug 11	$0.16
BigStar Entertainment	Aug 3	$10.06	June 28	$0.13
Egreetings Network	Dec 17	$16.25	Sept 26	$0.28
E-Stamp	Oct 8	$33.00	Aug 4	$0.19
J2 Global Com.	July 23	$10.31	Oct 13	$1.13
PlanetRx.com	Oct 7	$36.50	July 12	$0.28
Quepasa.com	June 25	$18.25	Aug 3	$0.09
Talk City	July 20	$16.50	Oct 2	$0.16
Theglobe.com	Nov 13	$24.25	Sept 27	$0.28

Forbes, December 25, 2000

For a while tech stocks made it see that economic laws could be repealed, or at least broken without fear of punishment. The internet companies used to brag about a stock price that sounded like area codes – 209 or 303. But these days many dot-coms are trading at "drill bit" prices like 3/8 or 9/32. When a stock sells at drill bit prices, the end is near. Nasdaq de-lists companies whose shares are priced at less than $1. By late November, 154 of Nasdaq's 3,866 listings were trading at or below $1 a share. These are ten that took the plunge.

Six High Tech Stocks to "Buy" in July, 2000

Below is a letter written to a newspaper columnist in July 2000:[xcviii]

"I would like to toss the dice on six super, high-tech issues that have minuscule revenues today but have the potential to generate huge revenues four or five years from now and, consequently, significantly higher stock prices. If their technology is promising, the share prices of the fledgling companies should explode as revenues and earnings grow."

Name	07/28/2000 Price	12/31/2000 Price	%Gain
Accelerated Networks, Inc.	$20.06	$2.78	-86.1%
Ariba, Inc.	$107.63	$53.63	-50.2%
AudioCodes Ltd.	$49.13	$13.56	-72.4%
Next Level Communications	$ 89.88	$11.38	-87.3%
Powertel, Inc.	$ 86.06	$61.94	-28.0%
Sonus Networks, Inc.	$ 65.00	$25.25	-61.2%
	Average		-64.2%

The columnist gave a quick critique of each of the six companies. All of them had fallen sharply since March. He still strongly recommended not buying any of them. The cry from this investor rather than "Buy! Buy", should have been "Bye, Bye!" The six stocks on average are down 64% in only five months. Prospects of earnings are way in the future. It is dangerous to buy only because the stock is "cheap." The market is filled with "cheap" stocks whose P/E has shrunk from 125 to 60. This is what the market pundits on CNBC call "trying to catch a falling knife."

Major Technology Stocks

Not only the smaller, speculative technology stocks have suffered this year.

This table shows the performance of twelve well-known technology stocks that I picked at random early in 2000. The group averaged a decline of 46.3% for the year; Yahoo! dot-com had the worst performance at negative 86.1%.

Name	Quantity	12/31/99 Price	12/31/00 Price	%Gain	PE Ratio
Amazon.com, Inc.	119	$76.13	$15.56	-79.6%	n/a
America Online, Inc.	120	$75.88	$34.80	-54.1%	66.5
Cisco Systems, Inc.	170	$53.56	$38.25	-28.6%	94.2
Dell Computer Corp	178	$51.00	$17.44	-65.8%	21.9
eBay Inc.	146	$62.59	$33.00	-47.3%	290.9
Intel Corporation	220	$41.16	$30.06	-27.0%	20.5
JDS Uniphase	113	$80.66	$41.69	-48.3%	n/a
Microsoft Corporation	78	$116.75	$43.38	-62.8%	25.3
Motorola, Inc.	185	$49.08	$20.25	-58.7%	29.3
Oracle Corporation	326	$27.84	$29.06	4.4%	27.0
R F Micro Devices	266	$34.22	$27.44	-19.8%	80.6
Sun Microsystems	236	$38.72	$27.88	-28.0%	45.9
Yahoo! Inc.	42	$216.43	$30.06	-86.1%	79.5
Total Account Value				-48.5%	

Oracle had a positive return, 4.4%. Despite the declines, these stocks still sell at historically lofty P/E's. These companies must produce extraordinary operating earnings growth in order to justify their price.

Don't Fall In Love

The stock market is an uncertain place, regardless of how comfortable it seems. The best insurance is to diversify and remember that no matter how well a stock performs, it is not likely to last. People every day fall in love with their stocks. We hear comments like, "I can't sell that stock. It has been so good to me." As though it were a beloved family pet. You must remember that stock does not know you own it. It does not return your affection. It will do what it's going to do, and you are powerless to do anything except hold it or sell it. That should be an unemotional decision.

Reality Check

If everything appears to be going well, you are most probably not aware of everything that is going on.

A Corollary to Murphy's Law

A *Wall Street Journal* article[xcix] on the boom in technology stocks gives a good perspective on how the recent bubble grew for two years. The bubble's foundation was based on several myths, similar to myths of previous bubbles. While each bubble appears different, there is just enough variation in the specifics and just enough truth in the myth to disguise the reality. On March 13, a Merrill Lynch strategist said, "It's not Tulip Mania." What's clear now is that this has come unraveled and it was a mania.

The entire tech stock spike in prices occurred because people believed things that had no basis: tech companies could generate breathtaking gains in earnings, sales, and productivity for years; they weren't subject to ordinary economic forces, such as a slower economy or rising interest rates; tech companies' borrowing needs were small and they were immune to interest rate increases; some tech companies had near monopolies with unbeatable advantages; exponential Internet growth had just begun and, if anything, would accelerate; prospects were much more important than immediate earnings; and finally, the greatest myth of all - this time, things are different.

Where We Have Just Been

For the last two years   the market has been somewhat like the Starship *Enterprise*. We have boldly gone where no man has gone before – to a market P/E of well over 200. (It is ironic that one of the most visible television spokespersons for this era was none other than Captain James Tiberius Kirk himself, plugging priceline.com.) In retrospect, we may wish that we had not been so bold.

Fifteen year olds who once dreamed of owning a car are opening brokerage accounts. Adults who once left retirement planning to pension managers now watch stock shows over breakfast and manage their own money. Many people are mesmerized by the talking heads on CNBC, and nothing has done more harm than the average person getting what he believes to be sound investment advice from that source.^{c}

Investors have fallen into the delusion that stocks are safe. Some expect their options or blue chips to hand them retirement on a platter. Hold for the long term is a mass delusion too; the latest favorites won't beat the market in the years ahead. There will be another, final delusion – namely, that someone is to blame (other than the face you see in your mirror). You're still responsible for yourself. Tough markets separate serious, long-term investors from those who just want short-term results. We'll see how many of each type there are. [ci]

Where Will This End?

We have said for years that we cannot predict the market and it would be presumptuous and contradictory to tell you where we think the current market is headed. We can only draw parallels to what has happened in similar periods. We must bear in mind that this time really could be different; in fact each time is just a little bit different. If it were not so, then the market would be predictable and we would already have priced it at an appropriate level for the next ten or twenty years.

We do not make forecasts, but we do assess probabilities based on history and judgment. We've tried to build a case that this has been a bubble. Of course we can be wrong! The technology stocks, including the Internet stocks, can come roaring back in a renewed bull market. But probabilities do not favor it. If this market has the usual conclusion, we have not learned our lesson yet. Too many people expect this stuff to come back. A poll released December 21 showed that 29% of individual investors think it is a good time to buy, 4% think it is a good time to sell. Bottoms usually occur when there is more pessimism than optimism. On average, individual investors still expect 15% returns over the next ten years. They need more pain to lower their expectations.[20]

Going forward "survival in the stock market means no longer investing like a 22 year old, but learning to act like your grandfather. The game is not as easy as people thought it was over the past few years."

People are still putting money into tech stocks. They do not appreciate that this was probably a one-time phenomenon that we are not likely to see again. Over the fifteen months ending March 10, anytime the market fell was a buying opportunity. In the first three quarters of 2000, $64 billion of value funds were sold and $161 billion added to growth funds and $443 billion to Tech Funds. Buyers will wait until the three-year record is good for value, then they will pile into value stocks after they have run way up. The most beaten down area, small cap value has had $1.6 billion taken out this year. *Forbes* December 25 issue reports that a net $4.7 billion flowed into equity funds in the first week of November, the fourth up week in a row.[cii] Nearly 2/3 of it went into small-cap and aggressive growth funds which

---

[20] For the 10 years ended 12/31/2010, the S&P 500 returned 1.5 % a year, rather than the 15.0% investors had expected in 2000.

will use the cash to start buying once they think the market has hit bottom. Tech stocks will rebound at some point, maybe early 2001. But analysts say a lot has changed. Actually it depends on your time horizon, in the short term, tech is no longer seen as an ever-growing industry. In the longer run, nothing has changed. This is an economic sector that is like every other – its value depends on growth, earnings, and dividends.

If this is a true bear market, it is not likely to continue in the same sharp decline that we have seen in recent months. Bear markets do not plunge sharply and then recover rapidly. Rather, they give sharp rallies to rekindle the hope of the faithful and then drop again and again until they have worn down the patience and optimism of the most enthusiastic bull.

If markets get richly valued based on greed, the opposite usually follows. Markets sell off to an undervalued level based on investor fear and panic. So, we are likely to have a period when investors become sick of the stock market. Many will be so disillusioned that they will leave and never return. Strange as that seems now, we created two such generations of market skeptics in this century; those who lived through the 1929 crash and those who experienced the back-to-back bear markets of 1969-70 and 1973-74. At the end of each period, most people believed just the opposite of what people believe now. Today, most people believe that the stock market is the easy road to riches. Then everyone "knew" that you could not make money in the stock market.

To date, even with the 51% decline in the Nasdaq, there is only limited evidence of pain, suffering, or lack of confidence in stocks. We are beginning to hear a few stories however. At lunches and dinners, when people introduce the market as a conversation topic, it now is more likely to be about how it is not going quite so well. Most people still believe stocks are the place to be for the long run. And indeed they are. But any number of investors told me that they were still committed to a sound, disciplined, diversified investment program for the long run in early 1999 after our value oriented approach began to underperform. And a year later, in early 2000 the long run was redefined to mean two calendar quarters. If the portfolio had not kept up for a couple quarters, then it was time to move on to what had been working. At the end of market declines most people will not want to own stocks, and they certainly will not want to talk about them.

A full recovery may take years. Technology stocks in the late '50s and early '60s were the rage. They slumped in the fourth quarter of 1961 and took five years to recover. The Nifty Fifty rose from 1970 until late 1972. It was 13 years before some of them got back to their peak. This group included Xerox, Polaroid, Avon, GE, Walt Disney and Merck. Investors bought them believing that they were not subject to normal investment rules. As these stocks began to fall, people at first said the same thing they said in 2000 – that the fall was due to specific company problems. In twenty months, investors had not only abandoned the Nifty Fifty, many had abandoned the stock market in disgust, never to return. They missed the move from DJI 630 to 11,000.

There are not many investment experts whose judgment we respect. However, there <u>are</u> a few. I have already mentioned Bill Gross of PIMCO. I met Bill in 1978 when he was an unknown bond manager with a fledgling institutional firm in Newport Beach. Today he is known in the institutional investment community as the "world's best bond manager," a reputation he has earned. Another great manager is Gerald Jordan. He runs Hellman Jordan in Boston. I first met him when he was starting his business about 1978. As *Barron's* said in an article at year end,[ciii] "...this guy is a money maker.... a man who has been taking big bets and making big money for his clients for some thirty-plus years." Bearing in mind that he is hardly infallible, I still think he is well worth heeding. In an interview in the year-end issue of *Barron's,* he shares his opinion on the market.

It's the end of the madness. We are coming to the end of the greatest speculative period in the financial history of the world. It has been the most extraordinary five years. Certainly, in our lifetime it will never happen again. It makes tulip mania look like a street corner card game. But it is over. And the effects of it will remain for the next 10-15 years. For those of us who like trading markets, that's what we are going into. I would be stunned to see the Dow Jones Industrial Average get to 15,000 in the next five years. I think it is going to be like 1969 to 1982. (A flat market, no increase in the Dow Jones Industrial Average in that 14 years.)
Gerald Jordan, *Barron's*, January 1, 2001

Good decisions come from experience. Experience comes from bad decisions.
Attributed to Mark Twain

Humility
It is important to maintain a sense of humor about the market and to learn from each experience, no matter how painful. To that end, I can't resist sharing a song that was circulated on the Internet in late March. The writer certainly had a sense of humor, and despite the painful message, most Wall Streeters thought it was pretty clever.

Humble Pie

A long, long week ago
I can still remember how the market
used to make me smile
What I'd do when I had the chance
Is get myself a cash advance
And add another tech stock to the pile
But Alan Greenspan made me shiver
With every speech that he delivered
Bad news on the rate front
Still I'd take one more punt
I can't remember if I cried
When I heard about the CPI
I lost my fortune and my pride
The day the Nasdaq died.
So bye-bye to my piece of the pie
Now I'm gettin' calls for margin
'Cause my cash account's dry
It's just two weeks from a new all-time
high
And now we're right back where we
were in July
We're right back where we were in July
Did you buy stocks you never heard of?
QCOM at 150 or above?
'Cos George Gilder told you so

Now do you believe in Home Depot?
Can Wal-Mart save your portfolio?
And can you teach me what's a P/E
ratio?
Well, I know that you were leveraged
too
So you can't just take a long-term
view
Your broker shut you down
No more margin could be found
I never worried on the whole way up
Buying dot-coms from the back of a
pickup truck
But Friday I ran out of luck
It was the day the Naaaa-sdaq died
I started singin'
Bye-bye to my piece of the pie
Now I'm gettin' calls for margin
'Cause my cash account's dry
It's just two weeks from a new all-
time high
And now we're right back where we
were in July
Yeah, we're right back we where
were in July.

Anonymous *(Circulated by Email throughout the Investment Community)*
March 10, 2000 "The Day the Nasdaq Died" (With apologies to Don McLean
and the late, great Buddy Holly)

*Up until March, people at work, barbers, neighbors and every third person at a
party quickly and without prompting shared the fact that their portfolio had risen
30%, 50% or 100% in the past few months. In recent months, since Nasdaq has
fallen from its lofty highs, people don't feel the same need to update me about their
portfolio.*
      Robert J. Gitter[civ]

No one knows how this contraction in technology will end. That is not the most
important thing. Most important is for the investor to maintain a sense of
perspective. Markets go up and down. The market has the uncanny ability to make
us at times feel euphoric or despondent. Remember the words of Rudyard Kipling,
"Success and failure – treat both those imposters the same". It is easy to convince
ourselves that we have either succeeded or failed. Yet in the market, Kipling is
right. Both feelings are imposters for neither lasts long – each new day brings
challenges and rewards. At the beginning of each day, we have no idea what

measure of either will be delivered.

Lessons and Teachers

We started by writing about getting others to learn from our mistakes, not their own. It is important to learn by reading the accumulated wisdom of others, but it is equally important to choose carefully whose "wisdom" to seek out. It is generally better to get advice from someone who has been successful, rather than from someone who just wants to tell you how to be successful. To that end, I have listened most carefully to those who have had a long term investing record. Three great investors stand out in my mind, though there are certainly others. These three are Warren Buffett (whose Berkshire Hathaway needs no introduction); Sir John Templeton of the Templeton Funds; and John Neff, retired manager for the Vanguard Windsor Fund. All have had a conservative investment philosophy for decades. All are hedgehogs, not foxes. And as contrarians, it should be noted that each chooses to live far from the investment crowd. Buffett is in Omaha, John Neff is in Valley Forge, and John Templeton left the country and ran his business from the Bahamas.

It is appropriate to quote Warren Buffett. An interview with him appeared in *Fortune* on November 22, 1999.[cv] The entire article is well worth reading. It lays out an extremely clear picture of just what investing is all about, something very few people understand – despite the fact that hedgehogs like Buffett will tell you their *great* thing. That one great investment secret is that there is no secret. But to quote him:

What was at work was market psychology. Once a bull market gets under way, and once you reach the point where everybody has made money no matter what system he or she followed, a crowd is attracted simply to the fact that it seems a mistake to be out of stocks. In effect, these people superimpose an I-can't-miss-the-party factor. Like Pavlov's dog, these "investors" learn that when the bell rings – in this case the one that opens the New York Stock Exchange at 9:30 A.M. - they get fed. Through this daily reinforcement, they become convinced that there is a God and that He wants them to be rich.

CornerCap's Role

He who tries to pick long-term value stocks must surely lead much more laborious days and run greater risks to his career than he who tries to guess better than the crowd, how the crowd will behave.

Attributed to John Maynard Keynes

If you can keep your head while all about you are losing theirs, you are an unemployed investment advisor, Gunga Din.

(With apologies to Rudyard Kipling.)

Sadly, in the last year there has been much disillusionment between investment advisers and clients, with the disillusion going both ways. Certainly, many clients wanted far better returns than they got. But many investment advisers grew frustrated with clients who were quick to "pull the trigger" based on what the manager perceived to be much too short a measurement time of his performance. In some cases the managers' feelings were probably justified. One very fine large value manager, Beutel & Goodman, simply closed its doors as a firm. Likewise, Julian Robertson. He was renowned for the great results he had achieved in the Tiger Fund. Then the technology stocks soared and left him behind, like all true value managers. He got so much criticism from his investors that in the early part of the year, he liquidated his fund. Julian Robertson, like Warren Buffett, had made himself and his clients enormously wealthy. After two years of being second-guessed by clients, Robertson decided not to take it anymore. Ironically, events within only a few weeks of his retirement announcement proved him to be right.

Others in the industry took another approach in this period. They chose to give the customer what he wanted, whether or not they thought it was good for him. Consider John Bogle's critique of the way the mutual fund industry has behaved – much the same could be said of the rest of the professional investment community: [Mutual funds] have turned their remarkable record of innovation away from seeking creative ways to enhance the investment results to our shareholders and toward the rather less lofty task of bringing more assets. The marketing of mutual funds has become highly aggressive, far too much so for an industry which is not a modern–day collection of Procter & Gambles, Budweisers, and Coca-Colas, hawking "consumer products" for their "franchise brands", but primarily as a trustee for other people's money. In this business, investing is becoming the poor relation of marketing. We appeal far too much to the desire to accumulate substantial wealth with ease. We too often fail to adequately inform the investing public of the risks and costs involved, and indeed actively promote the hottest performing funds we have. [cvi]

Regardless of the market direction, CornerCap will continue to do very much as we have always done. Our goal is to provide a portfolio that is structured to meet our clients' long-term objectives. This means trying to achieve the highest return available with an acceptable risk level. In addition, we will address our clients' specific problems on income and estate taxes, over-all planning, and general investment guidance.

Over the years, we have assembled a management team that is dedicated to these goals for our clients. We recognize the importance of our client relationships and that we would not have a business without them. Each of our portfolio managers and our administrative and marketing staff subscribes to the philosophy that we are here to serve clients. One of the advantages of working with an organization the size of CornerCap is an opportunity to build long term relationships that make clients comfortable with us.

Rather than be disillusioned by investors, CornerCap recognizes that people will always have a tendency to make quick, probably ill-timed decisions. That is why they need professional advice in the first place. We gave our best shot in the last year or two at educating our clients. Sadly, no matter what case we made, some of them still opted for growth and technology stocks right at the peak. Their actions are like driving a car by looking in the rearview mirror. And the results can be about the same – a wreck. Now many are finding out their weaknesses. A few younger ones may learn a lesson that will serve them for a lifetime. For the older ones, this is the last lesson; their funds are diminished, and they have no time or means to replace them. Still, our job is to continue to educate investors, and to manage their expectations.

POSTSCRIPT

MARCH 2001

This report was completed at year-end 2000. In the first quarter, 2001, the market continued to provide volatility and drama. The market has pretty much followed the script outlined by contrarians during 1999 and 2000. It generally continued to decline. We have received a number of questions concerning the outlook for the market, and technology in particular. Our answer is the same as always – we don't know. While we know nothing, we suspect a lot. History does not hold much immediate hope for technology investors. I still hear investors' comments about "buying on dips", and "technology is good for the long term". This may be wishful thinking on the part of those who have been first stung by, and now hung with, technology stocks as they spiral down.

Since we traced the history of previous bubbles, we should focus for a moment on their aftermath. It is fair to say that the contrarians have been right – Warren Buffett, David Dreman, Jeremy Grantham. If you look back at their comments during 1999 and early 2000, they don't sound nearly so out-of-touch any more. The question is whether we believe them enough to act on their advice going forward. It is too late to benefit from what they said was going to happen to the tech bubble. But it is not too late to heed what they still have to say about the future. The best plan is to start fresh. Forget what has happened, and ask only "What do I do with these stocks today?" Some of the technology stocks are coming into an acceptable range, but many of them are still selling at historically high P/E's. We also must take into account that for the first time in years, many of these stocks are beginning to deliver quarterly earnings that do not compare favorably with prior quarters.

At some point, investors will simply grow weary of technology stocks. In perhaps two to five years, they will be just another "run of the mill" S&P sector as they once were. People will be no more interested in buying them for their special characteristics than they have in the energy sector since 1982. At that point, when the investing public has lost confidence and enthusiasm for these stocks – they will be worth owning again for the long term. We have no idea when that will be.

However an article in *The Wall Street Journal*[cvii] compares this bubble with the Dow Jones Average in 1929 and the Japan market in 1988. The comparison is not encouraging.

It was a bubble, and it did burst. . . . Everyone really wants to know, what next? . . . The current technology boom and bust is nothing new, just the latest in a long history of investment bubbles... These past debacles offer lessons for investors trying to figure out what to do...History suggests that, eventually, many of the pieces of a burst stock bubble get patched back together... But the recovery takes longer than investors hope—usually years, not months. Many of the stocks caught up in the bubble will fail to survive, and of those that do survive, all but the most robust wind up behaving less exuberantly than they did before...it almost always takes longer to repair the damage than most people expect... while some stocks do bounce back and soar again, it can be maddeningly difficult to figure out which will be the winners.

When technology stocks bottom out, they probably will have annual earnings growth expectations in the 15-20 percent range. And they will have P/E ratios that generally reflect that, probably 15-30. If this is true, then technology investors must suffer more pain before there is any gain. The pain may be short and severe, but we suspect that it more likely will be slow torture. Our best guess, again based on history, is that the technology stocks will have rallies and declines that begin to diminish, and that five years from now, their prices won't be much different than they are now. This is because the current prices still seem to reflect the anticipation of about five years of good growth, and if it comes, today's prices may already have it built in. At some point, stocks will be a bargain, but looking at the P/E's today, there will probably be more punishment before prices get to levels that offer good returns.

This also says something about market expectations in general - the overall market is still not likely to meet investors' expectations. In a recent trip by air, I noted that you could get Nasdaq market updates from the telephone in the seat back in front of you. In the air terminal food court, I listened to three pilots discuss the action of the Nasdaq that day, and at the boarding gate, a television was tuned to CNBC for the latest market updates. People still do not believe that the market is a tough business that requires professional skill. Few are destined to have the market make them rich. Until people reach the point that the market holds no "entertainment" value for them and they do not want to discuss it, the market will continue to disappoint. The conventional wisdom for a decade has been, "Buy on dips!" The market will probably go through a phase where it will be, "Sell on rallies!"

So how do you build a portfolio that makes sense for the long term if it isn't going to be with technology? I can only point to what we have done in the past. Tom and I have managed investments consistently over the years with the same value oriented style. It is certainly not the only style to manage money, but we have applied some basic principles consistently. (A) We <u>never</u> timed the market; we stayed fully invested in stocks. (B) We stayed diversified with only about 3-4% in any one stock and with many industry sectors. We never focused on any one sector (such as technology). (C) We always bought value stocks with low P/E ratios. No, it's not the only way, but it is a way that can give respectable returns without the concentration risk.

I reread the *Forbes* debate between Henry Blodget and Jeremy Grantham. I suggest you do the same. It is probably the bias of my age, but I think the main difference between them is simply about thirty years in age and eons of experience. At the time of the interview, Henry Blodget was thirty-four years old. He was twenty-four when the market had its last real correction during the Gulf War. He was twenty-one when the brief, but severe, panic of 1987 happened. He was eight years old when we had the last real bear market, 1974. In contrast, Jeremy Grantham has been in the investing trenches for four decades – he knows that markets go up and down. He has experienced the gut-wrenching feeling of seeing stocks decline day after day. Now sadly, millions of new investors can also share this experience. It will certainly make them wiser the next time around.

So hang in there. Stocks should still be the best game in town for the long run, but don't forget that the short run can be painful, and it can also seem like the long run if it isn't going well. Don't confuse the two.

ACKNOWLEDGEMENTS

This book is obviously as much a compilation of other sources as it is my own material. When I set out to write this over seven years ago, the purpose was less to provide original thought of my own, but rather to gather articles from many sources that bear on the major economic issues of our time. A number of people at CornerCap over the years contributed material that has been collected here.

A few people deserve special recognition for their contributions. Without their efforts and guidance this book would still be just a manuscript. Merriweather Raidle here at CornerCap is responsible for editing my draft and turning it into a publishable document. Joe Thompson created the cover and gave us its title, one that captured the major points of the book in a simple phrase that came from my Uncle Ken. And we are indebted to Angus Morrison, a long time friend of my family and an accomplished author. He guided us through the world of online publishing.

I would also like to thank all the readers of the original edition who encouraged us to follow through and complete a second edition.

ENDNOTES

[i] Jonathan Clements, "The Stock Market Isn't as Bad as You Think," *Wall Street Journal*, September 11, 2002, p. C1.

[ii] Chet Currier, "The lemming's choice/Fund Report," *International Herald Tribune*, June 5-6, 2004, p. 20.

[iii] Nathan Vardi, "Booby Prize," *Forbes,* September 16, 2002, p. 124.

[iv] Holman Jenkins, *Wall Street Journal*, July 17, 2002 p. A17.

[v] George Mellon, "Global View/Scandals Won't Kill Capitalism," *Wall Street Journal*, July 2, 2002, p. A19.

[vi] Randall W. Forsyth, "Up & Down Wall Street -Koz, Jack & Bubba," *Barron's*, September 23, 2002, p. 5.

[vii] Robert Frank and Rebecca Smith, "Power Outage/CEO Brings Scandal To Westar," *Wall Street Journal*, Feb. 21, 2003, p. A1.

[viii] Jesse Drucker and Theo Francis, "Pensions Fall – Not CEO's Bonus," *Wall Street Journal*, June 18 2003, p. C1.

[ix] Rich Karlgaard, "The Little Search Engine That Could," *Wall Street Journal*.

[x] Bruce Kelly, "Merrill a 'boiler room' during tech boom," *InvestmentNews*, August 19, 2002, p. 1.

[xi] *The Mile High Club*, Kinky Friedman, Simon & Schuster, 2000, p. 150.

[xii] "Who Really Cooks the Books?" Warren E. Buffett, *The New York Times*, July 24, 2002

[xiii] Bruce Kelly, "Enron analysts eerily saw phantom profits," *Investment News*, February 25, 2002, p. 1.

[xiv] Alan Abelson, "Up & Down Wall Street, The Anti-Analysts," *Barron's*, June 18, 2001, p.3.

[xv] Neil Barfsky, "The Market Game," *Wall Street Journal*, May 8, 2002 p. A18.

[xvi] Charles Gasparino, "Inquiry Into Salomon Widens," *Wall Street Journal,* August 23, 2002 p. A1.

[xvii] Holman W. Jenkins Jr., "Business World/How Much Business Purity Is Too Much?" *Wall Street Journal*, April 30, 2003, p.A17.

[xviii] New York, (Reuters), June 10, 2002

[xix] Holman Jenkins Jr, "Once Again, Who's to Blame for Bubble Mania?" *Wall Street Journal*, May 22, 2002, p. A27.

[xx] Jonathan Clements, "Rating a Broker? Listen to the Pickup Line", *Wall Street Journal*, October 16, 2001, Page C-1.

[xxi] Randall Smith, Charles Gasparino and Susanne Craig, "Broker Oversight or Tunnel Vision? Two Case Histories," *Wall Street Journal*, February 13, 2002, P. C1.

[xxii] Bruce Kelly, "Merrill a 'boiler room' during tech boom," *InvestmentNews*, August 19, 2002, p. 1.

[xxiii] "Who Really Cooks the Books?" Warren E. Buffett, *The New York Times*, July 24, 2002

[xxiv] *InvestmentNews,* John Kapitan, December 3, 2001, Page 12.

[xxv] "Internet Meets the World of M&A", *Wall Street Journal,* January 13, 2003

[xxvi] "Cisco Kidding", Quentin Hardy, *Forbes,* May 14,2001, p. 52.

[xxvii] Floyd Rogers, "The Spenders," Floyd Rogers, *Winston-Salem Journal,* June 13, 1989.

[xxviii] "When Dinosaurs Mate," Gary Hamel, *Wall Street Journal,* January 22, 2004, Editorial page.

[xxix] *Forbes,* July 22, 2002 p.196.

[xxx] "Mores/Absolutely 120% Positive", Owen Edwards, *Forbes,* September 10, 2001, p. 86.

[xxxi] *Investor's Business Daily*

[xxxii] Walter Olson, "Rule of Law/ A Spanking for the Trial Lawyers," *Wall Street Journal,* May 232, 2003, p. A10.

[xxxiii] Gordon Fairclough and Vanessa O'Connell, "Once Tobacco Foes, States Are Hooked On Settlement Cash," *Wall Street Journal,* April 2, 2003, pA1.

[xxxiv] Shelly Branch, "Is Food the Next Tobacco?" *Wall Street Journal,* June 13, 2002, p. B1.

[xxxv] J. Savitz, "Last Man Standing", *Barron's,* November 25, 2002, p. 19.

[xxxvi] Susanne Craig, "Ex-Technology Analyst Blodget Tries Comeback as a Researcher," *Wall Street Journal,* July 18, 2004, p. C5.

[xxxvii] Michael Waldholz, "Cloning Research Seems Scary, but New Science Often Does", *The Wall Street Journal,* May 2, 2002, p.D6.

[xxxviii] Mark Veverka, "The Real Dot.Coms," *Barron's,* December 24, 2001, p. 19.

[xxxix] Michael Totty, "Déjà vu," *Wall Street Journal,* July 15, 2002, p. R13.

[xl] Holman W. Jenkins Jr, "A 'Perk' Too Far in the Mutual Fund Biz/Business World", *Wall Street Journal,* Nov. 19, 2003, p.A21.

[xli] John C. Bogle, "Fair Shake or Shakedown?" *Wall Street Journal,* April 8, 2004, p. A14.

[xlii] Thomas E. Quinn, CornerCap Report.

[xliii] Ian McDonald, "Mutual Fund Math Puts a Sheen on Returns," *Wall Street Journal,* July 23, 2004, p. C1.

[xliv] Holman W. Jenkins Jr, "A 'Perk' Too Far in the Mutual Fund Biz"/Business World, *Wall Street Journal,* Nov. 19, 2003, p. A21.

[xlv] Warren E. Buffett, "Who Really Cooks the Books?" *The New York Times,* July 24, 2002.

[xlvi] Carol Loomis, *Fortune,* December 10, 2001 .

[xlvii] Thomas E. Quinn, "The Character of an Investor," *CornerCap Investment Counsel,* June 30, 2004.

[xlviii] Professor William Goetzmann of Yale University's Yale School of Management.

[xlix] Gregory Zuckerman, "As Bonds Rally, Now the Losers Are Emerging," *The Wall Street Journal,* October 9, 2002, p. C1.

[l] Gregory Zuckerman, "Beacon Hill Doubles Size of Hedge-Fund Losses," *The Wall Street Journal,* October 21. 2002, p. C4

[li] *Investment News* ~ June 11, 2001

[lii] *CornerCap Emerging Growth Fund Quarterly Report,* September 30, 2001.

[liii] Holman W. Jenkins Jr, "Business World/ A 'Bubble' Is Not a Crime", *Wall Street Journal,* Oct. 9, 2002, p. A19.

[liv] Burton G. Malkiel, "The Market Can Police Itself," *Wall Street Journal,* June 28, 2002, p. A2.

[lv] Burton G. Malkiel, "Remaking the Market/The Great Wall Street?" *The Wall Street*

Journal, October 14, 2002.

[lvi] James Grant, "Lower Stock Prices Will Cure What Ails the Markets," *Wall Street Journal*, July 9, 2002, p. A18.

[lvii] James K. Glassman And Kevin A. Hassett, "Dow 36000 Revisited," *Wall Street Journal*, August 1, 2002, p. A13.

[lviii] Carol Loomis, *Fortune*, December 10, 2001

[lix] Kelly Greene, "How Sick Is Social Security?" *Wall Street Journal*, June 28, 2004, p. R1.

[lx] Thomas R. Saving, "How are we to Pay for All This?" *Wall Street Journal*, September 22, 2004, p. A28.

[lxi] Paul Ryan, "Outside the (Lock) Box," *Wall Street Journal*, July 19, 2004, p. A15.

[lxii] "Medicare Drug Folly", *Wall Street Journal*, June 16, 2003, p. A14.

[lxiii] Regina Herzlinger, "Prix-Fixe Rip-Off," *Wall Street Journal*, June 13, 2003, p. A 16.

[lxiv] Philip K. Howard, "There Is No 'Right to Sue'," *Wall Street Journal*, July 31, 2002, p. A14.

[lxv] Letter to Editor *Wall Street Journal*, April 1, 2002

[lxvi] Daniel Henninger, "Wonder Land/Marcus Welby Doesn't Live Here Anymore," *Wall Street Journal*, January.10, 2003, p. A23.

[lxvii] Laura Landro, "Six Prescriptions To Ease Rationing in U.S. Health Care," *Wall Street Journal*, December. 22, 2003, p. A1.

[lxviii] George Melloan, "Global View/Untangling Anti-Terrorist Confusion? Lots of Luck," *Wall Street Journal*, July 27, 2004, p. A17.

[lxix] John H. Wilke, "How Outdated Files Hamper FBI Effort To Fight Terrorism," *Wall Street Journal*, July 9, 2002, p. A1.

[lxx] Robert B. Reich (former Secretary of Labor), "Nice Work If You Can Get It," *Wall Street Journal*, December 26, 2003, p. A10.

[lxxi] Joe E. Hilsenrath, "Producer-Price Drop Signals Change in Inflation Dynamics," *Wall Street Journal*, September 13, 2004, p. A2.

[lxxii] Daniel Henninger, "Wonderland/Why the Election Is a Tough Call," *Wall Street Journal*, October 15, 2004

[lxxiii] Rob Long, "You Mean Terrorists Don't Read Variety?" *Wall Street Journal*, Nov. 26, 2001, p. A18.

[lxxiv] Dave Barry, "Tobacco funds go up in smoke," *Syndicated Column*, September 16, 2002.

[lxxv] Warren E. Buffett, "Who Really Cooks the Books?" *The New York Times*, July 24, 2002.

[lxxvi] Carol Loomis, *Fortune*, December 10, 2001.

[lxxvii] June O'Neil, "The Trust Fund, the Surplus, and the Real Social Security Problem,", (Professor of Economics at Baruch College, City University of New York. Director Congressional Budget Office from 1995 to 1999.) April 9, 2002, SSP No. 26.

[lxxviii] "If the Spooks Can't Analyze Their Own Data, Why Call it Intelligence?" *Forbes ASAP*, October 7, 2001, p. 47.

[lxxix] Thomas G. Donlon, "Busting the Boom," *Barron's*, July 15, 2001, p.39.

[lxxx] David Dreman, *Contrarian Investment Strategies—The Next Generation*, Simon & Schuster, New York, 1998, p. 361.

[lxxxi] Charles McKay, *Extraordinary Popular Delusions and the Madness of Crowds*, Templeton Foundation Press, January 2000.

[lxxxii] James M. Clash, "Henry Blodget Debates Jeremy Grantham," *Forbes*, June 12, 2000, p. 320.

[lxxxiii] James K. Glassman and Kevin A Hassett, *Dow 36,000*, Crown Publishing Company, 2000.

[lxxxiv] Alan Abelson, "Up and Down Wall Street," *Barron's*, December 4, 2000, p. 4.

[lxxxv] Matt Marshall, "Does P/E Still Matter?," *San Jose Mercury News*, March 11, 2000.

[lxxxvi] James M. Clash, "Henry Blodget Debates Jeremy Grantham," *Forbes*, June 12, 2000, p. 314.

[lxxxvii] *"Analysts' Pick: Cisco Systems Inc.,"* CNBC.com *Technology Reporter*, Nov 4, 2000.

[lxxxviii] " Poof! 'Smart' Investment Ideas Go Up In Smoke, As Market Tumbles," *The Wall Street Journal*, December 18, 2000.

[lxxxix] John Paul Newport, "Time to Go Easy on Japanese Stocks?," *Fortune*, August 31, 1987, p. 97.

[xc] Mary Greenbaum, "Gauging The Market's Prospects," *Fortune*, January 10, 1983, p. 97.

[xci] John C. Bogle, *John Bogle on Investing—The First 50 Years*, McGraw-Hill, New York, NY, 2001, pp. 291-92.

[xcii] James M. Clash, "Henry Blodget Debates Jeremy Grantham," *Forbes*, June 12, 2000, p. 320.

[xciii] John C. Bogle, *John Bogle on Investing—The First 50 Years*, McGraw-Hill, New York, NY, 2001, p.7.

[xciv] "Market Laboratory," *Barron's*, January 1, 2001, p. MW66.

[xcv] Attributed to Pimm Fox, "Information Isn't Experience," October 2, 2000.

[xcvi] Andrew Bary, "Down But Not Out," *Barron's*, December 4, 2000, p. 36.

[xcvii] Elizabeth Corcoran, "Drill-Bit Dilemma," *Forbes*, December 25, 2000, p. 264.

[xcviii] Attributed to Malcolm Berko, *The Herald-Sun*, July 2000.

[xcix] "Reality Check—Here Are Six Myths that Drove the Boom in Tech Stocks," *The Wall Street Journal*, October 16, 2000, p. A1.

[c] "The Bull Turns 10, But Will It Reach 11?," *The Wall Street Journal*, October 10, 2000.

[ci] Jane Bryant Quinn, "Wave the Bubble Goodbye," *Newsweek*, April 24, 2000, p. 32.

[cii] Elizabeth Corcoran, "Day of E-tonement," *Forbes*, December 25, 2000, p. 262.

[ciii] Sandra Ward, "Powerful Trend—An Interview with Gerald Jordan," *Barron's*, January 1, 2001, pp. 31-33.

[civ] Jonathan Clement, "Getting Going," Robert J. Gitter, 'Silencing of the Lambs,' *The Wall Street Journal*, December 26, 2000, p. C1.

[cv] "Mr. Buffett on The Stock Market," *Fortune*, November 22, 1999, p. 212.

[cvi] John C. Bogle, *John Bogle on Investing—The First 50 Years*, McGraw-Hill, New York, NY, 2001, p. 148.

[cvii] Stephen E. Frank and E. S. Browning, "Bursting of the Tech Bubble Has a Familiar 'Pop' to It," *The Wall Street Journal*, March 2, 2001, p. C1.